MILES BREDIN

BLOOD
on the
TRACKS

A Rail Journey from Angola to Mozambique

PICADOR

First published 1994 by Picador

a division of Macmillan General Books
Cavaye Place London SW10 9PG
and Basingstoke

Associated companies throughout the world

ISBN 0 330 33033 0

TMM

135798642

A CIP catalogue record for this book is available from
the British Library

Typeset by CentraCet Limited, Cambridge
Printed by Mackays of Chatham PLC, Kent

When elephants fight it is the grass that suffers

Old Kikuyu proverb

ACKNOWLEDGEMENTS

This book is not intended as a definitive guide to anything. For a start, it is hopelessly out of date but with any book which involves current events that is a necessary evil – in Africa only more so. It can offer no more than an accurate portrayal of what was happening at the time of our journey and what had happened before.

Many people helped me assemble the facts and figures but I bear responsibility for any faults in them. Due to the unpleasantness of the governments we encountered, a few identities have been disguised in the book. Those who can be are thanked below. They are joined with the people to whom Harriet and I owe incalculable gratitude for assistance and hospitality along the way. Thank you all. We had a wonderful time.

Akwe Amuso and Anita Coulson of the BBC World Service; Prospero, Jim and Barbara Bailey; Benoit for getting us out of Zaïre; Catherine Bond; Ginny Bond; James and Virginia Bredin for dealing with the bank and showing as yet unwarranted faith in my ability to pay them; Lizzie Chushi and Daniel Simunda of Zambian Railways; Rosemary Collins, Aidan Sullivan and Richard Ellis of the *Sunday Times*; Tim Deagle from Frontline News; Simon Ferrand at the British Embassy in Kinshasa; John Flynn and all the staff of the British Embassy in Angola; Francois Gordon at the Foreign Office; Bob Griffiths, Gavin Howard, John Wainwright and Scott Ranft from the British Military Mission to Angola; Rafaella Gunner latterly of the EC; Anthony Harwood; Jon Hsuan and Speedie plus all at RST and TransAfric; Sam Kiley of *The Times*; John Liebenberg from NBC and Reuter Television; Deborah Logan; Philomena Lopez at Manica; Paul Lowe at Magnum; Rafael Marques from the *Jornal de Angola*; Andy

ACKNOWLEDGEMENTS

Marshall of the *Independent*; Carlos Mavroleon; Robin Miller; Peter Miller; Giles Milton and Sinclair McKay; Roger, Carlos, Felipe and Jacques at ICRC Beira; Lionel Shriver; Lorraine Taboney at Barclays; Bill Steven at the US Embassy in Kinshasa; Sandie Underwood in Gabon; Daisy Waugh; and Tim Willis.

Africa is the home of the acronym. Please do not shy away from them. Had I avoided them the book would be twice the length. Reading the bits that look boring gives substance to the more interesting bits.

Here is a guide for when you get confused:

AK47 I am not a subscriber to *Soldier of Fortune* magazine and do not profess to be a faultless weapons identifier. I find discussion of their merits extremely dull, but to help with future chapters: AK47s are semi-automatic assault rifles which make large holes in people but are often inaccurate. They are the most popular weapons in Africa. M16s and G3s which are the American and West German equivalents of the AK (military aid) make similar-sized holes but are more accurate, although less reliable when not looked after properly. RPGs, mortars and cannons make holes in buildings and should be given a wide berth.

ANC African National Congress (Zimbabwe)

APC Armoured personnel carrier

BCA Beira Corridor Authority

BMR Beira, Mashonaland and Rhodesia Railways

Boss *see* NIS

BSA British South Africa company

CFB Benguela Railways

CFM Mozambique Railways

CIA Central Intelligence Agency (USA)

DSL Defence Systems Ltd

EC European Community (was the EEC, now seems to have become the EU)

FNLA Angolan National Liberation Front

Forex foreign exchange

Frelimo Mozambique Liberation Front (ruling party in Mozambique)

GDP gross domestic product

GNP gross national product

ICRC International Committee of the Red Cross

IMF International Monetary Fund

JVC joint monitoring commission (Mozambique)

KANU Kenyan African National Union (Kenya's ruling party)

KK Kenneth Kaunda (former Zambian president)

MMD Movement for Multiparty Democracy (Zambia's ruling party)

MPR Popular Renewal Movement (Zaïre's ruling party)

MPLA Angolan People's Liberation Movement (the Angolan ruling party)

MSF Medecins Sans Frontières (Belgian or French aid agency)

NGO non-government organization

NIS National Intelligence Service (South Africa); formerly BOSS

NRZ National Railways of Zimbabwe

OAU Organization of African Unity

PF Popular Front (ZANU and ZAPU use it as a suffix)

Renamo Mozambique National Resistance Organization

RPG rocket-propelled grenade

RR Rhodesia Railways

SADF South African Defence Force

SAP structual adjustment programme

SPLA Sudanese People's Liberation Army

STD sexually transmitted disease

SWAPO South West African People's Organization (Namibia's ruling party)

UDI Unilateral Declaration of Independence

UHF ultra-high frequency (radio)

UN United Nations

UNAVEM United Nations Angola Verification and Monitoring Mission

UNDP United Nations Development Programme

UNHCR United Nations High Commission for Refugees

Unicef United Nations (International) Children's (Emergency) Fund

UNIP (no relation of UN) United National Independence Party (Zambia)

UNITA (no relation of UN) National Union for the Total Independence of Angola

USAID United States Agency for International Development

WFP World Food Programme (UN)

WHO World Health Organization

ZANU PF a merger between ZANU and ZAPU (the ruling party in Zimbabwe)

ZANU Zimbabwe African National Union

ZAPU Zimbabwe African People's Union

ZR Zambia Railways

Statistics also look boring. They should generally be treated with contempt. All figures in Africa are guesses – educated or otherwise. Where possible, I have used UN figures for how many people died in or how many people live in such and such a place. This is no reason to trust them. The UN's figures merely cost more to compile than anyone else's. It is almost impossible accurately to compile figures in Africa and numbers get rounded off in a very cavalier manner. None the less, my figures are as accurate as possible and, while not oracle, can be used as a pointer.

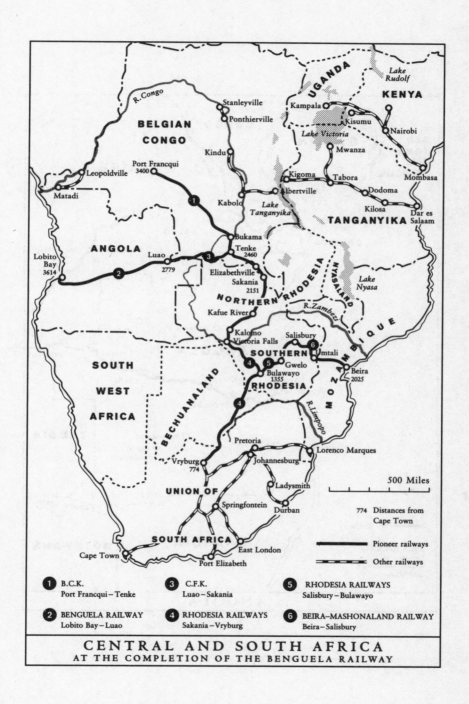

R. Congo

UGANDA
Lake Rudolf
KENYA

BELGIAN
CONGO

Stanleyville
Ponthierville
Kampala
Kisumu
Nairobi

Lake Victoria

Kindu
Mwanza

Leopoldville
Port Francqui 3400
Mombasa

Matadi

Kabolo
Kigoma
Tabora
Dodoma
Kilosa
Dar es Salaam

Albertville
Lake Tanganyika

TANGANYIKA

Lobito Bay 3614
ANGOLA
Luao 2779
Bukama
Tenke 2460
Elizabethville
Sakania 2151
NORTHERN RHODESIA
NYASALAND
Lake Nyasa

Kafue River
R. Zambezi

SOUTH WEST AFRICA

Kalomo
Victoria Falls
Salisbury
Umtali
SOUTHERN
Gwelo
Bulawayo 1355
RHODESIA
Beira 2025

MOZAMBIQUE

BECHUANALAND

R. Limpopo

Pretoria
Lorenco Marques

Vryburg 774
Johannesburg

UNION OF
Ladysmith

Springfontein
Durban

SOUTH AFRICA
East London

Cape Town
Port Elizabeth

500 Miles

774 Distances from Cape Town

━━━ Pioneer railways

━·━·━ Other railways

1 B.C.K.
Port Francqui – Tenke

3 C.F.K.
Luao – Sakania

5 RHODESIA RAILWAYS
Salisbury – Bulawayo

2 BENGUELA RAILWAY
Lobito Bay – Luao

4 RHODESIA RAILWAYS
Sakania – Vryburg

6 BEIRA–MASHONALAND RAILWAY
Beira – Salisbury

CENTRAL AND SOUTH AFRICA
AT THE COMPLETION OF THE BENGUELA RAILWAY

Zaïre's embassy in London is a grand stucco-fronted building on Chesham Place. It looks impressive from a distance. Someone, however, has stolen the nameplate, the flag and, apparently, the government.

'I would love to help you but I cannot give you a visa at the moment as we have no government,' the press attaché told us from behind his chaotic desk.

The rotting carpet of his office was almost entirely covered by empty crisp packets and crumpled pieces of paper – the waste-paper basket had become a wastepaper corner which looked set to take over the room. The lights weren't working. The embassy was enveloped in a fog-like gloom, yet he continued to attempt to help us.

'I will give you the number of the Ministry of Information,' he said. 'I have just sent a letter to them about you, but I don't expect a reply.'

Having searched through the rubble on his desk, he eventually settled on a file, but then his face fell. Two seconds later he broke into a wide smile and said, 'Of course ... we don't have a Ministry of Information any more, we have a free press.'

Stumbling down the stairs from his office, past the peeling wallpaper, the dysfunctional lights and the obligatory photographs of President Mobutu, we knew we were back in Africa. Zaïre was already living up to our expectations and we hadn't even left London. My photographer, Harriet Logan, has slept through artillery barrages, yet she was quite convinced we were going to die in Zaïre. It has that kind of reputation. It would be another three months before we realized how well Zaïre had earned it.

I was rather more Harriet's journalist than she my photographer. Having won the *Sunday Times*'s Ian Parry Young Photographer of the Year award for her work in Somalia and Sudan, she had announced that she would spend the prize money following a railway from Benguela on the Atlantic Ocean in Angola, to Beira on the Indian Ocean in Mozambique. She spent months preparing the journey and discussing the project with various film companies. But when it was time to leave she was the only one ready – none of the production companies was. Harriet wanted to be in Angola for the elections and knowing that I had just returned from Kenya and was going mad writing stories about the Wales's fast-failing marriage, she called me, and a few weeks later we left.

Until recently, I had been based in Nairobi where I ran United Press International's East Africa office. I had known when I had taken the job that UPI was in dire financial straits but had been unable to resist the temptation of calling myself a bureau chief. My time in Nairobi started with me covering the culmination of the Ethiopian civil war, pre-intervention Somalia and the Kenyan struggle for multiparty rule. It ended with me selling off the office furniture to pay UPI's debts, after which I returned to England still fascinated with the continent and looking for an excuse to return. Harriet's project seemed the perfect solution. The railway ran through some of the most interesting countries in Africa so we would be able to combine hard news with researching the tumultuous history of the line.

Cecil Rhodes never succeeded in building the Cape-to-Cairo railway that he had envisaged as a red route linking British territory from one end of the African continent to the other. The 2,760-mile stretch from Benguela to Beira, though originally intended as a branch line, remains as the only true monument to his vision. The railway runs from Benguela and its neighbouring port of Lobito, through the Angolan highlands to Zaïre's copper belt, where much of the world's copper supply lurks under the foliage. It winds down through Zambia with its own heavy mining industries, Zimbabwe with its coal and steel, to Beira, a recently rehabilitated port on the Indian Ocean. In 1892, a century before our departure, when Cairo still seemed a realistic goal, George Pauling started digging.

Pauling was a British contractor who could carry pit ponies on his shoulders. Born into genteel poverty, he had provided for his mother and all his siblings since the age of thirteen and had never failed on a contract. He was the stuff from which empires are built. His workers were eaten by lions and mosquitoes, and the locals and his engineers had to become hunters, naturalists and doctors on top of their normal duties. The railway, save for a few hundred miles in Zaïre, was built entirely by his company but was not finished until 1930, eleven years after his death. It was an extraordinary feat – the track crosses mountain ranges, swamps and virgin rainforests and passes through some of the most savage country in the world. Africa a century ago was as wild and dangerous a place as now.

We intended to follow the railway from the Atlantic to the Indian Ocean. When we left England in September 1992, there were elections pending in Angola, a government of national unity in Zaïre, well-publicized droughts in Zambia and Zimbabwe and a peace treaty had just been signed between the two warring factions in Mozambique. Things were looking good and even the most hardened cynics were being cautiously optimistic but, unluckily for southern Africa, we took along the four horsemen of the apocalypse as travelling companions. By the end of our trip the situation had changed: Angola was back at war, Zaïre's army had mutinied, Zambia and Zimbabwe were suffering from cholera epidemics caused by unpublicized floods and Mozambique was being short-changed by the UN who seemed to have learnt no lessons from Angola. Only 1,230 miles of the 2,760-mile railway was working and southern Africa was once again in crisis.

Nairobi is the place to get Zaïrean visas but after being rather too frank about the activities of Kenya's president in a recent article for the *Sunday Times*, I had been advised that it was unwise to pay even the most fleeting of visits to my former home. We therefore dispatched our spare passports to a South African freight company which promised that it could get us visas in Swaziland and deliver them to us in Namibia.

After thirty-three hours of caterers' strikes, delays and stroppy stewardesses, courtesy of Air France, we arrived in Windhoek, one of the strangest cities in the world. Namibia was the world's youngest democracy until Eastern Europe got so feisty and South Africa, its previous colonial master, has poured money into it. South Africa had not suddenly turned to good works in its abrupt adjustment from pariah to possible saviour of Africa. Namibia's mineral riches give it great potential. The money that has flooded in is investment not charity.

Long before South Africa's intervention, Namibia was known as German South West Africa and plentiful evidence of the German presence remains there. You can still buy swastika croissants in the bakers and they used to celebrate Hitler's birthday with jolly parades in the coastal city of Swakopmund, where lederhosen-clad Nazis and their large wives would march up and down, showing off their inbred and terrifyingly blonde children. The rest of the white community is broadly made up of former South Africans who were either involved in 'the struggle' or simply couldn't cope with the situation in their own country, and Afrikaners who thought South Africa was too liberal before the war. Sam Nujoma, the former SWAPO (South West African People's Organization) leader, who headed the fight against South Africa, is the freely elected president. Namibia does not look like it has been at war for the last twenty years because almost all the fighting was done in southern Angola. The South African defence forces have never been famed for respecting international borders and chose a guest country in which to fight Namibia's independence war.

Namibia, which gained its independence in 1990, is currently going through an odd phase. It is more like South Africa than any other African country – the poor blacks live in conditions far better than their northern neighbours and on a par with their southern. They have good roads, schools and hospitals; the economy is controlled by whites and it works.

The airport looks exactly like Stansted – ultra-modern with lots of exposed steel and colour coding. Modern though it is, it does not run to such accessories as taxis. Having missed the bus we had to call a hotel and have them send out a car for us. The next morning we discovered that our passports had not yet arrived so we missed the flight to Angola and resigned ourselves to a week in Windhoek. The town is surrounded by yellowy-brown mountains, making it an excellent place to invade as they are identical in colour to Airfix desert camouflage. Many modern high-rises – most of which are empty – surround a few remaining Germanic buildings that look totally out of place in the scorching heat and the arid landscape.

It is very like small-town America. There are lots of shopping malls and 'family restaurants' and the dissolute youth cruise in the evenings. The people, though, are different. Young white men sport 1970s footballers' haircuts and their girlfriends wear tie-dye as they drive up and down the strip in VW Beetles with exposed bottoms. The main street is called Independence Avenue by the government and Kaiser Wilhelm Strasse by everyone else, black or white. The mayor of Windhoek insists that it should retain its original name which fits in much better with other charming street names such as Goering Strasse. On the pavements you see expensively dressed blacks (not a common sight in Africa), one of whom we saw walking home with a tyre round his neck which, aware of the fire risk, not many blacks would dare to do a few hundred miles further south.

Sitting among the Kevin Keegan look-alikes in Le Bistro, Windhoek's hottest bar, we were getting frustrated. This was all very interesting but we were meant to be train-spotting in Angola and following the run-up to the elections, not people-watching in peaceful Namibia. We had been told the 'that's Africa, baby' joke* by the freight company when our passports had still not arrived; the people we were shipping our film through in Angola had sent us a fax saying, 'Cancel your trip as we are having elections', despite the fact that we were sending film to them *so* we could cover the elections; and the *Sunday Times Magazine* now wanted us in northern Angola to do a story about diamonds. Meanwhile, we were haemorrhaging money and in the wrong country.

During the five days it took us to get our passports back we did some research into diamonds and booked our plane tickets to Angola. The Central Diamond Mines building, which has a sign at its entrance saying, 'Please leave all firearms at reception', dominates Windhoek's skyline as its company does the economy. One of the aliases for De Beers, CDM provides Namibia with more than 30 per cent of its GDP and is proportionately powerful. De Beers is a secretive company which by controlling the supply of 80 per cent of the world's diamonds is in a position to dictate the price. Founded by Cecil Rhodes, of railway fame, it defies every economic law known to man by making billions selling an essentially useless and very common product. Diamonds are hard but not as hard as cheaper manmade alternatives, they are beautiful but not as beautiful as aquamarines, and they are difficult to mine but not as difficult as coal.

De Beers had just released some rather exciting pictures of

---

* A snake needed to cross the Limpopo but the current was too fast, so he asked a crocodile to give him a lift across. The crocodile replied, 'No, I'm not crazy. You'll bite me and then we'll both die.' 'No, I won't,' replied the snake. 'That would be mad. I have to get to the other side and I don't want to die.' After much persuasion, and against his better judgement, the crocodile agreed to act as a raft. 'Now you promise you won't bite me,' said the crocodile before they set off. 'Of course not. That would be crazy,' replied the snake. As they reached the centre of the Limpopo, the snake sank its teeth into the crocodile's back. 'Why did you do it?' asked the crocodile as they were both swept to their deaths. 'That's Africa, baby,' replied the snake.

illegal diamond mining in Angola and then immediately with-drawn them from the photo market and refused to discuss the problem with any but a few journalists. By doing this they thought they could force the Angolan government to take action to stop the practice. This skilful titillation of the press meant that for a while illicit diamond mining became one of the world's most sought-after stories. De Beers had admitted to spending $500 million dollars in 1992 buying up illicit diamonds so they might retain their grip on the market, and they thought that by being nice to the press and giving a few people access they could highlight a problem which was costing them a fortune they could ill afford. Illicit diamonds from Russia and Angola were wreaking havoc on a market which De Beers was supposed to control. A few journalists were allowed to interview De Beers personnel and then, when the interest was up, they slammed the door in order to keep the story alive. This method worked in that there was a lot of interest, but totally backfired because no one understood why De Beers should be allowed to have a monopoly.

We received the off-the-record treatment in Windhoek so, when we set off for Luanda, I had a vague knowledge of industrial diamonds from a former friend in London, my recently acquired De Beers knowledge and, by far the most interesting, the Wilbur Smith view – that diamonds are sexy and mined by people wearing dinner jackets who have private plane licences and interesting sex lives. None of these theories turned out to be true.

Angola was first colonized in 1575, since when the Portuguese have removed three million people from its shores and millions of carats of diamonds. When they left, instead of returning the country to the Angolans, they gave it to the world's superpowers to play with. In the sixteenth century, before it earned its current third world status, Portugal was the most important country on the map. In fact, it was drawing the map. When England was still squabbling with the Scots, Portugal was taking over the world. Angola was used as a labour pool for the bits of the world they had already occupied. Hundreds of thousands of slaves were sent out to their coffee fields in Brazil and to the sugar plantations in São Tomé.

A few centuries later slavery became illegal and the Portuguese were forced to stop trading. No longer having much use for their far-flung and hostile colony, most of which had not even been explored, they ignored it. But when the Pan-African independence movement started in the 1950s, the Portuguese government was just becoming aware of the stupendous mineral riches of Angola. It reacted to the independence threat by sending out to Angola 300,000 of its peasants. Angola is an enormous country so the Portuguese peasants had orders to spread out and proceate. They were neither quick nor fertile enough and a colonial war broke out in 1961, since when Angola has never been truly at peace.

Various rebel groups emerged, all of which have long Portuguese names. As in all African conflicts, it is easier to stick to the acronyms. The MPLA (Angolan People's Liberation Movement) was set up in 1956 and shortly afterwards the FNLA (Angolan National Liberation Front) joined it in agitating for independence. Both groups were working in exile but the MPLA, led by Agostinho Neto, pulled most of its support from the key area around the capital, Luanda. Holden Roberto's FNLA emerged from the north of the country and soon became based in and sponsored by the Congo (Zaïre). In 1966 Jonas Savimbi, a member of the largest tribe, the Ovimbundu, led a split from the FNLA to form UNITA (National Union for the Total Independence of Angola) and has been its political and military leader ever since. All of them wanted independence, but under different tribal and political systems.

The Portuguese won the early colonial war but the struggle continued and when, after the 1974 Portuguese coup, the new leaders said that they were going to divest themselves of their colonies, the three rebel groups met in Luanda to set up a government. The united interim administration took office on 31 January 1975 and the new war started on the first of February. It was going to be a different war though – east–west rather than north–south. It started off between the Soviets (with Cuban help) and South Africa. South Africa gave support to UNITA so that they could attack SWAPO (Namibia's independence fighters) and ANC bases in southern Angola. In 1986 the South Africans ended up fighting the Cubans in a battle outside Cuito Cuanavale which made both sides realize that they might be making a mistake since they didn't actually have anything against each other. South Africa wanted to destablize communist governments but Cuba wasn't exactly in their area.

With the arrival of the Reagan administration in Washington, it became a proxy fight between the Soviet-backed MPLA and the American-backed UNITA. Savimbi's UNITA controlled the south of the country and none of the towns while the MPLA as the legitimate government held the towns and not much of the country. Throughout the 1980s, the MPLA, who have a fully mechanized army, fought during the dry season, when it is easier to move around, and licked their wounds in the wet. The collapse of the Soviet Union, however, meant that the MPLA had to seek a truce. A peace agreement was signed between José Eduardo dos Santos, Neto's successor as leader of the MPLA, and Jonas Savimbi, the charismatic UNITA leader. Elections were called for 1992. Approximately 340,000 people had died to bring Angola to the same position it had been in thirty-two years earlier. We were off to see whether Angola's 500-year run of bad luck was going to change.

Windhoek airport had undergone a startling transformation by the time we arrived for our Angolan Airlines' flight to Luanda. Gone was the smiling efficiency of the previous week. In its place were some very stressed Namibian Airlines personnel trying to contain a mob of resolutely cheerful but totally uncontrollable Angolans. The check-in desks were invisible behind vast mounds of luggage, all wrapped up in masking tape.

Angola is so undeveloped that rich Angolans have to pay excess luggage if they want freezers and cookers. There are few shops and they tend to sell equipment designed by Soviets in the dark ages. The department stores and hypermarkets of Windhoek had been laid waste and their contents were going to bump us off the flight if we didn't move fast. Clambering through the rubble of soon-to-be-needed funeral wreaths, draining boards and car parts, we made it to the front of the queue and managed to get checked in. We knew that with the influx of journalists, PRs, UN observers and other parasites in time for the elections there were no hotel rooms in Angola, so were expecting to sleep on a friend's floor at the Meridien Hotel until we could find somewhere of our own.

On the advice of a Namibian television crew, we were first on the aeroplane so that we might be first off.

'At Luanda,' they told us, 'you have to follow your luggage from the hold to your hand or never see it again.'

Passing round our copy of Ryszard Kapucinski's *Another Day of Life* – a haunting book about the last days of Angola under Portgual – we discussed whether we were going to see a repeat performance in order to keep our minds off the flight. The plane was an ancient Soviet Ilyushin that looked as though it had been decorated by British Rail a long time ago and smelled like a fishmonger's. The vibrations were alarming throughout the journey and there was much applause when we landed. All the Angolans on the flight were going back to vote and were looking forward to the prospect of a novel and interesting experience. Uniformly fed up with the war, they were just getting used to their new and more enjoyable lives. The MPLA government had relaxed its fiercely communist stance and UNITA was talking sensibly. Luanda, apparently, was enjoying a revival – nightclubs had opened up and there was plenty of money circulating.

'I don't trust Savimbi though,' said Jacques, who had been studying in Windhoek for the last year. 'He's a bad one.'

Having successfully trailed our luggage, we were surprised to find that we had a reception committee at Luanda's crumbling Portuguese-built airport. Standing at the barrier was Katya, a Finn in her fifties who has spent most of her life in Angola and had recently made the change from government minder to head of the independent press centre. We had never been to Angola before, but those journalists who had remembered her as the person they were always trying to run away from were rather surprised by her transformation into a guardian angel. She ended up having many homeless journalists to stay at her house and if you ever needed anything she could generally arrange it. From visa renewal to cheap car hire she invariably knew where to go. We were lucky to be met by her since the journalists she was meant to be meeting had not turned up and we were able to take their rooms. She introduced us to Elder Tenente, a Mozambican Portuguese who had married Paula, an Angolan, and moved to her home country. They had us to stay in their house for the next two months.

Elder shoved us and our seven pieces of luggage into the back of his pick-up and drove us to his house. Paula and Elder lived with their three children and two Santomeans in a quarter of a house close to the centre of Luanda. Elder was stores manager of a diamond-mining company by day, but he also dealt in tropical fish. The fenced-over yard was full of bubbling tanks that made a spectacular breeding ground for mosquitoes. On the side he also sold cars and had converted his house into a hotel. The house slept four additional people in rooms that had been converted out of cupboards. It was completely self-sufficient. A pen housed some chickens, a large container in the dusty road outside was full of petrol and food, and they had a generator to provide electricity.

We spent many happy weeks there, grinning inanely at Paula who loved us and cooked us delicious dinners, to which, at the start, we could say no more than '*moite bom*' (very good) by way of thanks. All conversations had to take place through Elder who, having lived in South Africa for a while, spoke English.

'Paula says, what would you like for supper?' to which we would reply, 'Whatever you're having, but not too much.' Half an hour later, great pans of pasta and stews would appear which could have fed entire communities, and we would have to stuff ourselves under Paula's stern ey1. She thought we were wasting away. If we looked thirsty they would send the children out looking for beer. Like so many others, it was a happy home in a tragic country.

There was an atmosphere of great excitement in Luanda. In the short night-time trip from the airport we could already see the election posters that covered the town, the political T-shirts and the huge plyboard doves of peace exhorting people to join in the election process. There was no feeling of menace on the dark, pot-holed streets but the tension was tangible. Tall, thin figures swathed in rags lurked round fires by the side of the roads and from time to time a functioning streetlamp bathed its decaying surroundings in an orange glow. Something new and thrilling was set to happen in Angola. After thirty-two years of war they were going to have elections and start trying to live like normal people.

The immediate impression of the town is that it is incredibly dirty. The streets are piled high with rubbish and the smell of rotting vegetables becomes overpowering after rain, when the ill-maintained and ancient sewers throw up their grisly contents. There is seldom any electricity in the city, and in the intense heat food goes off very quickly and the smell pervades the alleyways. Householders' rubbish mounts up in the streets where it is sifted and recycled by the street children and other homeless. But underneath the filth and decay the town is graceful and beautiful – elegant old Portuguese houses have been taken over by squatters and have not been repaired for decades. Delicately carved wooden staircases lead up to the verandahs of the old colonial buildings which now house tens of families. The main streets of the city are lined with characterless modern high-rises which are falling apart faster than the older buildings, but the back streets are steeped in curiosities. Intricate carvings adorn the gates of gardens which have now become people's homes and stucco moults from centuries-old churches in secluded squares. In many places the street names have been changed to show appreciation to government supporters – Karl Marx gets a road, Lenin an avenue, but the old signs made out of hand-painted tiles which remember forgotten slavers remain.

Luanda is set on a lagoon with a fort at one end and a port at the other. The wide Avenida Marginale stretches along the waterfront, past the pink wedding-cake of the Central Bank which would not look out of place on Quai Branly next to the Eiffel Tower, out under the fort to the Ilha. The Ilha is an artificially created spit formed from a small island. It is lined with beaches, restaurants and a market where you can buy piri-piri chicken, beer, whisky and Marlboro. Almost anything which comes into the port gets stolen and will soon turn up on the Ilha or in one of the other markets around town. It is a vibrant and exciting place where the rich go to swim and eat and where the poor live and work. Journalists were able to do a good deal of their research while tanning at the Barracuda beach-front restaurant. On one side of the road you could do the amputee spear fisherman story, on the other you could convince yourself that buying the stunningly beautiful and scantily clad president's daughter a drink was important research. Isabella dos Santos's MPLA flip-flops were the most sought-after journalistic souvenir in Angola, but no one managed to get them. Her movements were monitored so closely that when she left a day ahead of schedule to return to her English university we all thought there was going to be a coup.

On our first day in Angola, Harriet had to go off with the *Sunday Times*'s Richard Ellis to photograph a UNITA rally and I went to get us accredited to the Ministry of Information. Angola was the first place I'd been to in Africa that had a press centre for the benefit of visiting journalists. There were fax machines, telexes, televisions and even a bar (although it always smelt of rotting meat). Usually, working out how you are going to file is the first challenge of any story. Many of my friends were there to cover the elections so I was able to gossip happily while filling out forms. It didn't take long to discover that every foreign correspondent in Angola – there were one hundred and seventy at that time – was trying to do the diamond story. We had some pretty formidable competition but also the advantage that, while we were interested in the elections, we were only commissioned to write about diamonds and trains so didn't need to keep a constant eye on the politics. This situation made for a very unhealthy feeling of paranoia, however, with no one sharing information. There was much whispering in corners, and inexplicable disappearances took on great import. After spending a day on the beach, we were happy to find we could rely on free drinks all evening from people trying to find out what we'd been up to during the day.

So began weeks of tarmac lurking, trying to convince someone to fly us up to Lunda Norte, the closed province in the north of the country where the Angolans mine their diamonds. We were only four hundred miles from the start of the railway but had to investigate the diamonds before we could get on with our main purpose. Almost daily we would drive out to the airport in our extremely stylish and very yellow convertible jeep which we had hired from Elder at fifty dollars a day. We were the envy of Luanda since not only did we look like extras in a Camel advertisement but everybody else was paying at least one hundred dollars a day.

Ever flying again after seeing Luanda airport is courageous. The burnt-out and cannibalized remains of planes litter the tarmac outside hangars that look like they have been looted. Oil is laid like Chocolate Spread over most of the apron and no one, no one at all, knows what is going on. When Harriet had to ship some film, it took six and a half hours and sixteen stamped forms before they agreed to take it, delay it and eventually send it to England ten days later. Heavily armed guards surrounded the airport twenty-four hours a day but anyone with enough gumption could drive right out on to the runway. We drove in every day for weeks to wheedle with pilots to fly us up to Cafunfo, the diamond capital, but no one would do it without the permission of Endiama, the state-run diamond firm, who didn't want us any-where near the place. On one day we managed to see soldiers from nine different armies at the airport – US, Canada, Nigeria,

Portugal, Britain, Holland, Ireland and, of course, the MPLA and UNITA.

Our first trip to the airport was made especially difficult. The president was due to fly in at any minute. Still with no authority to be there and laden down with cameras and notebooks, we loitered around to see what all the fuss was about. A red carpet was rolled out and pinned down with some green objects that looked like limpet mines. They couldn't have been, however, because no one was killed when the wind kept on sneaking under the carpet, causing it to whip the sweating dignitaries who waited to shake the big man's hand. Forty minutes after the line had been created, dos Santos's plane landed and blew the carpet across the airport with the back draught from its jets. Out stepped the grey-headed mestizo president with his cosmetic smile firmly in place. He walked down the steps, shook two hands and disappeared in an old Mercedes. The disappointed reception committee chased after the carpet then disappeared, grumbling sadly. Having caught this glimpse of greatness we started covering the elections in earnest. We had no one to file for but we could spend only an hour a day leaning on the diamond people and the run-up to the election was becoming increasingly interesting.

Luanda was plastered in posters. Dos Santos had hired a Brazilian PR company and the result was a very American-style campaign under the slogan of 'O *futuro certo*'. Dos Santos had bought massive hoardings on which he was portrayed grinning cheesily and looking about twenty years younger than he did in real life. No one dared to tear them down. There was one extremely sophisticated hoarding on the side of the square at Kinaxixe. The billboard revolved its three different messages: one a UN-sponsored public information message saying 'Vote for a new Angola', and two 'Vote dos Santos' messages. In the centre of Kinaxixe was a vast pedestal-mounted armoured personnel carrier crowned by an enormous dove of peace, and below it was the Café Democraccia where little booklets were handed out explaining, through cartoons, how to vote. The Café Democraccia was later blown up in a rocket-propelled grenade attack. The dove of peace was the symbol for the election campaign and appeared everywhere – on T-shirts, the nightly news and on many monuments around town. At Kinaxixe, the massive plyboard dove genuinely looked as though it was shitting on the APC below it.

The UNITA posters presumed victory. Their smiling portrait of Savimbi could have been taken in a photo booth for all its artistic merit but the UNITA cock, one of Africa's most powerful political symbols, was always in evidence. Everyone from Moi in Kenya to Banda in Malawi use the cock's crow to drown the voices of their detractors. Savimbi also had a PR – the American Riva Levinson who went on from Angola to Kenya where she tried to gloss over Moi's human-rights abuses to exactly the same journalists who hadn't believed her in Angola. Countless other parties had emerged but none had the budget of the two big boys, although there were some very creative ideas. One used the UN to get thousands of dollars' worth of free advertising by calling itself the UNDP (United Nations Development Programme).

In the run-up to the elections there were supposedly three powers at work in Angola: the MPLA government, UNITA, and the United Nations Angola Verification and Monitoring Mission (UNAVEM II), whose monumental failure will blight the participants' careers for ever. There were some excellent people working under Miss (not Ms) Margaret Anstee, who headed the mission, but it was chronically underfunded to achieve its ambitious aims and was mainly filled with highly paid incompetents. UNAVEM II never really had a hope. Margaret Anstee and her political negotiator Hugo Anson (whose brother was having a similarly bad year as the Queen's ill-fated press secretary during her *annus horribilis*) had to negotiate between two parties who had only stopped fighting each other through lack of funds, with almost no Security Council support and no military back-up.

UNAVEM was made up of unarmed soldiers, who handled the logistics of the situation, and diplomats from around the world.

Many of them had no common language which, added to their inability to force anything upon the protagonists, meant they failed in their most significant task. They had a year to set up a joint army and make the two sides disarm. Both parties pretended to disarm and participated in the joint army but were always able to marshal heavily armed and partisan troops whenever necessary. The UNAVEM military advisors knew this, but in the absence of Security Council support, could do nothing about it. Anstee never had a chance anyway. However good at her job she was, Savimbi was never going to take her seriously. A woman has a hard enough time fighting sexism in Europe but asking a woman to intermediate between two egos as big as Savimbi and dos Santos's in a country where women's opinions are regarded as worthless was quite absurd, but in the politically correct environment of the United Nations this could not be acknowledged.

The UN were based in an ugly building in an otherwise beautiful street that ran parallel with the Marginale. It was an alphabet soup of acronyms that became even more complicated than usual since everything was translated into Portuguese. The WFP (World Food Programme) became the Programme Alimentar Mondiale and Unicef (United Nations Children's Fund) the Funda – Nacoef Unidas Para a Infancia. The car park was scandalous. I am used to the fact that UN delegates always use fabulous four-wheel-drive cars for driving round town. Every car thief in Kenya used to be drawn, like poachers to a game park, to the UNEP (United Nations Environment Programme) headquarters in Nairobi, but at least people drove them there. The car park at the Angolan UN HQ was filled with cars gathering dust. There was even a fully equipped ambulance Land Cruiser which, by the time we returned to Angola in December, had collapsed on its now airless tyres and was fast disappearing under a thick layer of city grease. It still had the plastic on its seats.

It has to be said, however, that the UN were excellent travel agents – we flew all over the country with them (even to Namibia a couple of times). As well as its planes, UNAVEM had a fleet of

Soviet MI8 helicopters which were used to fly observers around the interior. They had Aeroflot markings on them and were flown by Siberian pilots who wandered around the country looking lost for months. The choppers were old anyway, but I think that the abrupt transfer from snow, ice and Russian to sun, sand and English must have been the main cause of the problems. They crashed with fearful regularity. We discovered after a few weeks that the safest 'airline' was WFP. They had six-seater Beechcrafts which we were told were being insured at $250,000 a quarter and which were flown by South African pilots. The WFP were also incredibly helpful – at one point they even put on a special flight to the central highlands for us. Bureaucratic wastage aside, this could explain why the UN spends so much in order to achieve so little.

On our first night out in Luanda we set off with Sam Kiley from *The Times* to Bob's Diner on the Ilha, which became one of our regular haunts. The restaurant was actually called So 8 but it was in the former garage of Colonel Bob Griffiths so assumed his name. He was the head of the British military mission in Angola and spent every day at the joint military commission mediating between the generals of UNITA and the MPLA who were meant to be setting up a joint army. The two teams got along famously and spent their days reminiscing about great bridges they had blown up but their friendliness was ruined by the machinations of their political leaders. A Portuguese military liaison whom we later met in São Tomé said, 'If the negotiations had been left up to the generals, Angola would still be at peace.'

The diner was a Chinese restaurant run by a Laplander called Anders and his North Vietnamese wife Kim who was a former anti-aircraft gunner. It had been set up with a hundred and fifty dollar loan from the British colonel that had been paid back on the opening night, and was the centre of all political gossip in Luanda. It can list among its celebrity clients many of the Angolan cabinet, countless ambassadors, Pik Botha* who drank so much

* The South African foreign minister.

for peace in Angola and the seersucker-clad former British liberal party leader, Sir David Steel.

You could never mistake Colonel Bob's profession – stocky and well turned out, he always looked totally out of place in Luanda, yet he succeeded in putting people completely at their ease. Despite resembling the hero of a thousand black and white war films (in which he would have been played by Kenneth Moore), he had no difficulty making friends with the bald and abrasive Sam, nor Harriet and I, who are scarcely army types. Compassionate yet realistic, he also knew more than most about the political situation in Angola and was free with as much information as he could be.

Driving home from dinner we were stopped at a road block on the Ilha bridge. Both soldiers were drunk and aggressive but Sam thought it might be amusing to take the piss out of them.

'Come on. Stand up straight,' he said to the soldiers as the rest of our car's passengers bowed and scraped.

The bridge is not a nice place to be stopped – it is unlit and has a body of water close at hand for swift cadaver disposal. None of us had yet mastered Portuguese, which irritates Angolans, but I had discovered that if I spoke French and put 'o' on the end of every word I could get by. We had Angolan press cards and were allowed to be driving at night but neither of the soldiers could read – although they weren't willing to admit this – and just barked orders at us to show more papers. Having silenced Sam and given the soldiers a couple of cans of beer we were allowed to pass and trundled home through two more road blocks.

It is difficult to drag me away from the television in London and crossing the river is something I do only with trepidation, yet in Luanda we went out every night, patrolling the deserted streets in our jeep and risking the road blocks which grew in number as election day drew closer. Luanda was like that – nothing could contain the festivity of the town. Despite the risks, every night we went dancing at the Club Aberto, drinking at the Surf on the beach or just out to dinner. The near-naked bodies that adorned the sand by day prowled the clubs by night, shadowed by the military observers, press and smugglers who paid the bills. Everything seemed more fun than usual and the slight element of danger only added to the highly charged sexuality of the town. Angola had a collective air of over-excitement and we became caught up in it.

By this time there were only four days left before the election and the whole country was geared up. Every member of the population had been given a T-shirt saying either MPLA or UNITA. Stickers had been stuck everywhere – on the roads, the buildings, the buses and, yes, even the trains. Wearing the T-shirt didn't mean a great deal as much of the population didn't have a clue what elections were anyway, but if the election was to be judged on T-shirts, dos Santos was winning hands down. He must have put millions into his merchandising and wasn't handing out only T-shirts but also head bands, kangas (African sarongs) and bracelets.

Many people were going to vote for whoever had given them the most kit so the MPLA was well in the lead. Harriet spoke to a woman at a UNITA rally in the FNLA stronghold of Uige, three hundred miles from Luanda, who said, 'I will vote for UNITA. They have given me T-shirts, hats, food, cooking oil and they are good for the country.'

Savimbi himself had said at a recent rally, 'Vote for me and get new trousers.' Earnest aid workers had told me that this had something to do with an old Ovimbundu folk story about trousers, but I never found a single Angolan to verify the theory.

Popular opinion had been that UNITA was going to win the election with a substantial majority. The MPLA had been running the country since independence and it was a hell hole. Millions of *dislocados* (displaced people) were penniless, fatherless and limbless. Agostinho Neto, the MPLA's charismatic leader, was long dead and had been succeeded by the less than entirely black and very plastic-looking dos Santos. Savimbi and dos Santos together looked like Action Man and Ken. Savimbi had been in the bush 'with his people' fighting for liberation, wheras dos Santos had been Minister of Planning in a country that hadn't seen a plan completed since 1975, and then Foreign Minister of a government with few foreign relations.

It all seemed pretty simple; but then Savimbi's past started catching up with him. When Fred Bridgland, a British journalist and authority on Savimbi, turned against him, it emerged that Savimbi had ordered the execution in Jamba (his wartime stronghold) of Tito Chingunji and Wilson dos Santos,* two of his most loyal comrades. Stories of gang rape and mutilation were pounced on by the government press and radio, then publicized all over the nation. This, when combined with the fact that all Angolans were utterly fed up with war and wanted to start living normal lives, did not bode well for Savimbi. He was a mite pugnacious for a country that for the first time in thirty-two years was beginning to enjoy peace.

Three days before the election we went to Savimbi's last rally in Luanda at First of May (Angolan independence) Square. Surprisingly, few people had bothered to attend despite the trucks cruising the streets nearby chucking out free T-shirts as they made their way Pied Piper-like towards the square (Luanda is not a UNITA area). Savimbi was late and the interim was spent by entertainers singing songs to an audience of logo-covered Angolans. The big man eventually arrived in a brand-new Mercedes which put dos Santos's to shame. He was protected by three dark-windowed GMC wagons which pushed their way through the crowd with the help of a squad of UNITA soldiers, who bludgeoned prospective voters to the ground when they got in the way. These US-aid wagons could be seen everywhere and were unnerving to say the least – you got out of the way when you saw one in your rear-view mirror. GMC jeeps induced particular nightmares in journalists who had worked in El Salvador. They had been the favoured form of transport for the Death Squads.

* Wilson is not related to José Eduardo. Dos Santos is the Angolan–Portuguese equivalent of Smith.

Savimbi levered himself out of the car wearing a very tight UNITA T-shirt, the central message of which was pulled out of all recognition by the great man's bosoms. He was supported by a tribal cane and attended by two amputees. This constructive use of amputees could have been a vote winner if he hadn't pushed them out of the way every time they got between him and a camera. Amputees are a significant minority group in Angola. He made what was intended to be a rousing speech which singularly failed to rouse the crowd and then disappeared again. I had been told about electrifying oratory of the silver-pistol-brandishing Savimbi and was sorely disappointed. He no longer had a visible pistol and was about as electrifying as Luanda's erratic power supply.

The next day's rally was much more impressive. Dos Santos was attending a soccer match in the city's stadium between his team and the Angolan Benfica. His lost, but the whole event was magnificent PR. People love football in Africa – so much, indeed, that Namibia was willing to send its national side to Angola in the midst of the fighting. It is surely only a coincidence, but a happy one, that the MPLA and AC Milan – the world's richest and best team – share a flag. By attending any match dos Santos was ensured a large friendly crowd. The streets around the stadium were jammed for hours before the game and at one point the police had to use live bullets – in the air – to stop people from being crushed. There was a national-holiday feel to the occasion since it was the Sunday before the elections and the rather nervous population – not many of whom had jobs anyway – were not going to work on Monday. Maximizing on this, dos Santos pressed flesh liberally and smiled at all the right people. He is a master of insincerity and had the crowd eating out of his hand. People like having the same interests as important men and women, so the crowd was made to feel somehow special that they were spending the afternoon doing the same thing as the president, even if he was in the air-conditioned communist equivalent of the royal box and they were sweating on the terraces.

We made a last-ditch attempt to get up to the diamond area before the elections by using our finely honed door-stepping abilities. Paul Lowe, a *Magnum* photographer, had moved into our house and we had joined up to do the story. He, Harriet and I spent the morning of election eve camped out in the office of Endiama who were still refusing to help us. We knew that both the people we needed to see were in the building and we were not going to leave until they saw us. After sitting in the waiting room for an hour and a half, listening to the World Service and making ourselves look as unattractive as possible, we eventually drove the receptionist to distraction and were ushered into the office of Noe Balthazar, the managing director of the state-run diamond firm. He was a tall, rich-looking mestizo, wearing a double-breasted cream silk shirt, and oozing charm. A political appointee who happened to have a cousin in the MPLA cabinet, he had his bets well hedged. He had lent the company house to Savimbi in order to be in with both sides. He could not keep his eyes off Harriet's breasts, which she obligingly thrust towards him, but even this was not good enough. He would see what he could do after the elections. Disappointed but not defeated we left and leaned on our other contacts some more. We had to have Balthazar's permission to go there but maybe if we could get someone else to ask him for us we might do better. In the time being, however, there was the small point of the election to cover.

Luanda was dead. Savimbi had returned to his central highlands stronghold at Huambo, dos Santos was lying low just outside the capital and the streets were deserted. Accordingly we went to lunch at the Surf where the British press corps had congregated, bemoaning the fact that there was nothing to do. The observers had been interviewed, UN flights to whacky places to watch the voting had been booked and there wasn't much to do save sunbathe and swim. We were a little behind after our morning at Endiama so we had a useful lunch, nodding sagely as everyone around us discussed the latest developments and we left well versed on the political situation.

That night there was going to be a party on the Mediterranean Sea, a large ship which had recently sailed into the bay and was setting up as a floating hotel. All the hacks had been invited. To get to the boat involved walking through a dark building site to the quay side which had been decked in flowers. The guests were greeted by Angolan beauties clad in mini togas and no underwear who guided the by now confused guests to the swimming-pool deck. We were all given small copper plates with the Macedonian emblem in the middle and 'To Angolan Democracy 27–10–1992 The Westminster Group' engraved on them. I'm told they made excellent frisbees, although mine is now an ashtray. We were very confused – togas, Westminister Group, Angola – what on earth was going on? I cornered the captain and discovered that the boat was a former Greek-island hopper, that the Westminster Group had financed the hotel project, and that they were 'overjoyed to be there in time for the elections'.

The boat resembled nothing more than a cross-channel ferry and had cabins to match, which they were renting out for $250 a night. A faint smell of puke pervaded the orange corridors which stretched from rusty bulkhead to scuffed stairs and up to the gaudy bar. The party was terrible and as we waited for some free dinner, we listened to the unavoidable speeches.

'We are glad to be investing in Angola,' said the master of ceremonies through a bemused Mozambican journalist who had been roped into the job of interpreter.

He then proceeded to give a fifteen-minute speech about Greek–Angolan cooperation. They were very proud of their investment in Angola, he told us. This investment consisted of an extremely mobile boat that took only dollars, which it later emerged was going to be the vehicle for the South African evacuation if the fighting started again. The ship, which soon became known as the Love Boat, went on to emerge as the biggest pick-up joint in Luanda and temporary home to Pik Botha while he failed to solve Angola's political problems.

We heralded the dawn of Angolan democracy at the Bar Aberto

where the press, United Nations and diplomatic community were mingling with the mercenaries, businessmen and diamond dealers who were the real life-blood of Angola, to the sound of Jim Morrison singing 'Light my Fire'. It was a surreal scene. Everyone had hand-held radios so that they would know if anything happened. Anyone who was anyone was on a radio network — stylish people were on two. Graham Martin, the director of Defence Systems Limited — a security firm with a difference — had five radios in his blue canvas bag. The bar was decorated in Africa-inspired metalwork. Bits of bicycles and old cars had been contorted into African masks and spears and could be viewed to the sound of modern European music. There was a gay barman with a Jean-Paul Gaultier haircut who was wearing a Boy T-shirt. The clientele was composed of beautiful black people and plain white people. We could have been in the Portobello Road. The only difference was that we were discussing real life in foreign languages rather than the latest foreign-language film in English. It was election day and, for the first time ever, the population of Angola was going to vote for the leader of their choice.

Up in Cabinda, the Angolan enclave in Zaïre where most of their oil comes from, they were not going to vote. This is the province where, during the cold war, American oil men guarded by Cuban soldiers ran the rigs while their country supported the war against the Cubans in the rest of Angola. The Cabindans were still fighting a secessionist civil war and had 'advised' people not to vote. In the rest of the country it was thought that Holden Roberto's FNLA would do well in his tribal homeland of Kongo but the main fight would be between the MPLA and UNITA. Prospective voters had to produce, as well as their identity cards, a finger, which would then be dipped in purple ink in order to vote. In Angola, the world's amputee capital, this was not always an easy proposition, and to cap it all the voters' choice was between the two people most responsible for their dismemberment.

CHAPTER TWO

We met John Swett, an American aid worker, at the Bar Aberto, who told us that the railway was working from the coast at Lobito to Kuito, where he ran a development project.

'I've been pulled back until after the elections but please come visit as soon as it's over. Not many people get to Kuito and it's a great place,' he told us.

This was good news for us because we had not imagined we would be able to get that far by train. Kuito is almost two thirds of the way across Angola and much further than the train had travelled for the past eighteen years. A long railway makes an easy target for a rebel group and UNITA had effectively closed it for the duration of the civil war. Zambia, which had previously sent half its exports out through Lobito, had been unable to use it since 1975.

Before leaving London we had negotiated for and received letters from UNITA's London representative. He gave us permission to travel with one of his commanders from the end of the railway to the Zaïrean border. A few months earlier, Isaias Samakhuva had laid out maps, showing where the train stopped, on the floor of his Clifford Street office. He knew where this was because UNITA had blown up the bridge.

'I will arrange for someone to meet you and take you across in boats,' he said, and swelling with pride he went on, 'You have to see the bridge. They said it was impossible to destroy.'

With a wide grin he went on to show us old black and white pictures of UNITA soldiers mining the railway.

Our plan was now to cover the elections, do the diamond story and head off to Lobito and the railway in about ten days. This decided, we observed the election full time.

The morning of voting had arrived. The doves of peace had been let loose on national television the night before and, less effectively, on the radio. By six o'clock in the morning what seemed like the entire population was queuing to cast their votes. Gangs of committed young men and women, wearing blue T-shirts with the dove printed on them, had been flown around the country by the United Nations to help with the election process. Observers from different concerned groups around the world had flown in to verify that things went smoothly and the international press swooped around in gangs to verify that the verifiers were doing their job. There was not a hotel room to be had in the country, so full was it of interested parties; surely nothing could go wrong.

We were in the fortunate position of not having to come up with photographs of Savimbi voting, Kate Hoey* verifying or Margaret Anstee monitoring, so we set off early in the morning to go and look at some normal voters who were not being so closely watched. Having slapped on the sun block and whipped off the roof we borrowed a tape deck from Elder and took the route south from Luanda. This was the road that seventeen years earlier the South Africans, who reached within a hundred miles of Luanda, had used to invade Angola. It was also the road on which seventeen days before a Portuguese family had been stopped and cut up into small pieces when they were returning from the beach. It's a beautiful journey which, after winding through the slums of Luanda's outskirts, follows the coast the whole way down to Lobito, where the railway begins, and beyond. We were filled with excitement when we actually crossed a railway and took a few photographs in case we never saw one again. This became a more and more wise precaution as our trans-continental journey progressed, but for the time being we were looking for polling stations and soon found one, unmonitored and functioning.

* A British Labour MP who was a member of the all-party observation group.

The *povo* (people) had been there since six o'clock and by the time we arrived at about seven, the sun was beginning to take effect. Angola is just below the equator and oven hot – consistently over 100 degrees Farenheit and often much higher. Long lines of people, clutching their registration cards, were waiting to do their democratic duty; among them many soldiers who were in a separate line of their own. A large table had been put out in the sun where sat a dove T-shirted helper, a UNITA representative and another from the MPLA. On the table was a baby-pink box for presidential votes and a baby-blue box for parliamentary ones.

The voters were called from the front of the queue, one at a time, when they had to produce their registration cards which were punched and checked against the voters' list by all parties. Every voter had their finger put in a pot of purple ink and would then go behind a curtain to make their vote on two sheets which had pictures next to the names for people who couldn't read. UNITA had its cock as a symbol and the MPLA had its flag and star. The votes were then deposited, under the eyes of everyone, in the appropriate boxes. This process, as you can imagine, took a long time and many who had been queuing on the first day didn't vote until the second.

People had been willing to admit who they were going to vote for on previous days but on the actual day of voting they had become suddenly coy. Whether this was because of the soldiers' presence, who were happy to say they were voting for the MPLA, or because of the sanctity of democracy we couldn't tell so we moved on to another polling station.

It was weird to see the army voting. African soldiers have such extraordinary power that voting seems like something they shouldn't need to do. The soldiers at this first polling station had been half demobilized – they were still in uniform but no longer had their guns and looked somehow naked without them. Most were conscripts and had been hanging around for months with nothing to do and no pay.

'We have to stay close to the assembly point because we get fed there and I can't go home until I have been paid,' said one soldier who, after two and a half years in the army, was unaware whether his family was still alive. There had been a lot of fighting around his home of Malange, some of which he had participated in.

It is difficult to sympathize with men who kill indiscriminately but these young soldiers, who had been given untrammelled power at such an early age, had abruptly had all their strength stripped from them and were having to make an accelerated adjustment to civilian life. They looked like confused children whose toys had been taken away. Now they were expected to make a decision about who they wanted to govern them, despite never having lived normal lives before. Angola, it seemed, was going to need another invasion, this time of psychiatrists – not only for the victims of war, but also for its perpetrators.

We carried on driving south where the country began to deteriorate. For the first twenty miles or so outside Luanda the roads are good and the slums are not too bad – as slums go. There is a diversion when you come within a mile of the president's house and after that, the country and road begin to decline dramatically. Much of the civil war was fought along this road. UNITA fought most of the war as a guerilla force. It had a proportionately small army – fifty thousand men to the MPLA's hundred and fifty thousand, which it used effectively by attacking only on its own terms. Outnumbered as it was, by using very few troops UNITA could cause chaos by mining roads and railways, ambushing convoys and generally harrying the MPLA's forces throughout Angola, without ever engaging in a set-piece battle unless they wanted to. By the time of the ceasefire, only four hundred miles of road in Angola – a country the size of France, Spain and Italy combined – was considered safe.

On the coast road, it is easy to see where the MPLA gave up defending the capital. There is a massive permanent checkpoint, like a border-control tower on the former Berlin wall, by the side of the road. After you passed that you were in the Badlands, and on the day of the election this was still an obvious demarcation point. A mile or two beyond the checkpoint a burnt-out Mercedes was slewed across the road like a text-book ambush. In an ambush of this type you are expected to slow down, go slightly off the road to skirt the obstruction, hit a land mine and get shot at by the surrounding troops. Luckily we were driving our Suzuki which being somewhere between a lawn mower and a Tonka toy was thin enough not to need to leave the road. In macho war-corresponent style I put my foot on the accelerator and using my driving skills learnt as a London mini-cab driver, flew past the burnt-out car at high speed. When we stopped at another polling station a few miles further on I discovered, somewhat embarrass-ingly, that there had been a crash the night before and a tow truck was on the way.

There were similiar queues here and still no sign of UN observers, but this time no soldiers, so I was able to question the electorate more closely. The majority of them, despite the fact that they lived beyond the point which the government was willing to defend, were going to vote MPLA. The MPLA tra-ditionally draws much of its support from the Kimbundu who live in the environs of Luanda, so this was expected. A few were going to vote UNITA and even fewer for Holden Roberto's FNLA. There was, though, no animosity between the opposing parties' voters. Democracy was a totally new concept for Angola but the *povo* had got the hang of it very quickly and seemed to like it. Admittedly, the people I was talking to spoke Portuguese as well as tribal languages, wore Western clothes, and had all been to Luanda, but they hadn't exactly been at the forefront of science and the twentieth century had largely passed them by. Its main manifestation, which none of them possessed, did indeed pass them by, for it was the car. Other than that they were living in the wattle and daub houses that their ancestors had lived in, on the same diet and with the same educational opportunities.

Angola beyond the cities is almost entirely undeveloped, and where it is, the work was done pre-1975 and has not been maintained since. These were country people – mainly subsistence farmers and fishermen – who were living the same life that they had done for centuries. The only change was that the armies who had spent the last thirty years fighting in their fields had been using more sophisticated weapons of late. It was this constant fighting that had so enamoured them of the democratic process. They wanted to have children with both legs who didn't have to go off and fight wars, get driven off their land and die for a country the benefits of which they had never seen. One young man in the queue, who shared his opinion with the rest of the people who were listening, was overjoyed.

'Now we can vote instead of fighting,' he said – predictably.

All around the country the election process was going equally smoothly. Reports filtering back to the press centre when we returned were very optimistic. Observers were saying in off-the-record interviews that there had been no fighting, no rigging and no intimidation. Even the deeply cynical journalists who had not believed that the election could go off without a hitch were impressed – bored but still impressed. With Angola being so peaceful the exchange rate to the dollar had plummeted and Luanda was becoming very expensive. An African election with no fighting or corruption may be a total surprise but that doesn't make it a story. The hacks were getting itchy feet and Somalia was beckoning in its own charmingly apocalyptical way. The Somalis know how to behave in front of the international press – badly. Angola was an important story because of the end of the cold war and the American involvement but they just weren't doing it right. The day was saved by the breakdown of the computer at the CNE (the electoral commission in charge of counting the votes). Surely something fishy was going on down there.

Everyone raced off to the CNE building, conveniently about a hundred yards from the press centre, to discover that there was nothing suspect at all. Instead some sort of power surge had blown the circuits on the computer and there wasn't even anyone to blame.

Security, however, had been stepped up in the capital – the Ninjas were on the streets in much increased numbers and the press centre was now permanently guarded by alert troops rather than sleeping policemen. The Ninjas, officially policemen, are the Angolan equivalent of the SAS – trained by the Spanish and armed to the hilt with everything from rocket-propelled grenades and machine guns to tanks and mortars. These menacing, Rayban-bedecked characters wander around Luanda wearing blue overalls like helicopter pilots' uniforms, with padded knees and elbows, and are so good at their jobs that they qualify for bulletproof vests – something I have never seen another African soldier wearing.

The population had also become slightly more hostile now that the voting was over. Angolans are naturally very warm but they are understandably paranoid about the press. When we first arrived we had encountered a lot of problems taking photographs. Angola had been pretty well closed off from the outside world for the past two decades and not many journalists had been in favour of the government side. As in many communist countries, the population had been nervous of talking to the press because of the possible repercussions, and this feeling was still evident. Coupled with this, the South African government used to send spies to Luanda disguised as journalists. With so many hacks in the capital, this effect had worn off over the past couple of weeks but curtly reappeared in the limbo time after the votes had been counted and before the results had been declared.

The CNE were unable to release results until after everything had been verified. This was a long and tedious process which involved holding up every voting slip to be checked by every interested party before it was officially counted. The national radio and TV stations were bypassing the checks and announcing approximate results as they got them. UNITA were quite obviously losing and things were beginning to get very tense. The journalists, who were desperate to get off to a new story, were in two minds as to what to do. Should they stay in the hope of death and destruction or were these delays going to carry on for ever? News editors on different continents were beginning to get frustrated – there was no news until the results came out and in the time being the story was getting expensive. The US marines were about to invade Somalia and all the Africa correspondents were over two thousand miles away from the action.

We didn't have this problem as we were there to take the railway but other hacks were beginning to trickle away. We still couldn't start the railway journey, however, because we had to do the diamond story first. Two days after the elections we went for dinner with Colonel Bob at the diner where the British parliamentary observers were also part of the party. They had been impressed by the elections and were heading off the next day. David Wilshire, a conservative MP, had managed to get himself arrested for taking pictures of soldiers, something you would expect MPs to know wasn't a good idea. He spent much of the evening trying to justify his behaviour, which had very nearly become a diplomatic incident. David Steel, in his tropical seersucker, was bouncing around trying to be interviewed, blissfully unaware that having been invited to observe the elections by UNITA, his integrity was in doubt and his opinion worthless. None of the official observers would speak to him either. It was rather sad. I checked in a newspaper library when I returned home and noticed that no one from the British press had mentioned he was in Angola at all.

Lunch on the beach the next day was interrupted by great excitement. *Le tout* Luanda was at the Barracuda. Graham Martin sat on a sun lounger topping up an already excessive tan and reading a Robert Ludlum, his radios squawking by his side; Rafaella Gunner, the European Community's PR whose excellent Portuguese, incredible contacts and enormous sense of fun were always a bonus, sat at our table; on other tables were assorted hacks, diplomats, soldiers and observers, all sunbathing and waiting for something to happen. The unofficial results coming from the radio were becoming increasingly interesting but the

MPLA still seemed to be winning and Savimbi was not taking calls from anyone, however important.

Akwe Amuso and Anita Coulson from the BBC – always first with the news – arrived clutching an explosive statement from UNITA. Savimbi had at last broken his silence and released a statement which was later denied, confirmed and denied again, saying words to the effect that the MPLA had rigged the election and if some sort of agreement wasn't worked out pretty damn quickly he was going back to the bush and God help Angola. Hacks were distracted from their beers and started looking interested for the first time in days. The electoral process, up until then, had been more like a council election in Taunton than the culmination of a thirty-year war and we were in dire need of a story. The British Embassy moved on to phase one of its evacuation plan and Gavin Howard, one of the British military advisors, insisted that we register as nationals, so the next morning we set off to the embassy to do our duty.

The embassy in Luanda is a pale blue and sandstone building drenched in purple and pink flowers which is hidden behind the fort that overlooks the bay. It has a spectacular view and was once a temporary home to David Livingstone. The embassy was guarded by Gurkhas from Graham Martin's Defence Systems Limited (DSL) who operate all over Africa and can do anything from guarding company personnel to training contract armies. They managed to make the embassy more British than any squaddy could and, by the time we left, used to recognize our car and greet us like long-lost comrades in arms. Union Jacks sparkled on the ranks of Land Rovers and the ambassador's gleaming Jaguar was being washed in the bright sunlight. We went in and filled out our registration forms under the Annigoni and chatted with Paul Sherar whose job it was to contact every British citizen in Angola and tell them to pack their bags.

'We advise you to have a bag packed and be ready to leave. Stay at home unless it is strictly necessary to go out,' he said, so we jumped in the car and headed to the beach.

At the Surf, Anita and Rafaella were busy listening to the radio results of the election. Every day the vote had been getting closer as the results from outlying provinces, who were mainly voting for UNITA, came in. The country was being driven insane by the very jazzy theme tune to the election results — one of those melodies that stick in your brain to such an extent you find yourself humming them while you brush your teeth. There had been a shooting incident at the press centre in which a passerby had been killed and a bomb had gone off at the airport in Cabinda. There were reports of UNITA picking fights with the MPLA in Huambo. The exchange rate had gone through the roof.

On every street corner in Luanda there were gaggles of women waving great wads of cash in bulky fans. They are a lesson in pure economics — through some extraordinary grapevine they decide the dollar rate, which changes hourly, but never rip off their customers. When we first arrived it was 2500 kwanza to the dollar. The news of Savimbi's statement had pushed it up from 1900 to 4100 in just a couple of hours. A soothing broadcast could have driven it right down again. In the Meridien Hotel, the smartest in town, the money changers came in with briefcases full of money and portable money counters for sorting the huge bundles of kwanza. There was a rash of counterfeit hundred-dollar bills going round Luanda and the big dealers were not going to be caught out. They had battery-powered ultraviolet machines with which they checked all foreign currency.

After lunch we went back with Rafaella to her office and bumped into a friend of hers, Rafael Marques, from the *Jornal de Angola*. Luck is too weak a word for what happened next. Rafael had been to Cafunfo before and dropped everything to help us get up there. We had been trying for three weeks, but in the course of one afternoon, Rafael and Rafaella got us invited to view the Luzamba diamond project and booked on to a UNDP flight to Cafunfo the next day. We were actually going to get there — despite all my disastrous efforts. I was made to stay in the car while the final rubber stamp was received from Noe Balthazar, who had taken an almost pathologial dislike to me. Pushed into a corner by the Brazilian director of Luzamba, he had to give us his authority and did. Rafael was going to come with us too, so our Portuguese was not going to be too severely tested. At six o'clock the next morning Rafaella, taking PR to new heights of perfection, picked us up and took us to the airport where we caught the flight to Cafunfo. UNITA had pulled out of the joint military commision the night before and the resulting tension meant fluent Portuguese was needed to get past the security at the airport.

In all we spent about three weeks in the diamond area. We stayed with RST, a mainly British mining company in Cafunfo where, hundreds of miles away from the nearest two-storey building, they had created an English pub with a guitar-shaped swimming pool. We led a schizophrenic existence. Our days were spent with a lively posse of Zaïrean diamond smugglers, with whom we investigated the illegal mines and the extraordinary lives of the people living in the region. In the shady world of the illicit diamond trade, we met ragged skinny children with thousands of dollars in their pockets and mysterious Algerian and Brazilian smugglers who were making millions, buying up all the diamonds while living in squalor and eating mealie meal (a revolting type of paste made from maize meal which is the staple food of most Africans). At night we returned to the comfort and safety of the British miners' houses where we became expert at playing darts and drinking South African beer. It was as though we were in a different country, so removed was Cafunfo from Luanda. Politics in the province of Lunda Norte were only a pretence – diamonds and dollars were all.

At the illicit mine of Kapemba, where thousands of miners had converged from places as far away as Namibia and Botswana, we saw avarice-refined politics. Above the illicit mine there was a burnt village which had been razed to the ground by a combined force of UNITA and the MPLA – probably the only time they have worked in harmony. They had asked the miners to return to their villages in order to vote, and when the miners refused, tried to force them by burning down their houses. The destruction had no effect. Literally on the ashes of the previous village had been erected a shanty town of Malthusian dimensions. Thousands of people slept within inches of each other in lean-tos, under tarpaulins and just on the ground. Prostitutes plied their trade along the avenues of the low-level town, strutting on the thousands of empty beer cans which carpeted the paths. Zaïrean smugglers sold ghetto-blasters off trestle tables for thousands of dollars each. A can of beer cost $15 and five men a day were killed in squabbles over lesser sums. Another five, on average, drowned in the river. No structure in the town – which must have housed 10,000 people – was over five foot tall.

In Cafunfo, UNITA and the MPLA were on speaking terms because to make money from corruption they had to ally, but by the time we arrived Kapemba was a UNITA mine. This had nothing to do with politics – just money. We arrived in the illicit mines with our Zaïrean friends and a diamond police guard. So incensed were UNITA by our and the guard's presence that they wanted to kill us – for ideological reasons, of course. The dispensation of beer and $3000 in small notes, however, soon put paid to their ideology and bought us a tour of the mines. After the failure of the democratic process, UNITA moved into the area in force. When we first went to the mine, out-of-uniform but still armed rebels showed us around. On our last visit a full commando unit from Malange had taken over. They had radio communications, were commanded by a full colonel and were armed to the teeth.

When we returned to Cafunfo we heard on the World Service that our friend Anita Coulson had been caught in the middle of a battle between UNITA and the police. Journalists were being held hostage in the Tourismo Hotel while UNITA, who owned the hotel, fought it out with the police whose main station lay opposite. The situation relaxed again in the capital but in the diamond areas it was becoming increasingly tense. A smattering of shooting at night was par for the course, but as the days went on, things began to look bad. The legal mines were meant to be a twenty-four-hour operation but every day now UNITA would come to the mines after dark and order the washing plants to be shut down. The lube truck which went around fixing the machinery was held up by armed men, the driver beaten and robbed. We spent the night in the pub where Jon Hsuan, the British general manager, and his senior managers took it in turns to stay up all night, listening to the UHF radio with which they kept in contact with their colleagues in Luanda and the British Embassy. No one moved without their hand-held radios which kept them in touch with their mining operations and colleagues. Their employees – under UNITA pressure – started to refuse to work night-shifts.

We got back to Luanda on Tuesday to discover that we were the only foreign journalists left in the country. Jon, the 33-year-old general manager, had to go down to South Africa so we played at being executives and flew back with him in the company plane – a very smart Gulf Stream with swivelling seats and picture windows. Tony, an enormous, bearded miner wearing Prestatyn rugby-club shorts, and Geoff, who was in charge of electrics, had challenged each other to a race round the airstrip so the whole senior management was there to referee and then wave us off. Bob, a former SAS man in charge of security, took me to one side and told me, 'Be very careful, particularly in Zaïre.' He gave me a list of people we could call on if we got in trouble. 'They'll look after you – just say you're a friend of mine.'

We had been cosseted in Cafunfo and had forged some unlikely friendships. It was with some regret that we left. The whole set-up was so fascinating. It had been like observing a parable at first hand. Cafunfo is what happens when greed takes over, yet in the middle of it all was this strange band of normal, uncorrupted British miners. They were paid huge sums to work there but were none the less an oasis of sanity in the centre of Gomorrha. Two days later UNITA took over Cafunfo and they were all held hostage.

Luanda was strained but still functioning. The police were on the streets in huge numbers. Long queues for petrol indicated the level of tension as people thought about escape, yet they still went to the beach and the clubs. Pik Botha was in town again, briefly, to try to sort out a truce but Savimbi had returned to Huambo and was not talking to anyone. The British Embassy staff had been told that they were not allowed out at night, so Gavin Howard used to make us have dinner at his house every night to save him from boredom. This involved running the gauntlet of road blocks to get from our house in Kinaxixe out to the Ilha where Gavin was living. Day by day it became more and more unnerving.

It reminded us again of Kapucinski who described in his book the Portuguese packing up their belongings and building crates as the South Africans marched up the road towards the capital in 1975. This time though there was no tapping of carpenters' hammers. The Angolans couldn't just run away and the few westerners who remained had aeroplanes at their disposal. By Thursday evening we were almost the only car on the streets. We spent our days organizing the railway trip. The last news we had received about the railway had been from the aid man who lived in Kuito, but we were not sure that the train could still be running and no one else knew either. On Thursday we managed to arrange with the UN seats on a WFP flight down to Lobito the following Monday. After two months in Angola we were actually going to see the train – running or not.

After visiting the UN we met Jon Hsuan who had just returned from South Africa. He had made a startling change of image. In Cafunfo he always wore shorts, Doc Marten's and short-sleeved shirts. UNITA had taken over his mines and all his workers were being held hostage. He now wore suits and ties and spent his time in consultation with ambassadors, politicians and generals negotiating for the lives of his employees. One of his workers had been killed by Zaïrean looters in the aftermath of the takeover. The rest of them were barricaded into their houses, having had all their radios and vehicles stolen.

UNITA had overrun the whole of Lunda Norte and did not want to let the miners go until they had the company's diamonds. In the centre of Cafunfo, RST had a plant where all their diamonds were sorted and UNITA wanted to get inside. Jon's employees had got the message that it was 'open the safes or die' time, but to do so they had to have four different key holders present at the same time – one of whom had disappeared. They eventually had to open their own safes with oxyacetylene torches so that UNITA could get into the sorting house. Meanwhile, the senior management had rigged up a radio in the pub. They had left a broken radio on full display for UNITA to confiscate, yet hidden behind the dart board in a priest-hole-type cupboard, previously used for storing beer, they had secreted another. It undoubtedly saved their lives.

By using the radio, Jon was able to find out exactly what was happening in Cafunfo, which helped him negotiate for his men's release with UNITA in Luanda. He eventually succeeded in obtaining permission for them to be freed from General Salopeta Pena, who twenty-four hours after giving the order was killed in an ambush. On Friday Jon flew up to Cafunfo in the company Gulf Stream, accompanied by a Hercules belonging to their sister company, TransAfric. They managed to evacuate all 232 staff without further mishap although the plane very nearly crashed on take-off. It was saved only by the skill of the world's most experienced Hercules pilot. It was the most overladen plane he had ever flown but he had to take the risk as leaving people behind was not an option.

By Friday morning the women on the street corners were offering 6300 kwanza to the dollar. This was not a good sign. The streets were empty. The idle rich were still on the beach but the Ilha was the quietest we had ever seen it. No one shouted and music was turned low as though everyone had their ears pricked for the first sound of shelling. Rumours proliferated but the bare facts were alarming enough. The night before, eleven people had been killed at the airport when UNITA had tried to occupy it and had blown up an ammunition dump. Elsewhere in the country there was fighting reported – in Lobito, Benguela, Huambo and Kuito – almost every station of note on the railway. The BBC put out a report that South Africa had invaded and then quickly withdrew it. We filled the car with petrol and headed out to the British Embassy to find out what the latest diplomatic wranglings had come to. We also bought a few crates of beer since it was becoming impossible to negotiate road blocks without them. Gavin and Bob had moved into the embassy and everyone was looking grey and worried.

The British Embassy in Luanda was superb. Headed by John Flynn (who deseves a knighthood), they were always the only people in town who knew what was going on. In constant contact with both sides, they had helped iron out many sticking points in the pre- and post-election chaos. The situation, though, was becoming too tense for even John Flynn to handle. Colonel Bob and Gavin suggested that Harriet and I move into Gavin's house on the Ilha. We lived close to a UNITA house and not far from the UNAVEM headquarters, which would be targets if the tension escalated. We agreed readily and arranged to move in that evening. Waving a cheery see-you-later to the Ghurkas we headed back to the press centre to make some telephone calls, which had suddenly become cheap since they were tied to a two-month-old dollar rate.

We tooled past the Hotel Tourismo and the police station to the press centre on the next corner. We were the only car on the road so it had not been a long drive. UNITA had a machine-gun post facing the police station and the police were staring venomously back across the square. Having parked the car, we nipped upstairs clutching our rucksack full of sandwiches and beer. All the restaurants and markets were closed and so, realizing that things were not as they should be that morning, we had started self-catering. The press centre was on two floors. The ground floor was a bar and conference room. The first had large plate-glass windows which looked down on the street outside, and banks of telephones and telexes.

I called home and said, 'Don't worry. We are perfectly safe, but don't expect to hear from us for a while.'

It was then that the shooting started. We rushed to the window from which we could see a squad of Ninjas advancing down the street towards the Tourismo, which was out of sight behind us, but in front of them. A rocket-propelled grenade bursting against the wall of the house opposite sent them scurrying for the doorways and calling for reinforcements. We were not going to see the railway for some time.

Also at the press centre were two Angolan staff and two American backpackers/freelance journalists called Alex and Matt who, having just left college, had been travelling around Angola for the last few months. These two had decided that Harriet and I were real journalists who did this kind of thing all the time and were gazing at us with awe as we identified weapons and watched the fighting from the relative safety of our eyrie. This was very good for us, since if they hadn't been there we would have been hiding behind the sofas and I would have nothing to write about. The two Angolans were wandering around clutching their heads saying '*mao, mao todo mao*' (bad, everything's bad), over and over again. Harriet and I shared out our avocado sandwiches and beer and we spent the next three hours sitting in chairs facing the window as the battle raged outside.

It was like having a wide-screen television. The Ninjas snaked about outside, zig-zagging from car to car, letting off bursts of machine-gun fire and even bringing up mortars. UNITA retaliated in kind and we watched in wonder as the buildings in front of us gradually disintegrated. The Globo Hotel sign on the corner became Glob Tel, then over the next few hours just el. Long streams of machine-gun fire would shatter the air as the Ninjas fired down the street, then UNITA would retaliate and silence would fall with the dust from the perforated plaster. Slowly, the droning of the television would re-enter our consciousness – a taped UB40 concert. The radio reported that the Tourismo was the source of the only fighting in Luanda and would soon be under control. In the time being, it quite patently wasn't, but the Ninjas were being reinforced. I went downstairs to show the Ninjas where we were and to tell them not to be frightened by our long lenses. One of the reasons that so many cameramen and photographers get killed is that their cameras look like weapons.

The Ninjas were still guarding us. Two of them, armed with a box of RPGs and a heavy machine gun, had set up in the lobby of the press centre and looked very relieved about it as their friends faced the barrage five yards up the street. The alleyway opposite was full of troops and the Nissan Patrols in which they moved around. One of them had bullet holes slashed across one side and two dead in the back. I moved our car a little further down the street. It was uninsured and had been perilously close to the corner.

Every time there was a lull in the fighting we tried to escape but then it would immediately start again. We were going to give Alex and Matt, who were stranded, a lift to their room on the Marginale and the two press-centre staff were going to stay overnight in the basement. We spent the interim making large signs for the jeep saying 'Imprensa [press] – please don't shoot' in several languages. Eventually, we felt able to leave and raced down to the car. The streets were deserted save for police, Ninjas and vigilantes who had been given guns by the MPLA. All along the Marginale, armed groups appeared from behind pillars and waved us through on our funereal progress of the avenue. Having dropped off Alex and Matt we drove to the Meridien Hotel at the end of the Marginale and up the hill towards Kinaxixe and our house. On the way, we did not see a single car or unarmed civilian. It was time to move into Gavin's house.

Elder and Paula were in a terrible panic. They had moved mattresses into the central corridor of the house and Paula and the children were crouched there, terrified. The war had never come to Luanda before and they had harboured what were, with hindsight, pathetic hopes for the elections. Elder was busy making the house secure and we felt like rats leaving a sinking ship.

Having plastered our bright yellow convertible with more press signs, we filled it up with our luggage and drove off into the dusk, as all around us gunfire ripped through the unnatural underlying silence. The fighting which had started at the Tourismo had extended across the entire city. We could now hear gunfire from the direction of the airport and over towards UNITA's headquarters in São Paolo.

We had to cross town to the Ilha but there was fighting in the square so our plan was to skirt round the edge, down to the Marginale which follows the bay, and out on to the island. We circled Kinaxixe and drove slowly down the hill towards the centre of town. The street has tall buildings on either side and another lane on the other side of the pavement for deliveries. Cars had parked all along the sidewalk. The only other vehicle on the street was a white Renault van which we followed in the hopes that it would draw any fire. The next thing we knew, it was reversing past us at high speed and we were being shouted at by an MPLA soldier who had appeared from the gloaming, brandishing an AK47. I tried to reverse back but on the steep hill the car kept on slipping out of gear.

Harriet began to scream abuse at me. 'Don't worry, I used to do this for a living,' I shouted. Bullets started raining down around the car and I became less calm.

A UNITA machine-gun nest on the top of the Tropico Hotel had spotted us and I couldn't get the car into reverse. Finally, I found first and did a U-turn. The bullets were getting closer and time had gone on to slow motion, like it does in a car crash. In a car with a 350cc engine, zigzagging could have put hours on to our journey, so I simply drove straight up the hill. Just as our assailant began to find his aim I spotted a gap in the parked cars and managed to squeeze through on to the pavement and into the lee of the high-rises. Continuing up the sidewalk I had to drive up the steps at the end – like *The Italian Job* in reverse – until we reached the relative safety of Kinaxixe. A change of plan was called for.

We headed for the Meridien where we knew well-protected UN personnel were staying. The Meridien is the only real skyscraper in Luanda, so there was a fine line between whether it was a target or a haven. We presumed it would be the latter, and besides, with night falling as fast as the city, there was nowhere else to go. It took us just over two hours to travel that last mile. On every corner impromptu road blocks had been set up by terrified civilians and policemen. Government forces had been handing out weapons to the *povo* who were backing the police. The MPLA's command structure was so bad that none of the boy soldiers knew what was going on except for what they could see; and by that time they could see tracer, mortar rounds and the beginnings of a fire on the roof of the Tivoli Hotel. We found it difficult to countenance, but they seemed to be even more scared than we were when we appeared out of the gloom at their road blocks. '*Nao, nao,*' they would scream at us, wildly waving their weapons and directing us off in the direction of more fighting. One would let us through and then another would send us back to where we had started and only our knowledge of the back streets saved us from despair.

At last, we arrived on the Marginale and started our slow drive down the front, with the sea to our left and a covered walkway supported by pillars to our right. Since we had dropped off Alex and Matt, the MPLA had handed out more weapons – surly ex-combatants and 'have a go' civilians lurked behind every pillar. A small square within sight of the Meridien was being guarded by a group of teenage policemen who appeared, cowering from their hiding places, and ordered us from the car. Press cards clutched in our sweaty little hands, we slowly unwound ourselves from the jeep on to none-too-steady legs which had now been filled with adrenalin for nearly three hours. Hands in the air, I explained that we were 'Imprensa vamos Meridien', forgetting that all Angolans call the Meridien Hotel the Presidente and *vamos* is what you say in Spanish when you want to go to the *playa*.

It was at this point that the first mortar landed in the square and we all hurled ourselves to the ground. This did not amuse the chief youth who, pointing his rifle at us from his starfish pose in a flowerbed, made us stand up again as the mortar rounds rained down. Ears ringing, Harriet offered him a cigarette, which pleased him although, sensibly, he wouldn't stand up to accept it and didn't want us to get too close. We were eventually allowed to pass having given them all our cigarettes and, just as we thought we were permitted to go, a lighter. Rounding the corner to the Meridien we discovered that they had blocked off the entrance, but once again we managed to inch through a gap between parked cars and catapulted ourselves on to the forecourt. Natural homing instincts directed us to the bar and we were by no means the only pigeons in need of a drink. We had made it, but the doves of peace which had been let loose on election day had been shot dead.

Roosting in the bar was a group of frazzled-looking business-men in unpressed suits who had imagined they could make just one more buck before leaving. Foreign embassies had been advising their nationals to depart the scene for many days and the people left were the real hard core. A few UN people, some oil men, a couple of DSL minders looking after the oil men, and there at the end of the bar was David, an Algerian diamond smuggler from Cafunfo. He and his Namibian girlfriend, Estelle, had flown out of Cafunfo on a Swiss-registered plane leaving all their partners behind. On the same plane, they told us, the UN team had escaped, just when it was going to be needed. UNITA were in full control of Cafunfo and David was trying to hire a plane so he could go back and buy all the diamonds that they had stolen from RST. Unable to leave the hotel for the next three days, he sat in the bar bragging to the other mystery men that he was on top of the deal of the century and telling them that he had made millions out of Cafunfo. Undoubtedly, he was going to make even more money out of it, since he had left all his partners behind to take their chances with UNITA, and would no longer have to share.

Having installed ourselves on the sixteenth floor, in a room with a spectacular view of the city, we sat down and started making calls. The British Embassy were pleased to hear that we were safe. From our hotel we could see right across the city to the embassy on the hill by the fort. Up to the left there was mortar fire landing on the Tropico where we had been turned back. Behind us, on the other side of the building, a battle was raging at Savimbi's house on the Miramar, and in the square below the British Embassy, all hell was breaking loose. Tracer was screaming across the bay and around the city centre like fireworks. Luanda was looking rather festive.

'This is not a civil war. This is serious conflict,' was the embassy's official line. Maybe we had a better view.

We were in a tricky position. The international lines were only working for incoming calls. No one knew we were at the Meridien and we were spending $300 a night of our own money to stay there. It was essential to find someone to pay our expenses. The brilliant Sam Kiley eventually tracked us down and I started filing for *The Times*. The BBC found us and then CNN. There was a problem though. There was a twenty-four-hour curfew so there wasn't much we could say, and it was the weekend of the American presidential elections so there wasn't much anyone wanted us to say. We had been in Angola to take the railway so were not as *au fait* with the political situation as we should have been. We failed miserably at getting permission to leave the hotel and without it we weren't willing to take our chances. All exits to the hotel were guarded and there was a shoot-to-kill policy to enforce the curfew. CNN patched a call through to Harriet's mother who was not worrying about her daughter at all. A friend of mine had called her a few minutes earlier from Sarajevo and told her, 'Miles is the biggest coward I know. Harriet will be fine.'

The Brits signed us up as quasi-honorary consuls and gave us the job of finding all the EC and Commonwealth nationals who wanted to evacuate to Britain. This was an excellent job as it meant we had a legitimate excuse for grilling people and therefore had the combined intelligence of the Meridien's network of guests to keep us up to date. The British Embassy informed us of all the latest diplomatic negotiations and from our hotel window we could actually see what was happening. We went to bed that evening having filed for *The Times*, CNN and the BBC. No one would pay our expenses but we were at least breaking even if you didn't include the lobster that we had for supper.

In the morning, evacuation was the word on everybody's lips. The Love Boat was all steamed up and ready to take people out. The Portuguese, French and British were all planning evacuation flights and residents of the Meridien were desperately negotiating to get on flights to places they wanted to go. During the night, the radio and television mast had been blown up which started rumours that UNITA had won. Taking over the news media is always a key event in any coup. It was in fact a last gesture before their total destruction in Luanda but it didn't seem that way then. In the course of those three days UNITA was totally wiped out in the capital.

A middle-aged Portuguese man kept on pulling me to one side in the bar and filling me with information he claimed to have received from the Portuguese Ministry of Defence. 'UNITA have taken over Lobito and Benguela and are advancing on Luanda,' he would tell me, begging me not to betray my sources.

I was never able to confirm any of his stories and in many cases my information contradicted his. I never deduced who he worked for and what he was trying to achieve, but he disappeared mysteriously and didn't leave on any of the normal evacuation flights.

The hotel carried on working as normal throughout the curfew. Freezers full of food were depleted but there was always smoked salmon on the table and CNN and the movie channel in our room. We spent much of our days staring out of the window trying to work out who was winning. The fighting went on and on as UNITA, pinned down in their bases, were pounced on by the Ninjas. RPGs and mortars were tearing into Savimbi's house on the Miramar which was above and behind the hotel. With a long lens we could just make out little blue figures scurrying around on the hill below it. Attack helicopters darted over the city, looking terrifying but doing nothing. On Saturday the government claimed to have retaken the Tropico in the Battle of the Hotels but loud bangs and flames from that vicinity tended to discount this.

Three unarmed men were executed on the Marginale outside the bar in full view of half the hotel's guests. In scenes reminiscent of a whale cull, they were kicked down into the water and shot by the soldiers who were guarding the lobby. Blood stained the sea as their bodies jigged with the force of the bullets, driven deep into the water only to resurface explosively like freed buoys. The corpses floated around in an eddy below the bar for two more days.

Two British citizens, David and Eleanor Chambers, had been kidnapped by UNITA and the embassy was trying to extricate them. The American chargé and his staff were pinned down in their embassy which was a few doors down from Savimbi's house on the Miramar. In the meantime we were stuck in the hotel and becoming rather frustrated. Harriet got rather keen at one point and tried to leave, but was thankfully repulsed by the guards at the hotel's back entrance. Since it was they who had performed the execution she obeyed. Aidan Sullivan, the picture editor of the *Sunday Times*, had told her that he would never employ her again if he saw any of her pictures from Luanda. On the eve of the US elections it was not worth the risk – no one would care and no one would buy them.

Gavin called us at one on Monday morning to say that a ceasefire had been agreed and that any fighting still going on was just a communication problem. The British, the only people whose radio net was working effectively, had been deep in meetings and negotiations with Anstee, Savimbi and dos Santos. They had arranged the release of David and Eleanor Chambers and were trying to get the American Consulate's staff out of Savimbi's back yard. Margaret Anstee was in the British Embassy throughout the fighting and so all negotiations were administered through the Brits.

Later on CNN woke us up and Harriet was able to do a wonderful live broadcast. Having told the news desk about the ceasefire, she was put on hold until it was time to be interviewed. We watched the screen as Bobbie put together the link which went roughly like this:

BOBBIE: Here's Harriet Logan from the *Sunday Times* live in Luanda. We hear there is a ceasefire in Angola. Can you tell us a bit about that, Harriet?
[*Alarum within as mortar hits next-door building and heavy machine-gun fire rains down from stage left*]
HARRIET [*from floor*]: I think it's fair to say, Bobbie, that the ceasefire hasn't worked.

As Monday morning progressed, the noise from outside grew gradually quieter until at about lunchtime all hell broke out again. From our sixteenth-floor vantage point we could see two tanks and some APCs moving along the Miramar and spraying the surrounding streets with covering fire. They drove along the Miramar, down the hill from Kinaxixe and on to the roundabout behind the hotel. We then lost sight of them until they arrived on the Marginale. Crouching inside the APCs, which were open from above, we could see groups of whites sitting on the floor. Thinking they must be hostages, we raced down the sixteen floors to try to get photographs and interviews. The lifts were not terribly reliable so we took the stairs on which I very nearly knocked over an MPLA guard. He must have thought he was under attack as we thundered down towards him. We arrived in the lobby just in time to see the fleet arrive in the square between the port and the Meridien.

Out of the APCs jumped the entire staff of the American Consulate, looking rather frayed at the edges. Despite having truck-loads of communications equipment – satellite dishes, radios and telephones – it had once again taken the intercession of the British Embassy to get them out. They had destroyed all their equipment when they thought they were about to be overrun and had relied on one hand-held British radio from that point on. From the toilets of the American Embassy where they were hiding, they were patched through to the British Embassy, to Brussels NATO military command, to George Bush himself. On his last day of office, when he was ordering military strikes on Iraq and sending the marines into Somalia, Bush also had an entire rapid deployment force of 2,500 men on standby to invade Angola. In retrospect, Bush's resignation speech was extraordinarily self-composed considering the pressure he was under.

Mary Speers, the perky US press spokesperson, described how they had been pinned down in their compound throughout the worst of the fighting and had suffered 'three days of terror'. Mortar shells had landed on the embassy and constant small-arms fire had kept them crawling around on the floor for the duration. They set up an office on the top floor of the hotel, from where they released a statement to the press – me – saying, 'We owe our lives to the discipline shown by both UNITA and the Ninjas.' America's perfidious interference in Angola's internal politics had once again caused them problems and they didn't know what to say, so they thanked everybody and evacuated as soon as possible. RIP new world order.

On Monday night it was announced that the curfew would be lifted from twenty-four to twelve hours, so bright and early on Tuesday morning we were out on the streets in our still well-marked jeep. Not many other people were taking advantage of this new-found freedom so we were able to fly around the eerily quiet streets examining the destruction. Corpses were the only obstructions to traffic flow. First stop was the Hotel Tourismo where we had witnessed it all starting. Molten heaps of metal outside indicated where UNITA had parked their GMC wagons. All over the town these cars were still smouldering where they had been left – American taxpayers' money going up in smoke.

The Tourismo was a shadow of its former self. Not a window remained intact and the road outside was littered with UNITA flags. Where the UNITA banners had flown, they had been replaced with triumphant MPLA flags which now adorned the wreckage of the hotel. Opposite, the police station's pale blue plaster was freckled with white holes but it was clear who had won. The water tanks in the Tourismo had been burst and a steady stream of water was pouring down from the broken first-floor windows. The MPLA soldiers guarding the remains agreed to give us a tour after a few cans of beer and much 'boy, you really showed them' had been shared out.

The building stank of death but all the bodies had been removed. Half-finished meals were still in the rooms and bits of blood-stained uniform were lying all around among the empty bullet casings and UNITA propaganda. It was easy to see where the main fighting had gone on. In one room facing the street, empty boxes of large-calibre machine-gun bullets were stacked neatly against the back wall. The front wall had ceased to exist – victim to a well-placed RPG. After a perusal of the damage we set off to look at Savimbi's house. As we drove past the press centre we almost ran over Rafael who had spent the entire weekend stuck in his office – in between the press centre and the Tourismo. He looked his cheerful normal self, despite the fact he had spent the last three days at the epicentre of the battle. Being Angolan does great things for your *sang-froid*. Within seconds Rafael was in the car and giving us a guided tour of the ruins.

With his *Jornal de Angola* credentials we saved a fortune in beer as we toured the destruction. São Paolo, where UNITA had its headquarters, was devastated. Vigilantes at road blocks tried to bar the way but were no match for Rafael's persistence and our bribery. You could smell the UNITA HQ from a couple of blocks away. Piles of charred and still-burning bodies lay outside in the street attracting flies and dogs. Blood-stained UNITA membership cards littered the floor of the offices and round every corner was another corpse. UNITA had held out till the bitter end and the siege had been finished only by hand-to-hand combat. The rest of the town was the same. Everywhere there were the forlorn and friendless shoes which always adorn sites of recent and sudden death. Wherever UNITA had been, strong, precise attacks from the Ninjas had cut out the cancer. A UNITA flat in the square below the British Embassy had been clinically removed. The neighbouring buildings in the square were untouched but the UNITA flat on the top floor had been amputated from the top of the house. Tiles from the roof were scattered all over the square and the window frames, where expertly aimed RPGs had entered, stood out like black holes from the façade.

Savimbi's house on the Miramar was the main focus for rejoicing. It was very difficult to get to since the TV transmitter had fallen on to three houses and blocked the street. Road blocks and unexploded ordnance prohibited entry from other angles. By the side of a parallel street was a car with four bodies inside. It had been crushed, almost beyond recognition, by a tank. We eventually walked through to where the Ninjas were showing off their booty. A line of civilians carrying chandeliers, lampshades and tins of food guided us to the spot where the Ninjas were encouraging people to loot. A squad which had led the attack on the house showed us Savimbi's cane which they were proudly displaying to all and sundry, and allowed us to enter.

Inside the elegant hall, blood-spattered shepherd boys, depicted on blue and white Portuguese tiles, looked on the devastation at their feet. There was blood all over the place and much UNITA memorabilia. Place cards from pre-election dinner parties were strewn around the dining room, where as we entered looters were trying to remove the table. Sheets of UNITA writing paper blew around in the wind created by the implosion of a couple of strategic walls. As we left, we discovered a baggage label belonging to Noe Balthazar who had lent the house to Savimbi. He no longer had a house with which to curry favour. Total victory had gone to the MPLA and they were showing their magnanimity by treating two UNITA prisoners surprisingly well. These two had been left behind, manning a machine-gun post, when their generals tried to run away and were now sitting under guard outside Savimbi's house looking very relaxed. Once again the soldiers were making friends but the politicians were causing problems.

Having dropped off Rafael we drove on through the creepily still streets to the British Embassy. Positioned next to an MPLA barracks and not far from the Tourismo, the embassy had been in the thick of the fighting yet you would never have known. The Brits were being British and it was quite a relief. Gavin had run out of real cigarettes so our popularity soared when we arrived laden down with Marlboro. We had filed for that day and had already written about the Chambers' miraculous escape, so were able to be sensitive when we bumped into their bandaged and fragile figures in the bowels of the embassy. They were having none of it, however, and needed to exorcise the horrors of their ordeal. They told us the whole story over lunch in graphic detail.

While tucking into a large fish that the embassy had found somewhere, David explained that he had an agreement with his neighbours – the Swedish Embassy – that he and Eleanor could jump over the fence if they ever had problems. Eleanor sat next to him looking shell-shocked with her arm in a sling. David continued, explaining that they had subsequently hidden in the garden for hours – the Swedes having removed themselves much earlier – while the MPLA and the UNITA had fought it out. Late in the night four men came to the garden gate claiming to be the police. 'You must let us escort you away from here. It is not safe,' they said. David opened the door to find that he had been captured by UNITA. They were taken to Savimbi's house and locked in a room.

'The house was under attack all night,' he said. 'An RPG hit the wall of the room we were being kept in.'

They were being treated well but during the night a UNITA commander wanted to interview Eleanor on her own, and David was bluntly told that if he did not allow this she would be killed. Two Bulgarians had also been kidnapped but were being kept in a separate room. The next morning General Salopeta Pena, Savimbi's nephew, entered the room and told them they were about to be taken to somewhere safer.

'We were put into a car in the drive of Savimbi's house with Salopeta Pena and Chivukuvuku' (UNITA's foreign affairs spokesman).

Some UNITA troops, realizing that their generals were trying to escape, crammed into other cars and the well-packed convoy of three vehicles flew out of the gates – straight into an ambush. The entire length of the Miramar was lined with police as they hurled along it – all shooting into the cars. Their driver persevered but was finally killed a mile or so later. Eleanor and David were saved only by the fact that everyone around them had been killed. The corpses provided cushioning and potection from bullets and bumps when they left the road and hurtled over a cliff at eighty miles an hour. Eleanor had her wrist broken in the crash and David had half his ear ripped off. 'When we crawled out of the car, the MPLA vigilantes thought we were UNITA supporters and carried on firing at us,' elaborated David.

They were eventually taken to a police station where they had to be protected from the mob. Twelve hours later they were taken to the military hospital for treatment. An APC arrived to take them there. Three captured UNITA soldiers had been stripped and tied to the roof. As they toured the streets, vigilantes were invited to shoot at the men on the roof. 'We arrived at the hospital to find them full of holes but still alive. I don't know what happened to them.'

David and Eleanor were then kept at the charnel house/military hospital for another day – denied permission to contact anyone. David managed to make a phone call alerting his business partner to where they were but was severely told off when caught. An Angolan television crew saw them in the hospital but refused to believe them when they said they were being held hostage. They were discovered by David's partner and taken to the British Embassy – frazzled but miraculously alive. They and the now crippled Chivukuvuku were the only people from the cars who had lived and they were able to provide confirmation that almost the entire UNITA command structure in Luanda had been wiped out. Salopeta Pena – the man who gave the order to allow RST to leave Cafunfo – had been UNITA's chief negotiator. Savimbi had a point when he refused to negotiate after this – look what the MPLA had done to his last negotiating team.

Gavin said that we could move into his house as originally intended and gave us boxes of army rations to keep us going. The embassy were seeing the lull as a window of opportunity in which to evacuate and were not taking any chances. The fighting continued in the rest of the country and if it started again in Luanda, the Meridien would be a natural target. We had paid already so spent a last night at the Meridien where our fellow guests were all preparing to leave the next day. The British, the Americans, the French and the Portuguese all had planned evacuations.

Early the next morning, after being reprimanded for stealing croissants at breakfast, we followed the American contingent to the airport. Theirs was to be the first flight out. They had recovered their bulletproof jeeps and arranged an escort from the MPLA. Promptly at nine, the American party sped off to the airport led by an MPLA patrol with its lights flashing and siren blaring. Incongruously, all the American vehicles looked like they had been borrowed from UNITA. The US had provided UNITA with the same vehicles they used for diplomatic protection so to interested onlookers it appeared as though a UNITA delegation was being escorted to the airport. We brought up the rear in our tired little jeep which had great difficulty keeping up with the others. A police vehicle raced up and down the side of the convoy, checking at junctions and then returning like a dedicated sheepdog to chivvy us along at the rear. We arrived in a fanfare of sirens at the airport to discover that the American plane had not yet landed.

The Brits were there already. The British evacuees had been

told to meet in the car park at 7 a.m. and to bring a packed lunch. They had. By the windows of the departure lounge were drawn up three Land Rovers, one of which had a sign saying RAF Brize Norton hanging on the door handle. Gavin was seated at a portable desk ticking off names and making sure everything went to plan. He was letting the side down a little, dressed as he was in a pair of shorts and a T-shirt with a duck on the front and the words 'not playing with a full duck' on the back. Bob, of course, was resplendent in immaculate white ducks and a Turnbull and Asser pinstriped shirt. Unable to go home and change during the fighting they had been stuck in the embassy with no change of clothes. Bob had stood up well to this, Gavin had not. Diplomatic sources tell me that Margaret Anstee looked very charming in John Flynn's gardening outfit.

The Americans left with much ado on a plane with the same markings as the one Savimbi had been using. 'We are leaving with great ambivalence,' said Mary Speers. 'There's work to be done here. We'd like to help this country go forward to a peaceful future. We have left nine people here to help them find a peaceful process.'

She and the other Americans were waved off by the skeleton staff that remained at the consulate. This staff consisted of some very obvious CIA men and a rather lost-looking chargé. The new embassy was on the top floor of the Meridien (except it wasn't really an embassy since they still didn't recognize the government). As they left, a fleet of Renault baker's vans appeared carrying the French contingent, and their dogs and tennis racquets. They appeared to be going on holiday.

With an opportunity ahead to get film out on the evacuation flights, we went off to see how the hospitals were bearing up and what was being done with the bodies. Rotting bodies of looters had been left in the streets as an example, but we had seen very few military corpses. They were all being taken away in secret. We headed for the main civilian hospital – the beautiful pink stucco Rosina Machel. Our noses soon guided us to the al fresco morgue that had been set up in the car park around the back. Piles of civilian cadavers wearing UNITA T-shirts were festering in the sun by a chain-link fence. No one was going to come and claim these bodies for fear of being associated with the enemy. So while the non-UNITA supporters' bodies had already been reclaimed by their families, these remained as another grim example of how in Angola your dress sense could be your downfall. As far as we could see, anyone wearing the wrong T-shirt had been shot. The few people venturing out had become dedicated followers of fashion. A vote-dos-Santos T-shirt was not only *de rigueur*, it was also a life preserver.

Back at the airport, the French were just leaving – by Hercules – and the Portuguese were soon to follow suit. The French had followed racial steroeotypes to the last. Their pilot had been a very sexy girl wearing Vuarnet sunglasses and a skintight flying suit and they were flying to Pointe Noire, the legendary mercenary base in the Congo. The Brits were still in the car park, settling down with their sandwiches. Harriet packaged up her film and gave it to someone going back to London and we sat down to await their departure.

Ther was nothing else we could do in Angola and we had decided to leave too, as soon as we could. We were in negotiation with TransAfric to get on one of their evacuation flights to São Tomé. A freight airline that specializes in delivering to war zones, they had millions of dollars' worth of stores in Luanda and had decided to remove them to their base in São Tomé in case of any more fighting. No one would be flying down to Lobito for a while as it was under siege. Everywhere else along the line was in a similar state – Benguela, Huambo and Kuito – so we decided it would be best to go to Zaïre and start the railway journey from there. We could come back to Angola if things ever calmed down.

By now everybody had moved through to the unmanned departure hall and was waiting for the arrival of the plane. George, an Angolan who worked for the British Embassy, was busy mastering the controls of a truck with stairs on the back so that people would be able to board the plane.

This was Bob's big moment. 'I've always wanted to guide in a plane,' he said as he marched to the centre of the apron.

A shining white RAF Tristar landed on the runway and taxied towards Bob's immaculate figure. George drove the steps over to the plane and in perfect synchronicity the powder-blue ambassadorial Jaguar pulled up to the bottom of the steps. Gavin drove up to receive a suspiciously large trailer load of 'emergency rations' and the SAS team who had arrived to protect the embassy discreetly exited the plane and the airport before anyone boarded. We were not meant to have seen them. Everything worked perfectly. We may no longer have an empire but we sure know how to evacuate. The British, who had one piece of carry-on luggage each as requested, queued in an orderly fashion and flew off back to England. We suddenly felt very lonely.

We returned to the embassy where Gavin had come over all shifty. We had to own up to the fact that we knew the SAS had arrived and weren't going to tell anyone. Gavin, discreet as ever, just ignored us and carried on with his work. The large, fit-looking figures whom we kept bumping into in the corridors were never mentioned again. We moved into Gavin's house and spent the curfew watching videos of *Wall Street* and *The Blues Brothers*. The next day we were going to leave whether any journalists had arrived or not. Hacks were still trying to organize cowboy flights into Luanda but we could not afford to wait for them. International interest in the story had returned to zero and we had a railway to find.

The next morning found us camped out at TransAfric's office – an air-conditioned container – at the airport. If we went to São Tomé we could go from there to Gabon where we would be able to get Zaïrean visas and fly on to Zaïre. TransAfric was a hive of activity but we couldn't get on a flight until the next day so we went to see our friend Dennis at the UNAVEM hangar. Maybe he would have a plane heading our way. Dennis was a Canadian major in charge of flight coordination for the UN. One of his men had malaria and another had broken his arm. He had to organize the entire UN's evacuation with only half his normal staff and was beginning to show the strain. He was sitting at a table in his office/bedroom playing with a bullet. 'War is no fun. I've had too many of these babies inside me to think that,' he told us morosely.

Dennis, in common with many other Canadian soldiers, had led an eventful life in the army. In the absence of anything else for them to do, the Canadian government sends its soldiers to every hell hole on earth to participate in peace-keeping missions. Dennis had been to them all and had an impressive collection of T-shirts to prove it. One of his more unfortunate staff was a Nigerian major who was stuck in the middle of the Angolan civil war and had only two other options. If he wanted to leave Angola he could go peace keeping in Somalia or Liberia. He was staying put. The UN were not flying anywhere of use to us, so we decided to go and say goodbye at the embassy. On the way out of the airport we bumped into Piementel Arujo, one of the men who flew up to Cafunfo. We asked him what all the smoke was up to the north of the city.

'Oh, they're frightened of cholera,' he said, 'so they're burning all the bodies. I think this is good.' Resigned, we decided we had better go and see what was going on.

We followed the smoke to its source – a military base on the outskirts. No amount of beer would allow us into the compound but they had a hell of a fire blazing inside. We could see two enormous bonfies – bodies, tyres, bodies, tyres. A siren distracted our attention and a Red Cross ambulance drove past – in its wake a huge lorry overflowing with corpses. It was a large sand truck with a swinging tailgate through which parts of people's bodies were sticking out. It gave the impression of indicating right since the arm of one of the corpses close to the cab was hanging stiffly over the side. The smell was appalling – people were vomiting by the side of the road as we passed through the slums. Harriet and I drank beer and chain-smoked while breathing only through our mouths as we followed the abominable convoy.

We drove on and on out of the city until we reached the bush and set off down a track which led through endless mounds of mass graves. When we arrived at a gap in between graves, we discovered a contingent of masked Red Cross workers gathered round a front-end loader. We photographed as the truck unloaded its contents. Since it was a sand truck, the driver had to upend the trailer then race forward jerking to a halt so the bodies would unblock the tail gate. Torn corpses slithered on the greasy floor of the trailer. The JCB pushed the bodies into a pit where angry flies fought for positions and buzzed up in a furious swarm as fresh food came their way. The workers choked back their vomit as they continued their grisly task and Harriet and I stumbled around taking photographs.* It took a long time to wash off the smell.

Goodbyes at the embassy were sad and prolonged. The British Embassy in Luanda had been a shining example of the genre. Active, well-briefed diplomats had kept control of what could have been a disastrous situation. Without the British Embassy in Luanda, the United States would have had to send in troops to Angola to protect their diplomats from a rebel force which they had been covertly supplying. Although it would have taught the Americans a lesson, it would have been expensive in both lives and dollars. The United States should be deeply indebted to the British Foreign Office. On a more personal level, we also had benefited enormously. Knowing that the embassy was there gave us a great sense of security during a week of great insecurity. As we left Andy Henderson gave us a card, having scrawled on the

* The photographs were never published. War has been sanitized – computer graphics and human-interest stories are what the public is given. The truth is censored by the breakfast test. If a photograph cannot be faced over bacon and eggs, it doesn't get published, so the public is conditioned into thinking of war as more glamorous and exciting than harrowing.

back, 'Please take care of these refugees from Angola.' It later came in very handy.

By two o'clock the following afternoon we were in a packed Hercules en route to São Tomé. Sharing our accommodation were two spare engines for the plane, various parts and a party of schoolchildren who were Santomean dependants of TransAfric workers. These black equivalents of Saint Trinian's students raced around the plane jumping over engines and pushing against emergency exits for the entire flight, but nothing could cloud our satisfaction. Lying in an engine cradle in the back of the plane, Harriet and I considered what other job could be so interesting. In the last couple of months we had been at the centre of a multi-million-dollar smuggling operation, we had witnessed the beginning of a civil war and we had interviewed fascinating people, who in other circumstances we would never have been able to meet. It was like being Tintin. By seven o'clock that evening we were sipping Mai Tais on a powder-sand beach while the waves lapped around our feet. We still hadn't found the railway but it was going to have to wait a while.

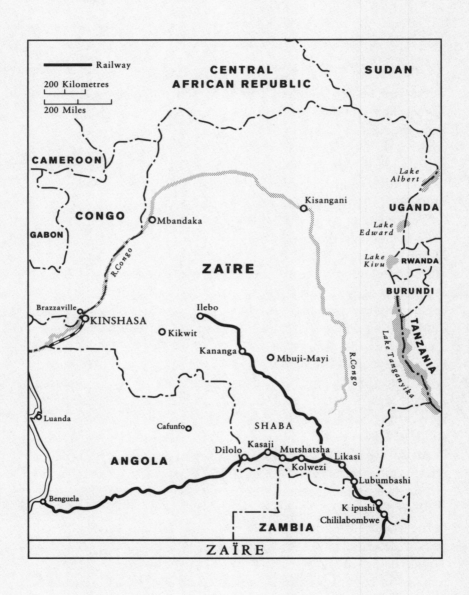

ZAÏRE

There can be few better places to which to evacuate than São Tomé. The fact that we had just flown to a point 2,000 miles from the railway didn't bother us too much. We reckoned that we could start the journey in the middle and work our way to the edges when it was possible. In the time being, São Tomé seemed like an interesting place to visit. Not many people have even heard of it.

We landed on a Hong Kong-style runway in the sea and stepped from the industrial bowels of the aircraft into bright sunshine. Jon Hsuan was there to meet us, standing with the grandparents of the schoolchildren. The spotless airport was vibrating with sound as the girls of Saint Trinian's became over-excited and the massive engines of the Hercules wound down. Jon hurled us through immigration, where we had to register as refugees, and through to the front of the airport. We sat down at the same time as the Hercules engines were turned off. Immediately a noisy silence descended. Insects and birds chirruped and squawked against a background of total quiet which you seldom experience in the west – no buzzing of electric wires, no motorway noise – just stillness. It was the first time we had heard it since we had arrived in Africa, two months earlier, and it had an immediate therapeutic effect. Unconcerned by the absence of a car to take us from the airport, we slipped straight into the rhythm of the island and sat.

From the airport's empty car park you could see the high peaks of the island – dressed in ruffs of cloud, a perfect white beach that lines a deserted bay and the brazenly picturesque town of São Tomé. In an overgrown field by the airport stood the rotting remains of some CanadAid Constellations that had been used to transport food to the starving of Biafra thirty years earlier.

Perched on the headland is the perfectly preserved fort that used to house the Portuguese governor. São Tomé is littered with the remains of ancient civilizations which betray its past as a pivotal economy. It is now slowly and peacefully returning to bush.

It has had as extraordinary a history as Angola. In the sixteenth century it was the world's biggest sugar producer and a vital sorting point for slaves. The mainland slaving capital Ouidah (of Viceroy fame) was an enclave of and used to be administered from São Tomé until 1961. The islands faded into obscurity when the West Indies took over sugar production and then in the nineteeth century returned to the world stage as an important coffee producer. Now its 120,000 citizens are among the world's poorest people and produce virtually nothing. High up in the mountains, clapboard plantation houses crumble. They look down on disorderly ranks of coffee bushes that are being pushed back by the counterattacking rainforest.

The volcanic islands of São Tomé and neighbouring Principe, which together form a country, were founded in the 1470s but were not exploited immediately. The mountains are uncommonly tall for the small area of land which they crown. This gives the islands a mad but pleasant climate, where one bay will be bathed in sunshine while the next one is being soaked with fresh warm rain. They can be humid and wet yet they can also be blisteringly hot. Subject to extreme micro-climates, none of the weather lasts for very long.

All the miners from Cafunfo had been evacuated to São Tomé, where their sister company TransAfric is based, so two weeks after our final farewells in Angola we met up again. They looked absurd. Many of them had been forced to strip before being allowed to leave Cafunfo and none of them had been able to take with them more than what they were wearing. So, all around the island, enormous miners were to be found wearing identical Hawaiian shirts and shorts. These were the only clothes they had been able to find in the country, except for MPLA and UNITA T-shirts. The Santomean government – which has close links with

Angola through their shared Portuguese heritage – had bought up hundreds of T-shirts from both sides. They handed out the MPLA shirts at the official party when the results were announced, and now the UNITA ones were gradually appearing in the market. Wearing a UNITA T-shirt in Angola by that time had become tantamount to committing suicide. In São Tomé, it was neither a fashion nor a political statement, merely something to wear.

We spent two weeks living it up in São Tomé, flying around in helicopters and private planes, visiting the only resort on the islands – also owned by RST's mother company – and making plans to go to Zaïre. São Tomé is so tiny that it was once fined by FIFA for not sending a team to a World Cup qualifying match. The government refused to pay the fine since no one had told them they were meant to and, anyway, they had neither a football team nor a pitch. Ambassadors ride mopeds in São Tomé, and their accessibility meant that getting visas for Gabon (the only access point to mainland Africa) was not a problem. Leaving paradise, however, was.

Arriving in Libreville brought us down to earth with a sickening jolt. X-ray and baggage-weighing machines adorned the hi-tech airport which could have been a satellite of Paris's Charles de Gaulle. In the bank at the airport they had a swipe machine which refused my credit card, leaving us penniless in the third most expensive city in the world. The *Sunday Times Magazine* had not paid back our expenses, which caused us problems for the rest of the trip. Instead of having thousands of dollars in cash with which to oil our way round Africa, we were left with a bouncing credit card and a British cheque book. In every country our first challenge became persuading someone to cash a cheque for us.

We checked into a sordid hotel on the beach – the cheapest we could find at $150 a night – and set off to find some cash. Gabon – a former French colony – has an economy based on oil. It is peaceful and allows foreign companies to exploit its resources with little government interference in return for a share of the cake. This has led to a situation where shops in Gabon look the same as French supermarkets – except for the prices, which are astronomical. You can get foie gras, smoked salmon and vintage champagne with ease, but it's best to organize a mortgage beforehand. Harriet and I could not afford to eat in the doubtless excellent restaurants so decided to have a meagre picnic – it cost us $70. During the four days in Gabon we spent the majority of our time drinking bottled water at $8 a go on the beach. Having bought Zaïrean visas on our first day, it was the cheapest place to sit and wait for the plane.

Our Swissair flight took off from Libreville in the middle of the night. All boarding passengers were searched by the airline's own security staff on the steps of the aircraft, but having passed that test were treated like royalty. Our Air Gabon flight had not turned up and we had managed to get on to Swissair at the last minute. Delicious food was served, champagne, current newspapers and magazines. Smiling stewardesses attended to our every need as we watched soothing cartoons and settled back into the first world.

Kinshasa came as a brutal shock. We were later informed that it is somewhat reckless to arrive in Kinshasa without arranging for someone to meet you at the airport. Arriving at three o'clock in the morning, we were told, with no *protocol* is bordering on insanity. There were about ten other people disembarking at Kinshasa and they were all pounced on by *protocols* at the plane's steps. *Protocol* is the name given to the foot soldiers of corruption who are paid by companies and embassies to do the bribing at the airports, banks and at all points where the west has to meet Zaïre. They are the torch bearers in the heart of darkness.

Luckily we had our own torches since the airport was in almost total darkness. Occasional gun battles over the years combined with endemic theft had left the airport unlit. There was still electricity but officials carried their own lamps which they moved from plug to plug as they hurried from counter to office to luggage carousel. As we stumbled into the arrivals hall our passports were taken away by an official and Harriet and I split up. I followed the passports, she followed the luggage. We were travelling on tourist visas and it was important that our baggage – which betrayed our professions – was not examined too closely. Journalists are not welcomed in Zaïre.

The airport, whose tall ceilings were pock-marked with bullet holes and whose floor was a mass of rubbish and broken glass, was bustling with people. Taxi drivers, wasters, soldiers, policemen, porters and airport staff all vied for the privilege of stealing our luggage. Unless we paid someone we were never going to see it again. I employed a taxi driver, a policeman and an immigration man to ease our way through the formalities. By this time I had lost all track of our passports and was taken off by our immigration man to a dark office where I had to declare my wealth and my intentions, fill out a long form and pay a negotiable adminstrative charge to ensure the passports' return. Frozen in my torchlight were three fierce-looking Austrian ladies travelling on Red Cross passports. Dressed in Birkenstock sandals and Indian fabric dresses surmounted by ostentatious crucifixes, they argued with their *protocol*.

'We are here to help your country, not to pay bribes,' said the moustachioed leader of the team. 'We have worked all over the world and never paid bribes.'

'Then you will never leave the airport.'

I paid up and left them in the dark.

The next step was to reclaim our luggage. We had carried on as much as we could but two rucksacks had been put in the hold. Through the black rubber curtains at the back of the static carousel, a fight could be heard. Our team policeman grabbed me by the arm and pulled me through. About twenty people were throwing luggage around in the dark, searching and fighting for the bags which they had been paid to receive. I sat on the sidelines, tracking our cases with the torch. The policeman followed the beam of light and disappeared. After ten minutes he returned, beaming and clutching our bags. He had entered the mêlée as a rather tatty-looking policeman; he left it looking like a survivor from a plane-crash – disorientated but triumphant.

Harriet was still sitting where I had left her. She was far from forlorn. Sat atop our pile of camera bags and rucksacks, she was listening to her Walkman and snarling at anyone who tried to hassle her. I had to change some money to do the next lot of bribery and was marched off to the remains of the airport restaurant where the bar was being used as a bank counter. Illegal money-changers sat on one side with great cases of cash and I and my entourage stood on the other. I swapped a hundred-dollar bill for a plastic bag full of neat blocks of zaïres (I was ripped off, I should have had two) and set off to customs. An enormous Zaïrean stood behind a desk with dollar signs tattooed on his eyeballs.

'You'll have to pay this man,' said my immigration officer, as he heaved our luggage on to the desk, 'otherwise he'll search your bag and steal things.'

It is a rather disconcerting Zaïrean trait for bare-faced thieves to accuse other swindlers of treachery. I tried a new technique.

'We are refugees from Angola,' I said.

'Oh, my brother is in Luanda. We have heard nothing. Do you know what has happened to the Zaïreans?'

'He's probably at the embassy. There are hundreds of Zaïreans there. Don't worry. The phones aren't working, so he wouldn't be able to contact you anyway.'

Pleased with this news, he didn't even look at our bags. Now all we had to do was get into town. I felt as though I had succeeded in taking on Zaïre and winning. I knew that Zaïreans were about as popular in Luanda as UNITA and that their embassy's compound was full of stranded smugglers. The ambassador had charged them all $75 to register for evacuation and then disappeared with the cash.

We descended the steps to the dark and empty car park where our jalopy awaited us. Another policeman stopped us on the steps for a bribe and I carelessly gave him a bundle of zaïres. I was getting cocky. I paid the others off at the car and Harriet, the driver, his *petit* (a small but none the less fifty-year-old man) and

I jumped in. We had survived the airport and it had only cost $100. We were then surrounded by six angry soldiers led by a captain. His combat trousers were held up by some string and a mountaineering clip. In the centre of the clip hung an enormous pistol, crooked in his right elbow was a skeleton-butt AK47. The pistol was the largest I had ever seen and was called a Desert Eagle. When I returned to England I discovered that it is the most fashionable gun in New York. Made by the Israelis, they fire bullets normally reserved for heavy machine guns and are mighty expensive. Arnold Schwarzenegger uses one in *Last Action Hero* and I still cannot understand where our captain had found his.

'You are the people responsible for corrupting this country. Why did you give that policeman money? How can we mend the economy if you westerners bribe people? Get out of the car and open the boot,' he shouted, toying with his enormous weapon.

I looked for help to our driver who just waved me on – apparently as terrified as I was. I got out and begged. I speak gutter Parisian French badly but well enough to plead forgiveness. Surrounded, as I was, by six well-armed men in a dark and deserted car park, I think the adrenalin would have inspired me to speak Sanskrit had it been necessary. After a tense ten minutes we were allowed to leave but just as we were, one of the soldiers jumped into the front seat and sat on top of the *petit*. Our driver started to circle the car park. Dark, indeterminate yet menacing shapes loitered round fires on the edge of the area.

'Give me money,' said the soldier to me.

'But your boss has just told me that I will be sent to jail if I do.'

'Give me money,' said the soldier.

'Give him money,' said the driver, the *petit* and Harriet.

I did, and the driver drove straight back to the officer in charge. Harriet and I exchanged, 'Well, it's been great working with you' looks and the car stopped. The soldier got out, shared the money and we drove into Kinshasa. The entire episode had been no more than psychological torture. We longed for Swissair.

So unnerved were we by our arrival that we re-routed to the

Intercontinental, where the night manager helped the taxi driver to rip us off and then checked us into a $260-a-night room with no water.

Down in the south of the country lay the railway for which we had been searching. Lubumbashi, the heart of Zaïre's copper belt, was our immediate goal. From there, the railway runs east to the Angolan border and south to Zambia. After months on the road, we were at last in the same country as a functioning railway. Zaïre had been Pauling's first goal when building it. Right at the centre of Africa, Zaïre had been unable to yield its riches to the hungry west before the advent of the trains. The new fashions for cars, electricity and plumbing in the early twentieth century meant that there was an insatiable demand for Zaïre's copper, which was then swiftly transformed into piping and wire before being sold at huge profit for the Belgians and the railway builders. They also made a fortune from the rubber plantations which fed the hungry motor industry.

Zaïre has had an unhappy life. It is only a little smaller than India, yet King Leopold of Belgium used to own it. It was not a Belgian colony, but the king's private property. In 1884 Leopold set up a trading company under the guise of a philanthropic mission headed by Henry Morton Stanley – a journalist with even fewer morals than is normally expected. Leopold spent twenty-three years raping the Zaïrean interior. He administered it so inhumanely that the Belgian government was forced by the world community to relieve him of his personal fiefdom and take it over as a colony in 1908. The region was then run almost as ineptly and unjustly by them and handed over at independence to a new government which was totally unprepared for it. No African had held rank higher than sergeant major in the colonial army and civil servants had been subject to a similar system. The fact that Zaïre had not been allowed to develop past this stage by the colonial government meant that a non-commissioned officer, Joseph Desiré Mobutu, was, within a year of independence, governing the country by decree, with the wholehearted support of Belgium and the CIA. Since 1960 he has either held power or allowed others to hold it for him while personally retaining control of the army.

Mobutu is the personification of every horror story you have heard about African dictators. A policy of Africanization led to his name change. His is now called Mobutu Sese Seko Kuku Ngebendu Wa Za Banga which loosely translates as the immortal red-hot chilli pepper. He calls himself 'the dignified redeemer' and insists that his portrait is on the wall of every church. His wealth is estimated at $6.3 billion and he has been known to hire Concorde for visits to the dentist. He has murdered and tortured his opponents and allowed Zaïre – which ought to be one of the richest countries in the world – to become an economic joke. On the other hand, he has managed to keep Zaïre united, which considering there was a civil war within five days of the Belgian handover is truly impressive.

He is absolutely corrupt, but to the tribal African mind this is no bad thing. The tribal system, which has worked in Africa for centuries, has always meant that a man should look after his family, his clan and then his tribe. Mobutu has done this and is therefore admired. His family live in palaces. Fellow members of his tribe receive sinecures. His home town of Gbadolite – previously a one-chicken village in the centre of thousands of square miles of impenetrable rainforest – is now the proud site for an international airport, a splendid chateau and a massive conference centre, all deserted.

Mobutu is an African success story. The fact that he has achieved his riches by reducing his country to ruins is anathema to the west but makes perfect sense to the average unschooled African. In fact, by African standards he is quite humane. He is ruthless when necessary but he prefers to corrupt his enemies rather than kill them. While we were in Zaïre, Mobutu and the sometime opposition leader Nguza Karl-i-Bond were conspiring together to create ethnic tension in the south of the country. A few years earlier, during a period of detention without trial,

Karl-i-Bond's testicles had been wired up to the mains. An Amin or a Bokassa would have flipped the switch, grilled them and had them for tea, but Mobutu, by only moderate use of the current, created a new ally. Throughout his reign, he has allowed opponents the rope with which to hang themselves. In 1990, under pressure from the west, he even allowed multiparty democracy – as long as all opposition parties supported *Mobutuisme*.

A national conference was set up, led by Archbishop Monsengwo Pasinya, to oversee the transition to multiparty rule. Since then there have been countless governments and no action. Mobutu controls, and pays personally, the Isreali-trained presidential guard of 10,000 men – the DSP. A faction of the DSP known as *les hiboux* (the owls), since they work so effectively at night, operates as a death squad to maintain the writ of the president. Meanwhile, the national conference appoints prime ministers for the president to ignore. Etienne Tshisekedi was the man of the moment when we were in Zaïre. He has lived in and out of exile for decades and is a sworn enemy of Mobutu. Tshisekedi and fellow members of his alliance, the Sacred Union, debate in Kinshasa and then make decisions which the president overrules by force. Shortly before we arrived in Zaïre, Tshisekedi fired the governor of the central bank. Mobutu reacted by sending troops and tanks down to the bank. This dual system of government had continued for two years and brought the country to its knees. Neither side can made decisions. They can merely overrule those of their opponents.

The British Embassy in Kinshasa, in common with many other embassies, is within a stone's throw of the Congo river. Kinshasa and Brazzaville (the capital of neigbouring Congo) are separated only by the river, and diplomats spend much of their time messing about on it. If there is rioting in Brazza, you go to 'Shasa, and vice versa. All embassies have their own boats and people trained to use them for midnight evacuations. The British Embassy was no exception to this rule, although the purpose-built building could have held off an attack for months. Tall security walls and gates surround the compound in which there is the embassy, a few Barratt-style houses for the diplomats, a flower-bordered swimming pool and the British Club (complete with darts board and a bar). Visitors have to park outside the gates as all the parking spaces are taken up by bulletproof vehicles and rubber Zodiac boats.

We were regarded with great suspicion when we arrived in torrential rain at the gates, since all British nationals had been advised to leave Zaïre long before we had arrived. A quick flash of Andy Henderson's card saying, 'Please take care of these refugees from Angola', however, earned us more preferential treatment. We were invited to the British Club that evening and therefore spent the afternoon looking for alternative accommodation and ascertaining at the cost of $100 each that we had hangovers rather than malaria.

We had been adopted by Martin, an Australian who had been at the British Embassy in the morning. He was running a pig farm on the outskirts of the city and devoted his day to showing us around Kinshasa. Running a pig farm in the west is, I imagine, a relatively simple task, but in Zaïre it was not. He spent most of his life currency-speculating, in order to buy feed before the money in his rucksack became worthless. He took us to a tin-roofed but open-walled restaurant close to the river from which a Lebanese man ran his financial empire. In Zaïre and neighbouring Zambia, Lebanese businessmen have at least partial control (many would say total) of the money supply. Money made from Mandrax production and dealing in South Africa, Zambia and Zimbabwe is laundered through the diamond trade in Zaïre, which is in turn supplied by illegal gems from Angola. It is an industrial operation: much of southern Africa's population is addicted to Mandrax.

'The Lebanese own all the money here,' Martin told us. 'You must always change money with them or you could end up anywhere. If you do it on the street, the money changers will more than likely inform the police who will arrest you for illegal currency dealing. Also, buy small notes as they are much cheaper than big ones.'

Intrigued, I asked, 'Why?'

'Since the roads don't work and currency has to be flown around the country, larger notes are more valuable as they don't weigh so much.'

In 1991 the government was still minting one-zaïre coins. When we arrived in 1992, there were approximately two million zaïres to the dollar. When we left, there were seven million. It was impossible to change money legally because all the banks, having run out of cash, were closed. Zaïre was falling apart. In 1991 there had been serious rioting in Kinshasa and across the country which became known as the *pillage*. Expats, Zaïreans and diplomats all spoke of before and after the *pillage*. Evidence of it lay all about.

Burnt-out shops had never been repaired and entire sections of the city were no longer lived in. Binza, the Kinshasa equivalent of Belgravia, was like an abandoned movie set since no one dared lived there any more. A Belgian Embassy couple had been living there the year before when their house was invaded by a drunken mob of soldiers who tied them up, stripped them and started looting. One of the soldiers, realizing that he was in the presence of a Belgian diplomat, bent over and asked if his brother's visa had come through yet. A group of leper-aiding nuns were turned over by their own patients. The next day the same patients complained that there was no food or medicine. The *pillage* had been a moral breakdown from which Zaïre is unlikely to recover. A year on, there were still makeshift stalls outside the army barracks where soldiers sold air-conditioning units ripped untimely from the walls of the hotels.

Seen from above, Kinshasa is a beautiful city. From our bedroom window at the Intercontinental we looked out over the river towards Brazzaville. Tall and imposing buildings lined the main streets, giving an impression of prosperity and peace. All around were green trees and wide avenues. We could see the stadium which Mobutu built to host the 1974 world-heavyweight championship between Muhammad Ali and George Foreman. Up close though, Kinshasa was another matter. We were soon to side with Foreman's manager who, having promoted the fight as the 'Rumble in the Jungle', was asked afterwards what he thought about Zaïre. He is reported to have replied, 'All I can say is, thank God my parents got on that boat.'

The wide avenues were full of holes, the buildings which had impressed us so much were either empty or squatted. Shops, restaurants and offices were few and far between. The streets were thronged with dishevelled soldiers, policemen, hookers and touts. Zaïre, a country at peace, had the appearance of being under occupation. The soldiers and the police were not the defenders of the prostitutes, beggars and refugee look-alikes. They were the enemy. The military had not been paid for months and had to mug to survive. Protection rackets were their only hope of finding something to eat. They had started the 1991 looting because they had not been paid and they were just revving up to start the 1992 looting. We had left Angola in the throes of a savage civil war. It was estimated that 10,000 people had been killed during the weekend we had spent at the Meridien.* Yet Kinshasa held infinitely more menace.

After an afternoon of bar research with Martin, we set off for the British Club at the embassy. We were the first to arrive, so played darts in the pagoda-enclosed bar which overlooked the pool. Safely behind razor-wire-topped walls, we stashed our rucksack of cash behind the bar and relaxed. First to arrive were the close protection team – six British military policemen who worked as bodyguards for the chargé Kaye Oliver and were the embassy's last line of defence. They were all wearing tight-fitting

---

* By who, I don't know, since all the bodies were buried as secretly as possible with no records kept. However, it was doubtless many thousands. Only 9,000 people were killed during the entire siege of Sarajevo yet this 10,000 went almost entirely unnoticed.

T-shirts with 'Close Protection Team' embroidered on their bosoms. Moustachioed and well-muscled, they had that indefinable something which identified them as British squaddies rather than the chorus line of *La Cage Aux Folles*. They were soon followed by Simon Ferrand, the most junior of three diplomats at the skeleton-staffed embassy.

At first sight, Simon looked like a London estate agent. A fresh-faced 25-year-old with a public-school voice and an immaculate pinstriped suit, he fools those he meets into taking him at face value. Behind the jovial exterior, however, lurked an agile mind which could think in three or four languages and understood more about the intricate power games around which Zaïre revolves than anyone else we came across. He was an invaluable guide, not only to the nightlife of Kinshasa, but also to its political life.

It was he who had invited us and under his arm he had a newly arrived copy of the *Sunday Times Magazine* for which we had provided the cover story. I had written the piece in the middle of the night while an ammunition dump blew up nearby and Harriet had never seen her photographs, so we were feeling rather pleased with ourselves. This was also rather useful, in that it proved to all members of the British Club that we were pioneering journalists, rather than the slightly down-at-heel bums we resembled. We were, of course, like Simon, in disguise.

In the course of the evening, a motley collection of pilots, bankers, diplomats and shady businessmen turned up. Harriet was the only woman and correspondingly popular. Kaye Oliver was on holiday so we would not be able to have a meeting until her return. One of the pilots offered to help us out by arranging a flight down to Lubumbashi, and the communications man at the American Embassy offered to arrange a briefing for us about the copper belt. Our train journey was not going to be as simple as we thought. In Lubumbashi, we soon found out, Mobutu was cleansing his ethnics and he was not going to want to be seen washing them in public.

We ended up on a grand tour of Kinshasa's nightlife which didn't finish until six o'clock the next morning. Kinshasa is famous throughout Africa for its kwasa kwasa music and its nightlcubs, so we were rather excited by this. As things transpired we were not to see the real nightlife of Kinshasa but the sanitized Euro version.

'We used to go out all over the place before the *pillage*, but it is too dangerous now,' Simon told us as we walked into yet another club that resembled nothing more than a disco in a Spanish seaside resort.

The doors of the clubs were all guarded by soldiers, armed with tripod-mounted machine guns. The first one had been the site of a shoot-out only the night before, when a Lebanese diamond dealer had pulled out an UZI to settle a dispute over the bill. The night we went, all customers were politely encouraged to leave their weapons at the door. The guards, who were paid by the club's invariably foreign owners, also demanded payment for guarding cars while the owners were inside, but John, one of the RMP (Royal Military Police) bodyguards, had a useful technique for avoiding the bill. He challenged them to – and always won – press-up competitions.

After dark, the pavements of central Kinshasa are peopled only by prostitutes and soldiers. For five cents the prostitutes, who besiege every car on the roads, will rub their genitalia against the windscreen. For ten cents they will give you the secret to their model-girl figures – Acquired Immune Deficiency Syndrome, the slimmers' disease. It is known simply as Slim in many parts of English-speaking Africa.

Zaïre is said to be the home of AIDS and circumstantial evidence for this is abundant. The facts, however, are not so clear-cut. As anyone who has ever had to pay for an AIDS test will know, they do not come cheap. Treating it is even more expensive. A year's course of AZT – £1900 – is three hundred times the per capita GDP. Few aid agencies are willing to waste money on testing penniless Africans in order to prove a rather convenient theory.

Therefore, many people in Africa have been written off as AIDS sufferers, when in fact they are suffering from entirely curable diseases or malnutrition. One of the results of this has been that millions of dollars of aid money has been poured into prevention campaigns, surveys and the purchase of condoms. The prostitutes of Africa are starving, since no one dares sleep with them any longer. AIDS is prevalent in Africa but it has not been proved to be the biblical epidemic one hears about. The effects of AIDS are monstrous, but so are those of curable tuberculosis, which appears independently of AIDS and is largely ignored by the aid agencies.

All of this is true but it is not the whole story either. AIDS is not carried by all Africans (as some newspapers claim), neither is it carried by none (as others claim). People who blithely claim that AIDS could be a blessing in disguise as the solution to Africa's population explosion are not only possessed of diseased minds, they are wrong. The disease is actually fuelling the population explosion because African men are staying with their wives through fear of infection from extra-marital alliances and hence having more children. AIDS is seriously a devastating disease for which a cure must be found, but the last thing Africa needs is for its workforce to be told that it has an incurable and fatal disease. The resulting apathy to which this often false news contributes can only be destructive. It also encourages people to die. Many Africans, together with other people who hold mystic beliefs, have an unnerving capacity for sitting down and dying of their own accord when they feel the time is right.

One of our ports of call was Savannah Anna's, a nightclub which used to be the haunt of air crews and businessmen. The businessmen have mostly cleared out and the airlines can no longer get insurance to leave planes in Kinshasa overnight, so we were the only fresh flesh there. Harriet and Simon abandoned me with John – one of the close protection team – while they went to use a satellite telephone. They did not return for two hours and John and I were left – the only men – with two hundred radiant women who wanted to sleep with us.

Shorts were probably not the best thing to be wearing. Crippled, both by embarrassment and by the fact that I could not stand up without my hands in my pockets, I did a little research. I bought the girls drinks, I tried to indulge in polite conversation, but John and I were the only men in a room filled with two hundred prostitutes who had seen the possibilities which my shorts offered. It was a strenuous two hours.

Virginie, whose hand I extricated from my shorts and held tightly, had no home. She worked the clubs at night and foraged for food during the day. She had been educated in a mission school but her behaviour totally belied her upbringing and speech. Understanding that this fool foreigner wanted to talk to her, she regaled me with horror stories about her life in the capital. But while telling me about the French priests who had educated her, her hands wandered all over me. It was like being groped by an underaged nun. It served me right for trying to find that old journalistic standby – the wise hooker.

'My family lives about one hundred miles outside Kinshasa,' she told me. 'My father used to have a shop, but he and my brother were killed in the *pillage*. My mother looks after my sisters but I have not seen her for over a year.'

The sixteen-year-old Virginie had been sent to Kinshasa to fend for herself, but arrived to find that it was in a worse state than her native Masia. Having come to the city she was caught in a snare. She could not earn enough money to leave and she had to betray everything she believed in to stay. Kinshasa is home to millions like her – trapped urban homeless. Huge shanty towns, housing hundreds of thousands, surround the grand deserted buildings in the centre of town. The conditions are appalling – floods bring cholera, as does drinking the only available water. Rape and murder are endemic. Food is increasingly scare.

Zaïre is immensely fertile. As well as its mineral riches, the fruits of its soil could feed half of Africa. Despite this, it can no longer feed itself. Mobutu's rape of the economy has led to a situation where farmers are unwilling to sell their food because the money they receive for it will be worthless. The kleptocratic state has forced them back to subsistence farming. The transport system has also broken down. The railway was never important to Kinshasa itself, but at independence the capital was well served by roads and the river. The Belgians left Zaïre with 145,000 kilometres of all-weather roads. By 1992, according to someone who did it regularly, it took twenty days driving eighteen hours a day to get from Kinshasa to Lubumbashi in an off-road vehicle. The journey, which takes two hours by plane, is only possible in the dry season.

The river was not much better. The Congo (renamed the Zaïre by Mobutu) is the largest river in Africa. It stretches from the Atlantic coast, in a huge wide loop through the interior of Zaïre where you can still find outbreaks of bubonic plague, and down almost to Lubumbashi. It has been the lifeblood of the area for centuries. In the 1890s Conrad trundled up and down the river in his steam boat having nightmares about the natives, but one hundred years later the boats no longer work. These great steam boats were like mobile supermarkets which housed thousands of people who traded with the forest dwellers along the way. Dancing attendance to the ships were a constant stream of pirogues. Monkeys were swapped for maize and maize for batteries as the years progressed. Stanley killed hundreds in order to open up this great highway, yet ninety years after his death the only regular traffic is the pirogues of prehistoric times and the waterski boats of the expats.

Harriet and I had both travelled by pirogue before. They are uncomfortable, wet and dangerous, so we went out on the river in a ski boat. The Club Nautique is home to about fifty ski boats, variously owned by companies and individuals based in Zaïre. It is hemmed in away from the main river by the floating homes of thousands of Zaïreans, so in order to enter the stream you have to motor past people's sitting rooms. The channel is almost blocked by the Kolomi, a sunken river steamer. Its bridge, which tilts at a drunken angle, is still above the waterline and is home to at least two families. Every weekend a small flotilla of speed boats races out of the club en route to upriver picnic sites. Vast clumps of weed and water hyacinth float down, detached from the never-ending greenness of the banks. At Stanley Pool above Kinshasa, the river is almost fifteen miles wide, but the very enormity of it takes away its grandeur. The floating islands, which indicate the current, are all that identify it as a river rather than a lake. Sand banks appear and disappear from week to week and on these, too, people live. After a ten-kilometre sail upstream we found a good picnic spot on a sand bank mid-river. Within fifteen minutes a man had paddled out to us in his pirogue to demand payment for the picnic site. He lived there in order to avoid theft on the mainland.

As the light began to fade everybody rushed back to the yacht club so that they weren't caught on the river at night. Smugglers and bandits own the river after dark and the expats club together to deny them rich pickings. When the boats have sped back to within sight of the Club Nautique, many people stop for a last beer midstream before floating down, docking the boats and joining a convoy back into the centre of town. Damp Zaïreans watch from the banks and the rotting boats that are their homes as the last stragglers come in (often towed by friends if there has been a problem with a boat). The expats jump into their Range Rovers and Land Cruisers, lock the doors and windows and head back into town. Some go to guarded and mostly unoccupied blocks of flats, reserved for expats. Others head for embassy compounds, or the American club where we watched Windsor Castle going up in flames on CNN while the few remaining diplomat wives squabbled over plans for a party. Yet more go to company compounds, guarded by mercenaries, and a rare few go to their own houses. Those with detached houses do not sleep easy, despite the full petrol tanks, guards and high walls.

Few Europeans dare venture out without a hand-held radio. It is not just the aid groups and the embassies who take these precautions. Mike, who worked for Grindlays Bank and lived in one of the empty apartment blocks, had one with which he could speak to both the British and American embassies. Martyn Purdie, the pilot who was arranging a flight down to Lubumbashi for us, had a hand-held scanning radio with which he could have picked up Squidgy and Camilla (the telephone conversations of both the Prince of Wales's mistress and his wife had recently been intercepted by a radio ham). The ultimate accessory, however, was the mobile phone. Zaïre's telephone system has decayed to such an extent that it is not worth repairing. The rich have introduced a mobile phone system which only enables them to call other mobile phones. The poor, or anywhere outside Kinshasa, are deemed not worth calling.

All these accessories do not make for a happy life. The expats were living in an entirely different world to the rest of the population – segregated by justified fear. The two worlds seldom, if ever, met. At the Club Nautique, I did not see a single black client. At the Centre Hequipage – a riding stables which would put any yard at Lambourn, the centre of the British racing industry, to shame – we saw one. But he was a colonel in the DSP who was being taught how to ride with a sword in his hand. Many whites no longer go to the shops. There are not many left and it is easier to send a *protocol* or to have things sent from abroad. In the barricaded international banks, the smallest decisions have to be made by expatriates in the hopes of avoiding corruption. In the surviving bars and restaurants where whites dare to tread, Europeans often wait at table.

'After the *pillage*,' explained an American Embassy official, 'I couldn't bear to speak to any of my Zaïrean staff for three weeks. People who I had helped suddenly turned into monsters. I saw people I knew, looting and destroying. I came here with all the proper credentials. I wanted to be posted to Africa but I hate the Zaïreois now,' he explained as we hurtled down the street, windows up, doors locked and horn blaring at anyone in the way.

George was a right-on university graduate who had passed all the lie-detector tests, thought racism was disgusting and had wanted to help the third world. After two years in Zaïre, he could have been mistaken for a member of the Klan. 'This country has been so destroyed that ordinary Zaïreois will do anything for money. It is the only way they can survive. There is no food, no money, and no hope. Everything we have tried to do here has been stolen or destroyed.' George had even fired the maid who came with his apartment thus rendering her homeless and penniless.

Many expatriates had not walked on the streets for months, and even driving a car had become dangerous. Further along the river from the British Embassy was the parliament building which drew troops from miles around. The road between the two was guarded by soldiers who had recently taken to stopping and robbing cars with diplomatic plates. Normally plated cars were fair game – hence the convoys – but this had been a new departure. There was a lull while we were in Kinshasa, since through sheer coincidence and terrible luck for the Zaïrean muggers, the last three cars they had stopped had belonged to Special Forces personnel from the German and Italian embassies. Special Forces men get bored in places like Kinshasa because they have to be constantly alert, yet are not allowed to shoot people unless strictly necessary. Being mugged is their equivalent of winning the lottery and their crippled victims had obviously put the word around.

The soldiers, however, had not disappeared. The parliament building was the venue for the national conference and attracted much interest. The soldiers had not been paid, so they were blockading the building until they were. In the confused state in which Zaïre had found itself, buildings had become the focus for discontent. Mainly through lack of coordination rather than any lenient philosophy, Zaïre has a free press. Mobutu is openly referred to as Satan in the papers and occasionally takes revenge by sending round *les hiboux* to kill journalists and blow up printing presses. For the main, however, the press reports what is going on, with a strong opposition bias. Unlike many African countries, where the World Service (open only to those with expensive radios) is the only source of factual news, in Kinshasa, many people know the facts. They therefore understand that there is not much that Tshisekedi can do while Mobutu remains in power.

Regardless of this, they blockade the parliament over which Tshisekedi presides because it is a symbol. They cannot go to Gbadolite, from where Mobutu governs, because it is hundreds of miles from Kinshasa and totally inaccessible. They cannot go to the Intercontinental where the real decisions on day-to-day running are made because it is the only building which everyone has an interest in protecting. It has never been looted. So when they are blockading the president's opponents in parliament they are actually demonstrating against Mobutu. When the parliament does something Mobutu dislikes, *he* blockades the parliament and fights erupt between the regular army and Mobutu's private army, the DSP. The DSP always wins.

Zaïre is a complicated place. The former British Liberal Party leader Jeremy Thorpe tried to explain it soon after independence at the time when the UN were suffering heavy losses in southern Zaïre. 'We are, after all, in a very involved situation. There are two prime ministers, Mr Lumumba and Mr Ileo, both of whom apparently have arrested the other. There's the president, Mr Kasavubu, and he's sacked Mr Lumumba but has in turn on paper been arrested by Mr Lumumba who has arrested him back. General Lundula is in charge of the troops but he's been sacked although appointed by Mr Lumumba and General Mobutu has been put in his place but he's also in theory under arrest by Mr Lumumba. The Baluba tribe are crying for Mr Lumumba's blood while Mr Tshombe is trying to have a tête-à-tête with Mr Kasavubu. That doesn't forget Mr Koinange or Mr Rajahswad Dayal who is the United Nations observer. Now that is the *dramatis personae*. I would say that any organization would have very great difficulties.' Thirty years later, if anything, it is more confused.

In Angola, we had met Ivan – an illegal diamond dealer – and his crew of Zaïrean partners. They were very dangerous people but they had looked after us well and indeed protected our lives on more than one occasion. Ivan had explained to me how Zaïre worked.

'Everything in Zaïre is finished,' he said. 'You have to look after yourself or you will starve. Kinshasa is the most marvellous city in the world, but it is not like Paris. You do what you have to do and pay people off if you are caught. I am buying diamonds here which I send to Kinshasa to be sold. I only allow my brother to do this as no one else can be trusted. If he gets caught, we pay a bribe and everything carries on. I sell to the Lebanese for dollars which then are flown back to me here, or to Paris or London. I pay for my family to be protected in Kinshasa and am investing my money in Europe. Everything goes through Kinshasa because in Kinshasa if you have the money you can do anything. My country is so rich. It has everything – diamonds, copper, food. I love it.'

Before the *pillage* Ivan had been a mechanic. When we met him, a year later, he was making approximately one million dollars a week. To the majority of Zaïreans, the *pillage* had been another nail in their coffins. Investors had fled the country. Money had gone so crazy that university professors could not afford to eat. But, to a few, it had been an opportunity. The breakdown of every system of government and justice had returned Zaïre to pre-colonial days, when warrior merchants and businessmen had been able to carve empires from the bush. This time, though, Africans had been able to join in the empire building. Pauling, the builder of our railway, and Ivan would have been rivals, but they would also have been friends.

Simon from the British Embassy took us on a tour of the *pillage*. The Okapi Hotel, in Binza, used to be the best hotel in Kinshasa. An enormous swimming pool looked over the city and out over the river to Brazzaville. Bands used to play in the elegant dining room where the food was world class. A few bums and a soldier were sitting in the lobby when we entered and – for a small fee –

allowed us to look around. Wild foliage was growing in what had, only a year ago, been the lobby. In an office lay an empty safe, the only thing too heavy to loot. The rest of the hotel was no longer there. Bare walls were all that remained. Floorboards, electric wires, light fittings, air-conditioning units, beds, tiles, partition walls – everything had been removed or destroyed. The car park was a mess of tangled metal where the hotel's fleet of hire cars had been accidentally blown up. Even the lights from the swimming pool had been stolen.

Elsewhere in the city, Simon showed us the old Firestone factory, the Toyota plant and the domestic airport. They had all been destroyed and, with them, all hope for Zaïre's reconstruction.

'This was all done in two days,' said Simon. 'Now people are being asked to invest here again.' Two days of wanton destruction had led to at least 80 per cent unemployment and a complete breakdown in the regular financial system.

Wall Street was an example of Zaïre's financial rebirth. A small bustling street, of the type one would find in SoHo or Soho, had been transformed by the money changers of Kinshasa into a temple to Mammon. It was a black market of extraordinary efficiency where you could change money in the most civilized way imaginable. Having been dropped off on the corner, I wandered into a busy club and sat at the bar. The tables were jammed with cheerful-looking people, gossiping and reading the newspapers, bulging rucksacks and cases on the floor beside them. Before I had time to order a drink, a mountainous but harmless-looking man came to join me. He was wearing a sharp chalk-stripe suit in brown and white which would have been perfect for a chorus member of *Guys and Dolls*. Heavy gold chains hung round his bull-like neck which separated a welcoming face from a cream silk shirt.

'Let me buy you a drink,' he said.

Well, this certainly is a first, I thought, as the barman gave me a beer.

'What money would you like to change?'

'Three hundred US, please.'

'I can do twenties at two point four, millions at two point two.'

'Fifties at two point four?' I asked.

'Deal.'

It had been the simplest transaction I had made in Zaïre – and I had bargained. I swapped three crisp bills for 14,400 pieces of soggy paper which I then had to carry around in a rucksack. My dealer joined me while I finished my drink and escorted me – for my own safety – back to the waiting car. Ordinary Zaïreans had invented an alternative system of banking which was more efficient, pleasant and safe than any bank in Africa. My dealer explained that the service had come about naturally. 'People were selling all their money to the Lebanese and we couldn't get any ourselves, so we started dealing here and paying off the soldiers independently. Now the Lebanese sell their money through us.'

Martyn Purdie had cashed a cheque for us and arranged a flight down to Lubumbashi on a plane which he could guarantee would be flown by an expatriate.

'It costs sixteen dollars to buy a 747 licence in Kinshasa, so it is important that you always check,' he told us. 'There are two Zaïreans who live in the United States and sit people's pilot licences for a fee. This is why I hate flying here so much. I gave my crew a test the other day and they just did nothing. We were sitting on the runway waiting for clearance and I said, "The right-hand engine is on fire. What should we do?" They sat liked startled rabbits for four minutes before someone said, "Turn off the engine." Anyone can fly a plane. It is for our knowledge of what to do in an emergency that we are paid so much. I have to fly the plane entirely on my own.

'Did you know that there is not a single working plane in the Zaïrean air force at the moment?' he continued. 'They had one repaired the other day. It was delivered back to Kinshasa, and the next morning someone taxied it out of the hangar and drove it into their two other functioning planes', he continued. 'Two of Air Zaïre's planes have been seized in Europe for non-payment of bills so they can't take their other planes for maintenance any more.'

Reassured by the fact that the skies over Zaïre would be fairly empty during our flight, we set off to the British Embassy to meet Kaye Oliver. She was the last Zaïre-based diplomat to have been to Lubumbashi and we were looking forward to an up-to-the-minute briefing on the political situation. We were to be sorely disappointed.

Lubumbashi is the capital of Shaba province (formerly Katanga) which until the *pillage* produced 80 per cent of Zaïre's wealth. Immediately after independence in 1960, Moise Tshombe led a secessionist movement in the province which was put down only with the help of the United Nations, Belgian paratroopers and the biggest UN loss of life until the Gulf War. The Belgian soldiers were there in 1960 to protect their nationals who were still running the mines, and have been regular visitors ever since. Secession was once more attempted in 1978 when the French joined in with the Belgians to maintain the status quo. The 1992 unease, though, was a different matter. Mobutu himself was inciting the violence with great effect.

By 1992, Mobutu, like Moi in Kenya, needed some evidence to back up his entirely legitimate claim that multiparty democracy leads to tribalism. In order to do this he appointed a Shabaian governor to the province – Kyungu wa-Kumwanza. Kyungu allied himself with Nguza Karl-i-Bond, of crisp testicles fame, and also a former prime minister and nephew of the exiled Tshombe, who returned to his home province of Shaba with Mobutu's blessing. Between the two of them, they had divided the province by refusing to recognize the government of Etienne Tshisekedi.

When the Belgians started mining copper in Shaba province they found two dominant tribes in the area – the Lunda and the Luba. In order to avoid nepotism and tribalism in their workforce, they imported a better-educated tribe from neighbouring Kasai to do the best-paid jobs. The Lunda and the Luba became the workers in the mines, the Kasaian Luba became the foremen. (To avoid confusion I will call the Kasaian Luba, the Kasai, and the Katangan Luba, the Katanga.) This has led to a century of resentment against the Kasai by the natural residents of Shaba which Karl-i-Bond and Kyungu set out to exploit.

Kyungu made inflammatory broadcasts on the radio under the slogan of '*chacun à son coin*' (each to his corner), in which he encouraged the Katangan youth to 'crush the Kasai like insects'. Large quantities of drugs and drink became available in the markets for mysteriously low prices, and the youth of Shaba went on the rampage. The homes and villages of many Kasai were razed by drunken youths while Kyungu ordered the Kasai to return to their tribal areas.

'The Katangese no longer accept the Kasaians here. Their presence is an insult. They are arrogant and don't hide it. It is not possible for the tribes to live side by side,' Kyungu had told Mark Huband of the *Guardian* a month or two earlier. An estimated two million Kasai had been ordered to leave the jobs and homes which had been theirs for a century.

When we visited Kaye Oliver, Medecins Sans Frontières (the Belgian aid agency) were reporting that 60,000 people had been forced from their homes and were living without food or shelter at a railway station in Shaba. However, Miss Oliver, in her infinite wisdom, decided that we – the only foreign journalists in Zaïre – were not worth briefing on the situation. In fact, she did not want us in the country at all, and told us we were on our own. This meant that in order to receive a non-biased judgement on the situation we had to go to the American Embassy (not famed for their lack of bias and guilty of some very dubious debt write-offs to guarantee support in the UN for the Gulf War), whose ambassador had visited the area a good three weeks prior to Miss Oliver. The contrast between the quiet efficiency of John Flynn in Angola who braved the battle for Luanda with only a Union Jack and a soft-skin Jaguar for protection, and Kaye Oliver in Zaïre who took a bulletproof Range Rover and four bodyguards to go out for lunch, was highlighted by the fact that even the Americans were horrified by her attitude.

'The European Community are meant to be doing something. [Britain was president of the EC at the time]. We gave $25,000 to MSF the moment we saw it, but motivating anyone else has been very difficult,' the information officer at the American Embassy told me.

Linda Gregory from USAID spent two hours – on a Sunday – briefing me about the troubles. 'There is terrible danger of a cholera epidemic if something is not done to contain the situation,' she told me. 'Tens of thousands of Kasaians have been forced from their homes and are living in railway stations and schools with no food, shelter or hygiene. Just over the border in Zambia there is a cholera epidemic and six weeks ago MSF were seeing the first cases of cholera in Likasi.'

The railway reference had not passed me by. The track, which had been built to get Zaïre's copper to the coast, was now being used to dispose of the people who used to mine the copper. Our only problem was that the administration in Shaba were not going to want us anywhere near this operation. We were going to need a disguise to see our railway. Bill, the chief of communications for the US Embassy, with whom we had been waterskiing, arranged for us to be helped by the American Consulate when we arrived in Lubumbashi. They had a skeleton staff of Zaïreans running the consulate, since it was rightly deemed too dangerous for American nationals to be based there.

Simon volunteered to take us to the airport for our flight down to the south. We were not going to make the same mistake twice and hoped that the presence of an accredited diplomat would make things easier at the airport. It did. Simon managed to get us checked on to the plane without paying a single bribe, but as soon as he left us we were pounced on. The well-armed guard who controlled access to the plane wanted a hundred dollars to let us pass. Twenty did the trick and got us on to a Scibe Air 727. Our minds were immediately put at rest as to the terrors of the flight when we saw our pilot lock the door to the cockpit. Martyn had sworn to us that the pilot held a genuine licence, and we knew he wasn't going to let the first officer have a go because the first officer spent the entire flight asleep on the three seats in front of us.

CHAPTER FOUR

Lubumbashi – after the heat and bustle of Kinshasa – is a joy. There were pleasant, unarmed people on the tarmac at the airport and we were actually welcomed to the province. Shaba has been the source of Zaïre's wealth for over a century, yet most of the money which it has earned has been lost to foreign bank accounts or spent on developing Kinshasa and the rest of the country. Lubumbashi is still a pretty little colonial town with wide avenues, stylish 1920s buildings and a veneer of peace. It even had a pleasing climate while we were in town – warm and dry.

Leaving the airport involved not a single bribe and as we entered Lubumbashi in the flat-bed of a pick-up, we heard a horn blow – a train's horn. We were at the heart of our railway and our odyssey could finally begin. The first thing we did was walk around the centre of town, looking for the railway station. People seemed to move at a slower pace here, and the weight of having to look over our shoulders, for fear of being mugged, swiftly receded. At the end of a broad and attractive street, we found the station. It was a white Art Deco building, with an elegant central arch, which seemed to have stepped from the pages of Babar. To compound the image, the word Lubumbashi had been stencilled over the still-visible original name of the town – Elizabethville. We could see trains waiting on the platform but they were well guarded and obscured by a ragged bunch of refugees and their baggage. (They were being forced to seek refuge and were therefore refugees, but in United Nations speak you do not become a refugee until you leave your country of origin.) The station was not open to the public, but at least it was there, and we were able to go to bed that night in the knowledge that we had seen our first train.

We had checked into the decaying but once grand Park Hotel, which has an atrium dominated by an ancient cactus taller than the building itself. The classical grandeur of the hotel had been somewhat obscured by a 1978 renovation in keeping with Mobutu's Africanization policy. The black and white photographs of great white hunters and colonial tea parties had been taken down and replaced with wood carvings of the death and destruction school, in which fearsome warriors could be seen impaling their equally fearsome foes. Brown, orange and yellow was the dominant colour scheme, which extended to polystyrene tiles that had been randomly appliquéd to the roof and walls. They had been sprayed with oil paint, producing an effect like that of disco lights which shine through a revolving disc of technicolour oil. We were almost the only guests, since the hotel had no water and the Sheraton at the airport did. We could not afford to stay there since, like the Intercontinental in Kinshasa, it was charging international prices for Zaïrean service.

After settling in and locking all our equipment in the cupboard, we had a long dinner in the hotel restaurant planning our deceptions for the following day. We had bought a new padlock and some chain in the market because someone had stolen the last lot in Kinshasa. The restaurant had been decorated like the African equivalent of an English pub. Horse brasses had been replaced by copper carvings along the beams and the room glowed in their reflection. Everything was made of solid copper — from the door knobs to the plates. Three waiters appeared to clear the table and serve the food since the crockery was so heavy that two hands were needed to pick up an ashtray.

In all our time in Lubumbashi, we never saw another customer in the restaurant, where every night a band came to serenade us while we ate. The troupe consisted of five men wearing assorted trousers and ancient, matching, black and red shirts: an organist, a trumpeter, a guitarist, a drummer and a clapper. They always started their set with *Je t'aime* (*sans* Jane Birkin), but also played requests. Having asked for 'Moon River' and 'Amazing Grace' on our first night, we became quite intimate with their "Uckleberry Flen' by the end of the stay. They spoke no English, yet having played venues as diverse as the Catholic church, the Sheraton and the Gecamines Christmas party, they had a vast and eclectic repertoire of half-remembered songs.

Gecamines, the state mining company, was fast becoming a half-remembered enterprise. For a start, the better-educated part of their workforce was being ethnically cleansed. The Zaïreans are world-champion looters (beating even the Somalis) and the *pillage* had been as destructive in Lubumbashi as it had in other parts of the country. The mines had been looted then flooded, the stores destroyed, and the railway alternately ravaged and neglected. What little copper Zaïre was able to produce now had to be driven in trucks from the Zaïrean copper belt to a railhead in Zambia. It then made the long and tortuous journey down to South Africa, rather than the much shorter trip to Lobito, which Pauling had envisaged and the Belgians (with Williams's help) had made a reality.

The bottom had fallen out of the copper market. This, combined with the extra transport costs and dwindling production, meant that Zaïre's copper income was drying up. Not many of the expatriates, who used to run the mines, dare to live in Zaïre these days and their Zaïrean replacements are generally corrupt and inefficient. The profits in diamond mining mean that expats will risk their lives to mine them. The same no longer applies to copper. South Africa had refused the last shipment of copper because it was not of the required purity. Zaïre could not afford to take it back or send it anywhere else because the extra costs prohibited it. Zaïre's basket-case economy is largely blamed on the Belgians for leaving Zaïre with a one-commodity system. However, copper-industry insiders disagree. First, the economy is not one commodity, rather one industry – mining. Alternatives to copper – zinc, bauxite, even diamonds – are plentiful. One miner I met in Lubumbashi blamed the entire mess on Mobutu's rapacious nature.

'Zaïre and Zambia,' he told me, 'used to produce a vast proportion of the world's copper, so when Zaïre gained independence it was able to dictate the price in the same way that De Beers does with diamonds. Controlling the supply means that you can name the price. Mobutu, realizing this, doubled and tripled the price of copper and held the world to ransom. This forced the copper-hungry west to innovate. Extraordinarily, a power-crazed dictator in Africa was responsible for a sudden growth in the plastics industry. Copper became impossibly expensive and plastic piping was the result. Now we all have plastic plumbing in our houses rather than the more efficient and originally cheaper copper, and the demand for copper has all but disappeared.'

There was not much of a copper industry left to look at. The same fate, to a lesser extent, had befallen the cobalt mines. Until a few years ago, Zaïre provided 40 per cent of the world's supply. Industrial diamonds were being mined now by illicit diggers. Tin, uranium, iron – all the natural products of Zaïre's fertile ground – were remaining where God had put them. The machinery to dig them up had been regularly looted or destroyed. The management behind the machinery had fled and the workers were being ethnically cleansed.

Mines look much the same wherever they happen to be and they were no longer using the railway to transport the copper, so we set off to the American Consulate to find out what was happening with the refugees. We could look at the mines after that and after we had made the necessary contacts to arrange a discreet visit. We were already attracting attention and had to be very careful of whom we spoke to, in order not to be exposed as journalists. The man who came to clean our room had eyed our cameras and flight cases of film with suspicion. Guy Guy, an enterprising beggar whom we had met at the airport, had, by our first morning, been to visit us three times. He, too, had asked us if we were journalists. Lubumbashi had not played host to many tourists for the past couple of years and informing, in Zaïre, is a way of life. The country, under the auspices of Mobutu's MPR

(Popular Renewal Movement) party, is divided into cells which form a pyramid – right up to the Big Man himself. Obviously, years of inefficiency, hatred of the ruling party and lack of communications were on our side, but the residents of Shaba had recently been united by the MPR governor in their hatred of the Kasai.

We hired a taxi driver whose last job, he claimed, had been three days earlier and set off for the American Consulate. He took us to an imposing-looking compound which bristled with satellite dishes and aerials and was guarded by what looked like a SWAT team. American culture had rubbed off on the local hire employees of the consulate, who all spoke perfect American, complete with late 1980s slang. Baseball caps, sweatshirts and hi-tops were the order of the day. Thanks to Bill's communications skills (he had just won the Communicator of the Year award from the US state department), we were expected and allowed to enter – as long as we got rid of our taxi driver who was causing a security alert by blocking the gates.

Inside the tall gates was a rank of GMC jeeps (which we immediately imagined to be UNITA mobiles), the boarded-up and battle-scarred consulate and a few smaller buildings. The office being used by the head of station was a small pre-fab, in which sat a group of lolling Zaïreans drinking Coke and watching *Raiders of the Lost Ark* on video. They were 'maintaining a presence', we were told. They wanted to help us to cover the tribal problems but feared a diplomatic incident if they lent us one of their cars, so arranged for us to hire a Gecamines Volvo. One of the consulate's laid-off chauffeurs was prevailed upon to act as our guard and driver. That way, if we encountered any problems, he could radio the consulate, who would try to get us out of the clutches of the governor. If we had no problems, their involvement would not be known.

After arranging a pick-up point for the next day, we were taken back to the hotel in a GMC – Savimbi style. Travelling in such grandeur instilled in us the nerve to go and worm our way into the railway station at Lubumbashi. We padlocked all our equipment into the cupboard again and walked down to the station, where we employed the train-spotter technique to get past the guards.

'We have come all the way from England to visit your railways,' we told the surly-looking captain barring the gates to the station. 'We work for British Rail and like to look at other countries' railways during our holidays.'

'You need to have permission from Kinshasa,' he snarled.

'We do,' I replied. 'Monsieur Tolombaye at PanAfric Railways has given us authorization to go anywhere on the railway. Call him up and check.' I was relying on the fact that the telephones don't work, since Monsieur Tolombaye was an entirely fictional character. After fifteen minutes of wheedling, we reached the final hurdle.

'My daughter is sick and I have no money. What am I to do?'

Formalities over, we saved his child from certain death by dispensing three packets of cigarettes to the captain and his men.

The platform was home to about two thousand refugees, whom we studiously ignored while showing great interest in the rolling stock. Soon we had blended into the chaos that was Lubumbashi station. Some railway employees appeared from under the verandah to show us around. They, in common with almost everyone we had met in Zaïre, had not been paid for months. Yet they were not like the residents of Kinshasa who, in the absence of cash, go wilding and stealing. They had been growing their own food (impossible in urban Kinshasa, but easier in less developed Lubumbashi) and living frugally. They continued to come to work, although there was nothing to do, out of a love of trains and a forlorn hope for the future. Lubumbashi is full of characters like them – lawyers in a lawless land, doctors with no medicine and miners whose mines have been closed. I was plagued by guilt, as they were genuinely interested in British Rail, about which I was able to tell them nothing. After a grand tour of the station, they told us that we could come back with our cameras if we could persuade the soldiers to let us take pictures.

We rushed back to the hotel to get Harriet's cameras, and shared them between us in an attempt to look like well-equipped tourists, rather than professional photographers. This was a fortuitous precaution since Guy Guy was lurking outside the hotel when we left, although he didn't approach us. The captain let us in again, but inside the station an under-employed corporal latched on to us. He was painfully thin, with legs like scissors and a grey complexion, which under World Health Organization guidelines would immediately have identified him as an AIDS sufferer. He wanted to sleep with both Harriet and me, before he would let us take any pictures, and we concluded it was worth a couple of million zaïres to avoid this. We can sneer at the WHO with the best of them, but we weren't taking any chances. Having passed over the cash, we set off again but the corporal, who had discovered a new source of income, would not leave us alone. We had already ascertained that he was bisexual, so Harriet gave me the task of flirting with him while she tried to get pictures of the refugees, in whom we were still feigning a lack of interest.

The corporal and I promenaded the platform, hand in hand, inspecting the trains. Graffiti, proclaiming that 'Mobutu égale misère' (Mobutu equals misery) adorned the sides of the carriages, drawn in the thick dust which encased them. No one could remember when they had last moved. Belgian, South Africa and Japanese rolling stock were all waiting on a train. The Zaïrean railway companies – SNCZ and OCS – had no money for spare parts, and even if they had would have been unable to get them. These donations from foreign powers were already obsolete when they had been sold cheap to the Zaïreans and parts for them were no longer available.

I nervously inspected the sleeper carriages, hoping I wasn't being too forward, as Harriet skulked around outside, sneaking shots of the refugees when no one was looking. The American 1950s-style brushed-steel carriages had been looted like everything else. All the seats and interior fittings had been torn from the walls. Our friends from the railway company were upset at what had happened to them.

'We tried to protect them during the *pillage* but there was such chaos that we had to look after our own families,' their leader, Jeannot, told me.

'But why were your family at risk? You aren't Kasai.'

'Everyone was at risk after a while. When it started, the foreigners and the big companies were the targets, but soon, all the boys had gone mad on drink and drugs. The DSP came and shot at everyone and then started stealing things themselves. When the Belgians came, it was dangerous for everyone, because they didn't know who was good or bad, but at least they were fair. The DSP didn't stay for long after the Belgians had arrived.'

Belgian paratroopers had been sent into Lubumbashi to evacuate the expatriates in 1991. They had managed to restore peace, merely by arriving. A tense stand-off at the airport – they didn't actually parachute in – had been solved by a fierce demonstration of Belgian fire power, which so terrified the rampaging police, soldiers and DSP that they had all returned to their barracks as fast as they could. Within two days of the Belgians' arrival in Kinshasa, they had been directing traffic, and much the same had happened in Lubumbashi.

The station had a charming, shady platform which was still in good repair, but the tracks alongside were beginning to disappear under the combined onslaught of grasses and weeds. I was surprised that any train could make it along the ill-maintained rails, but Jeannot assured me that only a week before a train had gone up to Kasai.

'These people on the platform,' he explained with a wink, 'are waiting for the next one.'

Harriet discovered that some of them had been there for three weeks, but neither of us were able to speak to them properly without arousing suspicion. My corporal already smelt a rat and was trying to extract more money not to expose us. I stuck to my

British Rail story as we ignored the heaving mass of refugees who littered the platform. We were not the only ones ignoring them. Hundreds of people had made their homes on the platform but they were all ignored by the rail workers, the soldiers and the police. They had become non-people.

Early the next morning, our American Consulate driver arrived to take us to Likasi, where the refugee problem was at its height. He was driving a large blue Volvo, which it emerged was the company car of one of Gecamines's ghost employees. Zaïreans really have corruption refined. You find ghost employees in many countries, from Northern Ireland to Peru, but I had never come across one with a company car before. We were hiring a car from someone who not only didn't exist, but also had the car, petrol and maintenance paid for by the company.

Likasi is about a hundred miles from Lubumbashi and totally different. The regional capital looked like a normal town, but in Likasi no effort had been made to cover up the fact that there was something strange going on. We were not in a position just to walk in and hope for the best. We would have stuck out like Amish in New York and been immediately arrested. Instead we went to the town hall to get permission to visit. Leaving our tell-tale equipment in the car, we walked into the disintegrating building to find the head man.

The guard at the door – who was more than a little surprised by our arrival – took us through to his boss, to whom we explained our situation.

'We have come from Britain where we work on the railways and would like to visit yours,' I lied. 'We thought that we ought to come and report our presence to the *commissaire urban* before going to the station, although we have permission from Kinshasa already.'

The official to whom we explained this was a bowed old man, sitting behind what looked like a school desk. Above the desk, we could see a minor civil servant wearing a tie, blue shirt with a frayed collar and a grey jacket. Below it he wore a pair of ragged surfing shorts, covering thighs which topped a pair of ulcerous shins and bare feet. The piece of fabric – with Mobutu's head screenprinted in the centre – which was tacked to the front of the desk, occasionally blew up in the wind from the open door and broken windows. Unaware of the breakdown in subterfuge, the official bobbed up from the desk to shake our hands on arrival and departure, without betraying his *deshabillement*. He passed us on to the man we wanted to see, who fell for our story.

The *commissaire urban* – a type of government-appointed mayor – was a smooth, wealthy-looking man who wore sunglasses indoors and a sober black mafioso suit. He apologized for not being able to show us around himself.

'I'm afraid we have a little bit of a war on at the moment so you are not seeing Likasi at its best,' he told us, 'but you are welcome to go wherever you wish. Thank you very much for having the courtesy to introduce yourselves. We do not see many foreigners here any more.'

Astonished by this reception, we walked stony-faced across the road and had a celebratory drink in the bar opposite. Then we went to the station.

Where the car park should have been, an impromptu market had grown up, where the forced returnees were selling salvaged household goods in return for food. A house to the right of the road had been taken over by the army and police, who were stopping people from going in and out. We had the necessary permission so were allowed in. We left the car and walked the final two hundred yards to the station.

The closer we came to the station, the worse the condition of the refugees. Many of them had been waiting for months, since being driven from their homes, and had long ago run out of food. They had erected small shelters from the rain and in almost every one there was a sick person, too ill to move, surrounded by their relations. On the outskirts of the camp, small children ran around searching for scraps and playing. At the station fence, lethargic women held scabious babies to their dried-up breasts while staring into space. Likasi was not like Sudan or Ethiopia. They had been suffering only for a few months, but the huge concentration of homeless people had led to death rates which equalled those then current in Somalia. Twenty of the 60,000 people at the station were dying every day (3.4 per 10,000). They were dying of infectious diseases, rather than starvation. Measles, one of Africa's biggest killers, was rife. The water supply was unclean and dirty water on empty stomachs had sent the dysentery rates soaring. In the quiet of the despairing centre, the terrible dry coughing, known as refugee flu, was the prevalent sound until people started to notice us.

The station was laid out like a low-level, open-plan office. When being driven from their homes, the Kasai had picked up everything they could and they had set up their recovered homes on the platform. Like Habitat home-starter kits, there was always something missing: a charcoal-burning stove but no bowls; a bed but no mattress. Old ladies sat in salvaged armchairs beside homemade beach screens, while their children and grandchildren sat on mats at their feet, waiting for a train to come. One train had been sitting in the station for ten days and was full of people. No one knew when it would leave, but having secured places were not going to let them go. The roofs of the carriages were laden down with pathetic goods that looked like the contents of skips but were the Kasai's only possessions. Broken pots and bicycles, mattresses and planks of wood were all tied to the sides or hanging out of windows. No one wanted to go to Kasai. Only a few of them had ever been there before and they knew they had no homes or work there, but they were terrified at the prospect of staying in Shaba. They sat with their meagre possessions waiting to be forced into the unknown.

On the embankment above and behind the station were about 50,000 even less fortunate people living under eight hundred and fifty nine-foot by six-foot, thin plastic tarpaulins. The tarps had been provided by Medecins Sans Frontières. ICRC were trying to provide food, but when we were there it had not yet started. The

UN were giving the problem a wide berth. The last time they had intervened in Katanga it had taken them four years, many peacekeepers' lives and one dead secretary general before they could extricate themselves. When the trains worked, they managed to move two thousand people a week in room for four hundred and fifty. Many died of asphyxiation along the way. But they were not working because the provincial authorities, having ordered the Kasai to leave Shaba, were refusing to pay for locomotive diesel and, anyway, the train drivers were on strike. Hope as well as food and water was in desperately short supply.

The ethnic cleansing had started in August 1992, shortly after Etienne Tshisekedi (a Kasai) had taken over from Nguza Karl-i-Bond as prime minister. Since then, the Kasai had been on the run. In September, many of them had found sanctuary in a military base; in October they had been thrown out of there and turned up in the grounds of Kikulu school. By October, almost the only sanctuary left was the extended waiting room which now surrounded Likasi station. It was now late November and all over Shaba Kasai were hiding in people's houses and in the bush, while those who could not were awaiting their fate at the stations of Likasi and the next stop Kolwezi. A Kasai religious group had set up to organize and protect them at Likasi station, but even this was ineffective, except as another form of totalitarianism.

We were soon approached by an officious refugee who didn't want us there. We had undermined his authority by not asking his permission. We were told that we could not remain at the station without the authorization of the religious boss so we dragged our persecutor off to help us find him. After a long drive around the town, from smart office to comfortable house, we discovered him in the car park of a church. He was taking a vast tomato salad out of the back of his Mercedes and would not stop to talk to us. The happy clapping of a harvest festival in the church was too tempting for him and he left us in the hands of one of his lieutenants. He told the minion that he was not to talk to us on the record, but he could escort us to the MSF base in the middle of the refugee camp. The minion took this very literally and would not talk to us at all, although he did want to be paid for his trouble. These were the good guys.

Monique – one of four MSF doctors at the camp – showed us around and begged us to write about the problem. This was the best indication of how bad things were in Likasi. MSF has suffered from a very bad press over the years and has countered this by being consistently foul to journalists. This was the first time that an MSF doctor had even smiled at me, let alone helped me do my job. Monique, a veteran of many an unpleasant situation around Africa, was close to despair. The dispensary was a small compound of wooden shacks surrounded by patient queues of long-suffering mothers cradling sick children. This was medicine at its most basic and pointless. There wasn't much that MSF could do. The causes of the illness were simple but man-made. The children were becoming ill through lack of food and sanitation and the administration was denying them both. Until the causes were eradicated, all MSF could do was treat the symptoms.

'Sixty per cent of the children arriving here are malnourished,' she said. 'We are meant to be doctors, but there is no one here to feed them, and no end in sight. The provincial government has banned Zambian food imports to Kasai, so even if we get them back to health here, they are being sent to a place where they also have no shelter and no food. We have managed to get enough funding for ourselves, but there are no other agencies to fill the gaps.'

Ethnic cleansing is a new cliché in the west but it has been fashionable in Africa for centuries. It is called tribalism. From Sudan, where the Nuer fight the Dinka, down to South Africa where Zulu and Xhosa are at each other's throats, ethnic cleansing is the norm rather than anything new. What horrified observers about Likasi was the sheer cycnicism of it. Both Karl-i-Bond and Kyungu – the two main protagonists of the policy – are married to Kasais. Etienne Tshisekedi was powerless to intervene and Mobutu was having fun fanning the flames.

As Monique walked us down from the crowded dispensary to the station, we saw a father wheeling a tiny coffin, strapped to the back of a bicycle, across the railway tracks. Small boys brushed him aside as they scrambled along the path. Parents of sick children along his route did not avert their eyes and showed no signs of sympathy. They had become inured to death and acceptant to their fate. A sight which would have brought tears to the eyes of far-removed newpaper readers was of no interest to the people whom it most affected. They were just sad and despairing.

One woman, who had been there for nine weeks and had recently lost a child to measles, greeted me from the entrance of her nine-by-six tent. All around her hundreds of other similar families were living in regimented lines under plastic tarpaulins supported by sticks. When it rained, streams would sweep right through the shelters, over bodies and blankets, stores and fires. Erected on the slope of a cutting, at the first sign of heavy rain, the entire camp would be swept on to the railway tracks. She told me of her particular experience.

'They came in the middle of the night and just burnt down the village. No one was killed, but we have nothing left. I was born in Shaba and have nowhere to go in Kasai. I have never even been there. Tshitsi (Etienne Tshisekedi's nickname) will not forget his people and the Lord will help us.'

There was going to be a lot of disappointment ahead for these religious zealots, but for the time being, their faith was helping them. It resulted in a stoic acceptance of the most appalling conditions and a great deal of community spirit. Famine and hardship break down tribal and clan loyalties to the point where families become insular. Young children – who have no productive use – are often allowed to starve in Africa when circumstances force it. But here in Likasi, families were sharing food with others. People had withdrawn to such an extent that the arrival of western journalists, laden down with shining equipment, cigarettes and sunglasses was of little interest even to perpetually curious children. When a man stole my cigarettes and lighter, under the nose of a group of people, he was castigated by the crowd and I was given a formal apology by a religious leader. The thief was ostracized and the fellow members of his tribe were ashamed.

The Kasai are the strongest tribe of the country's over two hundred ethnic groups, but in Shaba they were in the minority. There is no doubt that they do dominate the top jobs in Zaïre but the Kasais of Shaba were minor offenders. In other parts of the country, people need to speak Kasai in order to get ahead – the majority of these people did not speak Kasai at all. They regarded themselves as Shabaians and spoke the local language – Kiswahili. In the first Katanga (Shabaian) war they had even fought against the UN, Zaïrean and Belgian troops on behalf of the Katangese. The majority of Katangese had little objection to them. The horrific scenes we witnessed at Likasi station, which blurred further the woolly line between ethnic cleansing and genocide, were the direct result of three people's evil machinations. Mobutu, Karl-i-Bond and Kyungu had used a small group of dissolute, unemployed and impressionable youths to tear a province apart. Their actions had set worker against worker, kith again kin and further destroyed the economy of the nation. Furthermore, the will for secession, which they had let loose to achieve these aims, is going to have to be equally brutally crushed in the years ahead.

We returned to Lubumbashi marvelling at the duplicity of the triumvirate. Martin, our driver, understood what was going on and just wanted to keep his head down until the Americans came back. He was getting enough money on part-wages (from the consulate) to survive and was insistent that he would.

'I was studying for a scholarship before the *pillage*, and continue my studies at home,' he told us. 'If only I can get to America, I will be able to leave this country for good. But, to do that, things have to get better first, or the Americans won't be able to come back. Without their scholarship I don't know what I will do. They can't pay me for ever. I don't do anything any more.'

We arranged that Martin could take us out again to visit

Kolwezi, where similar scenes awaited us, before he dropped us off at the hotel. In separate parts of the lobby, both Guy Guy and the lusty corporal were awaiting our return. The two were resorting to blackmail by now, yet to give in to their threats and pay them would be to admit that they were right and we were indeed journalists. We managed to postpone our exposure by getting them drunk in the bar. The management of the hotel were not happy about this. We were lowering the tone of the establishment. We, like everybody else, had by this time not washed for a week, so felt justified in ignoring their complaints. After a day in a refugee camp and a week with no water, we would have donated vital organs in exchange for someone else's bath water.

We met Jean, an ICRC delegate, in the bar and discovered that he was trying to accompany a cleansing train from Lubumbashi to Kasai. He had been trying and failing to do this for a couple of weeks and was becoming angry. The trains rarely left when they had been authorized to do so and when they did, his permission to travel on them was withdrawn at the last minute. The endless toots from the station did nothing for his blood pressure as they never signified a departing train but he couldn't take that chance. He had a team of Zaïrean delegates, all dressed up in their Red Cross aprons as though operating in a war-zone hospital, waiting to do a study of the conditions. They arrived for a last-minute briefing, only to be informed that the train had once again been cancelled. No train had left for a week and the resultant concentration of refugees was becoming unmanageable. They were not allowed to leave the station and had long ago run out of food. There was something terrible about the silence at the station. Hundreds were crammed into carriages, others waited their turn on the platforms. None of them talked, in the hope that keeping their heads down would spare them further brutality.

Despairing of the situation, Jean took us out clubbing with an Air Zaïre pilot and his Swazi girlfriend. We went to Lubumbashi's top club, the Club Nouveau. It was an evening of pent-up emotion. The Air Zaïre pilot was desperate to get away from

Lubumbashi, where he had been stranded for two weeks awaiting parts for his plane. He was from Kinshasa and thought his compatriots in Lubumbashi were nothing better than peasants. He longed for the sophistication of the capital which we had been so glad to leave. He no longer had any clothes, money or possessions. Some soldiers had come to his room in our hotel at dead of night and – holding him at gunpoint – stolen everything in the room, including the sheets. Through the course of the evening he sat by the side of the dance floor, drinking the strongest beer available, while Harriet, Jean and I danced with his girlfriend.

Zaïreans love dancing and are incredibly good at it. Carolyn, the Swazi girl, tried to teach me to '*faire le kwasa kwasa*'. She was very beautiful in an imposing and regal kind of way. I spent the evening stumbling around the minute dance-floor with my head in her cleavage, while everyone else flew about us like competition ballroom dancers. Styles of dress varied but were always bright – enhanced by the ultraviolet light which bathed the mirrored bar and torn brown velour stools. One man, who resembled a portly penguin from the back, turned round to reveal that his otherwise black suit was adorned with green, red and yellow harlequin panels on its front. A large diamante Jesus brooch shone from his handkerchief pocket, in no way disguising that he was wearing a shoulder holster. Others were dressed like Michael Jackson in his *Thriller* days. The girls went for Lycra. The dancing was frenzied, the drinking Herculean.

A rumour was going around that the border with Zambia was going to close the next day. The Lebanese money dealers had released the five million zaïre note in Zambia and Tshisekedi wanted to close the border before it could reach the Zaïrean market. The five-million zaïre notes had been printed a few months earlier but not released to the public. In a convoluted and dodgy deal, the central bank had handed over all the notes to the Lebanese money dealers who promptly flew them out of the country. The dealers wanted to keep the dollar rate down in order to maximize profits when they did release the notes. The only thing that was keeping the dollar rate to two million was the fact that zaïres were scare. Releasing the note would push the rate to seven million in a matter of minutes and the Lebanese would make a killing.

They not only made a killing, they also caused more than one. The eventual full introduction of the note led directly to the 1993 rioting in which the French ambassador and many others were killed. Mobutu paid the army with the five million notes and Tshisekedi then told everyone not to accept them as legal tender. The army reacted by blockading all the appropriate buildings and going on the rampage. The DSP were sent in to deal with them and then went on the rampage themselves. French and Belgian paratroopers were sent in to deal with the DSP and after a few days it was estimated that Zaïre had lost another billion dollars' worth of infrastructure. They no longer have many billion dollars' worth of infrastructure left to destroy.

Harriet and I were rather panicked by the news. Guy Guy, the corporal and the chamberman were all on the verge of exposing us to the authorities and we didn't fancy the idea of a Zaïrean jail. Kaye, the British chargé, had already told us that she wasn't going to be much help if we got into trouble and as British citizens we couldn't rely on the Americans. We did not have enough money for the type of bribes it would take to get out of jail and no nearby friends. We went back to the hotel to think. The border was rumoured to be closing at two o'clock the next day, so we had to do it fast.

There was an angel in the lobby. We had met him before but presumed him to be another boring missionary. Over the next twenty-four hours, he made a startling transformation. Benoit had come to tell us that we should have our bags packed and be ready to leave by eleven o'clock the next morning. The rumour was fact and he too had to get to Zambia before the border closed. He could give us a lift as far as Lusaka in his Land Cruiser. We went up to bed feeling happier than we had for weeks. We had seen as much of the railway as possible, so didn't feel too guilty, and would be in Zambia the next day. After months on the road, we would be able to relax in a country where we were welcome. We had friends in Lusaka and we had even applied for Zambian press cards. When we reached our room there was a strange gushing noise coming from behind the door. The water was back on. We rejoiced in our cold baths and went to bed clean.

Guy Guy came to breakfast, blithely unaware how close he was to being strangled. Overnight, he had discovered some more penniless relations who were in need of our help. By this time his family had been decimated. He had a wife with leukaemia, a brother with AIDS, various children in need of education and a mother who needed burying. I bought him breakfast and arranged to meet him that afternoon. Zaïre had got on top of Harriet. Feeling mildly sick and uniformly fed up, she had refused to leave the room and was packing upstairs in preparation for our departure. Guy Guy was succeeded by the corporal who was beginning to get nasty and demanded beer at seven-thirty in the morning. The staff, whose pride had returned with the water, were furious. He was wearing a pair of threadbare combat trousers which exposed his wasted left buttock and an antique army shirt. I hit on the perfect answer. Gavin, the British colonel, had given Harriet a pair of army trousers in Angola when we were stranded with a battle between us and our wardrobes. They did not fit her and she hadn't worn them since. There is now a pathetically happy Zaïrean soldier in Lubumbashi, wearing a British colonel's fatigues. He left clutching them to his breast, prepared to meet us again that evening.

I returned triumphant to the room, where we hid on the balcony until eleven o'clock. Both of us wanted to keep our remaining contact with Zaïre to a minimum. Our room overlooked the street, where a party of soldiers had set up an impromptu road block. Every car that entered the road was stopped, transformed into a cash-point machine and then allowed to drive on. The three soldiers were wearing smart green uniforms, Sam Brownes and white puttees. The headman stopped the cars with a whistle, marched smartly to the driver's side, saluted and pushed an Uzi through the window. No one asked for a PIN number and cash was dispensed immediately. We basked in the sunshine and waited for our lift. When Benoit arrived he stopped at the road block and loudly berated the patrol. They got nothing out of him. No one did on the entire trip to Lusaka.

Benoit was a Belgian evangelical missionary working in central Zaïre, at the end of an interminable forest track, which he had built. He had been working in Zaïre for fourteen years and spoke one tribal language, Swahili, English and French fluently. At six foot four, with shoulders to match, he concentrated rather more on building bridges and roads than spreading the word, but through doing this had done more for the Zaïrean people than any straight missionary ever could. He was an awesome figure, in the true sense of the word. A Saint-George-style defender of the faith, he roved the country doing good by using his brain and his brawn. If something needed doing he would order a book and learn how to do it – from building bridges to breach births. He had taught his local tribe how to combine traditional birthing practices with hygiene. It required no new equipment and so they continued to do it when he was away. He disarmed and beat up soldiers who victimized his people and had enough natural authority to get away with it. To his local villagers he gave the things they needed in a manageable and sustainable way. I am sure he sinned every day, but only for a higher purpose.

In the course of the journey we discovered that before his vocation he had been in the Belgian special forces and had been involved in more covert operations in more places than Ollie North. He put this rather strange training for a missionary to good use in the bush and emerged as an honourable and impressive man. We were in the best of hands for getting across the border and as we left Lubumbashi felt like unaccompanied minors being looked after on a long-haul flight. As we travelled along the road to the frontier, Benoit floored the accelerator. None of us wanted to get stuck in Zaïre and anything could happen on that road. In 1977 the French had used it as a landing strip, where they rearmed and fuelled their MiGs for bombing runs on Kolwezi. H. F. Varian, one of Pauling's engineers, had been driven back by bandits there on a surveying trip eighty years earlier. Hence he built the railway only to the border and left the Zaïrean part to another company.

We were worried about crossing the border with all our equipment but Benoit told us not to panic and covered everything in the back of the vehicle with a tarpaulin. Just before the border we stopped and ate our sandwiches and drank coffee before heading off for the next ordeal. Benoit told us stories of pre-missionary missions he had done in countries we knew and understood, with astonishing and verifiable detail. To repeat them would be fascinating but would also betray his identity. Suffice it to say that we could not have been in safer hands.

As we drew up at the frontier, the guards were rubbing their hands with glee. This was no longer a busy border crossing and the pickings had been slim of late. They were to be disappointed. We left Harriet to guard the car and went through to immigration and customs. Benoit handed out Swahili Bibles to the less-than-civil servants and we were back at the car with the necessary stamps and papers in ten minutes. We drove on to the gate, where an officious guard came over to the vehicle.

'Get out of the car and open the back,' he said.

Harriet and I had heard this refrain in Kinshasa and were beginning to sweat. Benoit got out of the car, loomed over the soldier and said: 'Do you have a problem with the Church?'

'No. No. Are you a priest?' came the startled reply.

Benoit gave all the guards a Swahili prayer book. They demanded Bibles. Benoit refused, explaining that they were very expensive. The gate was opened and we moved into no-man's land with fifteen minutes to spare before the border closed.

We drove on towards Zambia. Zaïre looked beautiful. I almost believed the many people who have assured me that outside the cities it is actually a wonderful place to visit. A heat haze hovered over the black strip of road which bisected the bush and seemed to flow out of the interminable green of the faraway rainforest. Beyond our range of vision lay the great river and the jungle of central Zaïre, the mineral wealth, the fertile land and the forgotten people of the interior. It was the best view I'd had of Zaïre — receding in the rear-view mirror.

CHAPTER FIVE

Zambian customs needed no bribing. We even told the truth on our immigration forms, which always gives one a sense of security when entering a country. The fact that there were five road blocks between the border at Chilalabombwe and the first major town of Kitwe was no problem either. The troops guarding the road were heavily armed and doubtless dangerous, but also unerringly polite and well behaved. They were just taking the precautions deemed necessary by a country which shares a border with Zaïre. In their position, I would have built a wall.

Impoverished Zaïreans had been sneaking over the border for years and with the unrest in Shaba the problem had recently worsened. Car theft in northern Zambia is so prevalent that you feel nervous every time you leave your car. Vehicles are often stolen, stripped down, repainted and driven over the border before they have even been reported missing. The roads are not safe after dark, as bands of smugglers stop cars, shoot the occupants and take the vehicles over to Lubumbashi. Just after we left, two deputy ministers were stripped, robbed and left to walk home when they were electioneering in the area.

Truck drivers are often provided with armed guards by the government, and the big trucking companies have their own security staff. The government likes to blame this on Zaïreans but in fact it happens throughout the country. A friend in Lusaka, who imports from South Africa, described it as an occupational hazard. We came across him one afternoon inspecting a bullet hole in the roof of a Volkswagen. One of his transporters had recently been pulled over by armed men, who had tried to shoot the driver. The bullet narrowly missed the driver's head and passed through the roof of the truck and the base and seat of the

VW above before exiting through the VW's roof. Zambia seemed like heaven after Zaïre but it was still a front-line state with severe problems. Although Zambia itself has remained peaceful, it has been a base for rebel groups of many different countries. They brought weapons with them which have filtered down to the bandits who rule the roads.

When we stopped in Kitwe for a drink and something to eat, we had to go to absurd lengths to park the vehicle within sight of our table. Benoit was going back to Zaïre as soon as he had finished his business in Zimbabwe but we were all relieved to have made it over the border in time. Our only worry was cholera. There were posters on every surface telling the populace to be alert to the threat of cholera but once again this was a prime example of wasted aid money. UN-sponsored posters encouraged people to wash their food and make sure that their water supply was safe. Many Zambians cannot read that well for a start and in most places there *was* no safe water supply. No advice about boiling water was given and cholera was sweeping through the schools and townships. There is no point in washing food and utensils with infected water. We drank luke-warm coke from the bottle. None of us was going to mess with ice.

In October 1888, Lord Salisbury, the British prime minister, gave Cecil Rhodes's British South Africa Company a royal charter. This allowed Rhodes to make treaties and fight battles north of the Limpopo, with the sanction and authority of the British government, while retaining personal control for himself. Rhodes wanted the mineral rights to Katanga in what is now southern Zaïre and sent off expeditionary forces to forge treaties to that effect. Robert Williams managed to get there first, but by that time Rhodes's company owned a vast tract of land from the Transvaal to Zaïre. It became Northern and Southern Rhodesia and was administered by the BSA for twenty-five years before being handed over to the British colonial office in 1923.

Apart from being a politician, diplomat and businessman, Rhodes was a miner. Mines need railways and it was through them that he and Pauling had met in 1885. They were in constant contact over the years and Pauling & Co. built many railways in South Africa while Rhodes was still an MP. As prime minister in 1894, Rhodes called Pauling to Cape Town and asked him to become a founder member of the ruling council of Rhodesia. By the end of 1895, while his railways surged across the continent, Pauling had assumed the mantles of minister for public works (including railways), minister of mines and postmaster general. As is still the case in Africa, business and politics were as one. Africa was opened up by the slave business in Zanzibar, from where merchants set out to govern the interior. Today, Tiny Rowlands's Lonrho plc intervenes in peace negotiations in Mozambique and Sudan, only these days the merchant kings travel by aeroplane.

The protectorate of Northern Rhodesia gained its independence as Zambia in October 1964. Britain hurled it upon the world scene with a grand total of a hundred graduates and just under a thousand holders of secondary-school certificates. Its economy was tied to copper, which for the first few years after independence provided it with a good income but soon proved to be a millstone. By 1984 the real income of Zambians was half that which it had been in 1974.

Zambia's leader from independence until 1991 was Kenneth Kaunda, a lovable hulk of a man affectionately known as KK, who ruled it as a one-party state and played a mean guitar. He managed to combine respect for the Queen, as head of the Commonwealth, with a principled and very costly stand against white rule in neighbouring countries. He supported terrorist campaigns in Namibia, Angola, Mozambique, South Africa and Zimbabwe, which led to the razing of villages on Zambia's borders and the bombing, by Smith's Rhodesia, of his capital, Lusaka. He also brought the warring parties together in numerous attempts at peace. His rare combination of strong principles and a desperate urge to be loved led to Zambia's crippled economy and his eventual removal from power.

In 1991, 80 per cent of the population voted against him in a multiparty election. He fought the election fairly and was the first post-independence African leader to retire the political stage with grace and a semblance of credibility intact. The only remaining 'founding father' of black Africa was then Dr Hastings Banda of Malawi who was voted out of office in 1994. Kuanda tried to farm but has now had to return to Lusaka because he was not made welcome in the northern province.

KK is a grand old man who meant no harm, yet none the less has to bear responsibility for reducing the mineral-rich, fertile and economically powerful Zambia that he inherited to the pot-holed poverty trap it is today. He is generally acknowledged to have been incorruptible although this is within an African context. Evidence has emerged about secret deals with Pretoria and he certainly had many dealings with Lonrho, but then who hasn't? Moreover, two years of humiliating treatment by the new government, involving dawn raids on his offices and minute searches of his personal papers, has resulted in no charges being laid against him. After twenty-seven years of extremely difficult rule – whatever the whispers – this is an impressive record.

His policies, however, paved the way for less-principled associates, and have left his beloved Zambia gasping for economic breath. Zambianization of everything in the post-independence years led to skilled workers being elevated to managerial and directorial positions. This left the country with unskilled workers being managed by unskilled directors. His protests against white rule on Zambia's borders led to the severing of trade links and the necessity to build new transport systems, when the ones that went through politically incorrect countries already worked perfectly. He had to stop using the Copperbelt to Beira railway because, in order to reach the coast, his goods would have to go through Rhodesia or South Africa. He managed this by sending goods to Dar es Salaam on a dirt road known as the 'hell run' and then, as soon as it was completed, on the Tazara railway which had been built with the help of Mao's China.

Well-meaning agricultural subsidies were absorbed by the many inefficient parastatals, state-owned and -run companies, which he had set up. As in other African countries, the parastatals and one-crop economies have destroyed agriculture. In Kenya it is illegal to cut down a coffee bush yet they are not worth harvesting because the coffee board to whom one is obliged to sell seldom pays and never pays enough. Farmers have been forced to grow other crops in the shade of the bushes. In Zambia, as a result of similar practices and subsidies on consumption, poverty-stricken rural peasants fled to the towns. It was cheaper to eat subsidized mealie meal in town than it was to grow it. All the main towns of Zambia are on the railway line and by 1991, 50 per cent of the population lived in them. The rest of Zambia is all but deserted.

The teetotal Kaunda lost the election because of his drunken mismanagement of the economy. His refusal to accept foreign-aid-dictated reforms led to no support coming from the international community when he was trying his Africa solution. Frederick Chiluba, then a 38-year-old trade union leader, far to the right of Kaunda, became the new president and now has to reform the terminally damaged economy. He has grasped the concept of structural adjustment programmes (SAP) with religious fervour. SAPs are an IMF invention which force the liberalization of economies. Very simply, having an SAP involves setting up a stock exchange, floating the currency, removing subsidies, privatizing everything and firing half the civil service. It tends to beggar the nation concerned. IMF and World Bank experts sit down with local leaders and iron out a programme for change. In order to receive aid, governments have to keep to a schedule laid out by the financiers and previously agreed with local ministers.

In Zambia, billions have to be spent, privatizing everything that Kuanda had nationalized and trying to kick-start the economy. To do that, Chiluba will have to fire half the workforce, remove subsidies on everything and then win an election. He has two things on his side – Mandrax and God. Chiluba himself is as pure as the driven snow – a born-again Christian on a mission from God. The people who surround him and helped put him in power, are not. He owes them many political debts and will have to weigh these against his principles. Two members of his cabinet allegedly had connections to drug running and have now been forced to resign following donor pressure. They were not alone. Where most leaders have a kitchen cabinet, Chiluba has a medicine cabinet. The money which financed his campaign was, at least partly, the earnings from drug running.

We were entering a country which shows categorically the difficulties of being a principled African state. If you want to succeed in Africa, it helps to be a bastard. Ian Smith proved it in neighbouring Rhodesia and the monsters of Pretoria proved it in South Africa. Kaunda stuck to his beliefs in Zambia and was cheered by everyone except his countrymen. Zambia and Zimbabwe used to be two parts of the same federation but you would never believe it today. Ian Smith, by being ruthless in Southern Rhodesia, kept the economy going and left a thriving though by no means perfect country. Kaunda stuck to his principles in Northern Rhodesia – vacillating when harsh economic policies were necessary to pay for them – and totally destroyed his once-prosperous nation. Chiluba cannot afford to be a nice guy but, if Zambia is to have any chance at all, he must retain his Christian morals. The test of the next few years will be whether he can hang on to them when he's out in the desert. He's going to be tempted for much longer than forty days. I shudder to say it, but evangelical Christianity is Zambia's last chance. Zealots are meant to be incorruptible.

We were intending to spend the night in Kitwe before making our way down to Lusaka on the railway but there was no room at the inns so we drove straight through to the capital Lusaka. We drove through Ndola and the copper belt where giant vats of glowing slag mounted on rail wagons are poured on to the heap in an industrial firework display. An old friend of mine had recently married a prominent white landowner's son in Lusaka so we were going to stay in someone's house for the first time in a long while. When we arrived at two o'clock in the morning, however, we thought it might be best to wait until the next day before contacting them. Benoit was driving on to Harare that night, so we said our farewells over coffee at a Lusaka hotel. It had been a simple but interesting journey from the heart of darkness. Lusaka was hardly the city of light but it was a welcome change to be in a hotel with CNN, room service and hot running water, and where we didn't need to disguise our identities.

I went to sleep cursing the fact that I could not write a whole book about Benoit. He was a fascinating man. When we had stopped on the road for coffee in the middle of the night, we were approached by a gang of youths, pretending to have a breakdown but obviously set on stealing our car. Had it been Harriet and I alone, we would have been walking to Lusaka. Benoit, by striding towards them and offering to help them mend their car, shamed them into changing their plans. We drank our coffee, packed up our Thermos in peace and drove on, leaving them to hijack the next vehicle foolish enough to stop for refreshment on a deserted road in the middle of the night. Benoit will continue to walk through the valley of death like some avenging medieval angel and will doubtless die of natural causes many years hence, his certain ability to see right from wrong undulled by time.

We managed to track down Ginny Bond and her husband Robin Miller the next day. They live on a large farm on the outskirts of Lusaka where Zambianization had mainly beneficial results. Ginny works for the University of Zambia and spends most of her time up country, fighting against AIDS with a zeal which sits uneasily with her appearance. In common with her sister Catherine – the doyenne of the Nairobi press corps – she is a small and seemingly fragile blonde with a formidable brain. Ginny is studying for a doctorate in social anthropology and is an expert on African sexual practices. 'Dry fucking is the key to Zambia's STD problem,' she once told me. 'People use herbs and leaves to neutralize lubrication which in turn causes open sores that attract disease.'

While her conversation can be gory, her complete lack of embarrassment means that things which have to be discussed in order to be understood do not get swept under the carpet. In a country where the deputy minister of health claims that, 'In our intent to enjoy sex, we are killing one another,' they need people like her.

Robin, too, is a conundrum. He looks and sounds like a white African farmer should. He is enormous, looks good in shorts and can speak with a broad Rhodesian accent. Many would be horrified by the feudal nature of the Millers' farm, but they would be wrong. The Millers have invested hundreds of thousands of dollars in tourism which brings much-needed foreign exchange into their country. Robin's father gave up British nationality and is one of a very few white Zambians. Their farm is, against all adversity, one of the few capable of feeding the towns of Zambia, and Robin part-owns the only independent newspaper in the country. When we arrived he was suffering a backlash because the paper remains critical of the government although the government was, until rcently, the opposition. One of the country's key ministers, Michael 'King Cobra' Sata, was suing the paper which, like being sued by Slobodan Milosevic, was great advertising.

We had hoped to be in Zambia in time for their wedding but were – without explanation – three months late. Regardless, we were welcomed and we settled into almost a month based at their farm in Lilayi. Ginny and Robin's house had been our only definite visit on the trip and, to our surprise, piles of letters and parcels were awaiting us there. Shepherd's pie for dinner that night had never tasted so good. Harriet and I decided to get straight to work and spent the next day trying to organize our railway trip. Zambia has a veneer of efficiency. There are telephones, televisions, electricity and water. Sadly, not much of it works very well. In the Lusaka Zambian Airways office, they use the current telephone directory in place of lavatory paper. We could not get through to railway headquarters, so resigned ourselves to travelling, unnannounced, up to Kabwe – Zambia's equivalent to Crewe.*

We had applied for press cards months earlier and went to collect them the next morning. At the Ministry of Information – a huge and sparsely populated building full of unmatched furniture, small offices and contradictory signposts – the man in charge of press cards allowed us to search through a filing cabinet full of them. All our friends seemed to have uncollected passes in the drawers, and among them we managed to find ours – signed by the commissioner of police himself. Armed with this legitimacy we went to the railway station to book ourselves on to our first train. Not far from Robin's town office, the accepted way to approach the station was through a graveyard for redundant railway machinery, over the tracks and up on to the platform. The station master was impressed by our credentials and tried to get in touch with the PR department in Kabwe via the railway's separate telephone system. He, too, failed.

'I am sorry,' he said. 'You will have to drive up and see Mr Chaonsa. The telephones don't seem to be working.'

'Is there a train going up tonight?' I asked.

'You don't want to take the train,' he replied. 'It takes all night to get there on the express.'

We assured him that indeed we did want to take the train and over his protestations booked two first-class sleepers for that evening – at a dollar a piece. He had even offered to have someone drive us up to Kabwe himself and quite patently thought we were mad.

Robin, too, thought we were crazy to be taking the train. 'I can get someone to drive you up there tomorrow morning,' he said. But we insisted we were going to take the first available train. We were looking forward to it.

From what we could hear on the radio, things were calming down a little in Angola. We made a few telephone calls and

* British Rail's main hub.

discovered that we might be able to get down to Lobito and take the first section of the railway if the ceasefire held for long enough. The MPLA had announced that despite winning the election, they were going to set up a government of national unity in the hope of keeping the peace. To this end, they had offered a post in the new government to UNITA – the Ministry of Culture. I am sure they did not intend to be ironic but the peace offering was so insulting that it did not bode well for the future. By this time UNITA controlled more than half the country and all I could bring myself to write in my diary that night was, 'Oh my God'.

We booked tickets to Namibia for the weekend and set off to try to get visas for Angola and Mozambique. These visas are notoriously difficult to obtain. Zambia, though, is a laid-back and relaxed country. By the end of the day we had received both countries' visas and were marvelling at our good fortune. It had taken three weeks to get Angolan visas in London and we had needed letters from endless sources vouching for our reliability. In Zambia, all we did was explain that we had left the country during the war and wished to return. The advantage of telephones not working is that if you can convince one minor official of your needs, you are set. He cannot call his boss for confirmation. This technique worked at both Angolan and Mozambican embassies. We considered trying to get Iraqi and Bhutanese visas while we were at it but Bhutan was not represented and Iraq was no longer on such good terms with Zambia since the Avenue Saddam Hussein had been renamed Los Angeles Boulevard.

Our unfortunately named taxi driver, Manson, drove us from embassy to consulate at high speed, stopping only to pick up his children from school. He had supported Chiluba in the elections but was already growing tired of him.

'Look at him. He is in court today talking about corruption. KK would never had gone to court to give evidence. What kind of man is he?'

Chiluba had astonished his countrymen by appearing in the high court to give evidence in a corruption case against some of his associates. The west heralded this as a great step forward in accountability. His fellow citizens thought he was bringing shame on the third republic. Despite all their multiparty leanings, most Africans still like their presidents to act like chiefs and they were outraged by Chiluba's behaviour. 'As the president of Zambia, he should have to answer to no one,' thought Manson out loud.

Many others shared his view, and combined with the austerity measures needed to bring the economy under control, Chiluba was fast losing popularity. The turnout in the local elections had been laughably small and the MMD had lost much of the ground they had won in the previous year's general election.

Ginny was off in the south where she spent most of her time gathering information for her Ph.D. and living in a small village on the banks of the Zambesi. Having left most of our luggage at Lilayi, Robin took us to the Gymkhana Club for a drink before we took the night train. Zambia has none of the elitism of other former colonial circles. The Gymkhana Club is a dowdy institution where the privileged whites of Lusaka occasionally meet to drink. There is none of the snobbery associated with polo and riding that you would expect. The Club Hequipage in Kinshasa has a strict dress code. In Nairobi, riding has a definite class-based appeal and it is a source of great anger to some that the best polo player in the country is an African syce. In Zambia 1970s fashion and CND badges seemed to be popular and regional British or white Zambian accents were the norm. Anyone braying would not have been welcome among the darts boards and pool tables. Still, there were no black Zambians there except the staff. But the whites despaired of Zambia's demise and wanted to do something about it. An equivalent gathering of whites elsewhere in Africa would have been indulging in non-productive sneering.

Robin took us to the station at nine o'clock. We sat on the steps chatting with gem smugglers who were trying to interest us in their wares. Robin astonished them by telling them in their own language that the stones were glass. Barriers down, we had an amusing hour as they told us what they were up to. They lived in Kabwe and spent their time travelling round northern Zambia, buying stones from subsistence farmers and Zaïrean smugglers, then bringing them down to Lusaka to sell to the Lebanese. After an hour we told Robin to go home. He was still suggesting a lift but we shunned his offer and went off to the signal box to find out when the train was coming.

Huddled on the platform were hundreds of people, also waiting for the train. The station master could not give us a definite time for the train's arrival but did let us wait in the control room. He did not want to talk to us officially until we had been authorized by the PR department but was very friendly and explained to us how the glowing control panel worked. The panel was a rectangular box which showed the line and points in and around Lusaka. It was very high tech, and had been made by Siemens of Germany. The flashing lights indicated points problems. Every light on the board was flashing. The equipment, the station master explained, was a little too sophisticated, and had never worked. He had to send a spare locomotive along the line to tell the waiting express from Livingstone that all was safe and it could come through to Lusaka.

After a few minutes we could see the light of the approaching train. The voice of Chris, the ticket salesman who had secured us a first-class compartment, came on to the PA system.

'Have a very safe journey and trust in God,' he said.

The train which rolled into the station was already packed. No compartment could be found for us and the ticket collector was furious that he had not been warned of our arrival. Four well-armed soldiers were sharing a compartment and one of them offered to move out so that Harriet, at least, could get some sleep. She declined the offer.

The guard set about waking up everyone on the train in his attempts to find room for us. We jumped from foot to foot feeling sheepish, English and embarrassed. Eventually a bed was found for me in a compartment that I was to share with an Angolan missionary on his way to Mozambique. Harriet was to share a larger compartment with three Zambian grandmothers but walked down to have a final cigarette with me. We needed to discuss this momentous occasion. We were on our first train. The compartment and in fact the whole train stank of stale sweat. The second- and third-class carriages were like refugee camps on wheels. Coughing and groaning people tried to sleep, two and three to a seat. Pathetic bundles of possessions were rammed into the overhead nets, competing for space with small children and chickens. In the relative comfort of first class, the bunks were made of body-clinging, torn brown plastic. The lavatories had backed up and the corridors were full of seatless people with damp feet. A broken mirror with RR (Rhodesian Railways) etched upon it allowed Harriet and me to sit on the bottom bunk, yet still have eye to eye contact with the young missionary in the top bunk. His attempts to convert us were interrupted by a roar from the door.

'This is not Tanzanian Railways,' shouted the brocade-adorned guard whose evening we had ruined. 'Get back to your compartment, madam.'

Harriet skulked away while I faced the wrath of the conductor. I had been unaware of the reputation for loose morals of Tanzania's railroad system and tried to explain that, either way, Harriet's and my relationship was purely professional. Defeated, I returned to my bunk and assumed my position under the missionary.

He had found the Lord in Kuito and his converters had torn him from his home and sent him to Mozambique to spread the Word. His Portuguese would be handy, they had told him.

'I have never been outside Angola,' he told me. 'Is there lots of fighting in Mozambique?'

'It can't be worse than Angola. The ceasefire has held for six months now.'

'Who is fighting who?'

The poor boy had been uprooted and was about to be launched

upon a country about which he knew nothing. He was terrified, alone and, as I belatedly pointed out, going in the wrong direction. He got off at Kabwe and headed back the other way, unable to speak English and a long way from home.

We awoke in Kabwe, the centre of Zambia's railway system, and site of the famous Broken Hill Mine. Trains either go up or down in Zambia and this one was continuing up to the Copperbelt. The next day it would be a down train to Livingstone, on the border with Zimbabwe, and the crew would get a day off before repeating the process. This system, whereby on Mondays trains go up and on Tuesdays they go down, is meant to avoid head-on collisions. It fails. Trains get so delayed that they find themselves going in the wrong direction for the day. The results have been horrendous in the past, but as the trains are getting gradually slower and slower due to poor track maintenance, they are now more likely to kiss gently than lock wheels passionately.

It was four o'clock in the morning so the conductor, who was nervous about Zambia Railway's important guests, arranged an armed guard to take us to the hotel. The Elephant's Head hotel is not as picturesque as its name suggests – a modern building with a grey-painted bust of a tusker over the door which owes more to John Merrick than Michelangelo. After five minutes of banging at the door, we were shown to a room with hot water where we could wash off the grime we had picked up on the train. It was a two-bath job. Our first train ride finished, we pondered whether or not to hire a car for the rest of the journey. Having decided we wouldn't be able to get away with it we went to sleep.

The railway reached Kabwe – then Broken Hill – on 11 January 1906. H. F. Varian described, in his autobiography, the last rush to complete the contract. 'As a final exhibition of their skill, the last half mile into Broken Hill was laid with materials offloaded from the plate-laying train behind, carried forward by hand, and laid with such rapidity that the train passed over the newly made track without a pause, or even a slackening of the turning of the wheels.'

Benguela shunting yard, Angola

500 yards from our house near Kinaxixe: looters were left in the street as an example

Mass burial in Luanda

2ᵉ CLASSE

Members of the Luba tribe at Likasi railway station, waiting to be forcibly relocated

Boilermakers at Bulawayo steam sheds

Dawn at Bulawayo steam sheds

Victoria Falls

Zambian soldier guarding the Victoria Falls bridge

Rhodes had died four years earlier, when his railway was still surging towards Cairo, but this was the closest that his vision came to reality. Pauling was pulled up from South Africa in his private coach to celebrate the completion of the track. He was able to drink the beer which he delivered with men who had been building the railway the whole way up from Vryburg, 1,367 miles away. It had taken them only ten years to explore, survey and then drive the railway through virgin country. They got very drunk.

Varian was disappointed by Broken Hill and so too were we. He had built the railway so fast that the mine was only just operational when he arrived. 'The Cape-to-Cairo Railway came to an end in the middle of a burnt-out vlei, without even a buffer-stop at the rail terminus. Beside it stood a solitary telegraph post, and in this atmosphere of desolation it languished for several years,' he wrote.

Kabwe is still not an attractive town. According to people who measure such things it is the most polluted town in Zambia. If you took away the railway, the mine and the army, you would be left with two thorn trees and a wind-blown *duka* (shop). The town revolves around the three organizations and they are intricately linked. All parastatals used to be owned by two holding companies which had many army officers on their boards. The managing director of Zambia Railways is a former lieutenant colonel and the railway exists only to service the mines (until recently they had been owned by the same parastatal). Thousands of houses are owned by the three corporations, in which they put up their workers. The Kabwe Warriors (railway football team) play against the army in the mine's sports stadium. Each has their own social clubs (strictly segregated into junior and senior management and workers), magazines, shops and schools. Zambian industry is patriarchal in the extreme. Almost no one in Kabwe lives in a house which belongs to them. Instead they live in the long lines of company houses. With a new job comes a new home and a new set of friends and neighbours.

The centre of town is railway territory. From the station, where a tiled sign proclaims the circumstances of Broken Hill's founding, you can see the new railway headquarters. It is a massive slab of red brick with very grand gates, which has only been half completed due to lack of funds. The nerve centre of Zambia's railway system, it is appropriately set in an overgrown wasteland full of rubbish, in which an army camp has sprung up. Two cars on bricks furnished the otherwise empty car park. The old railway headquarters is beyond the Elephant's Head and there we found Mr Chaonsa, the head of PR for the railways.

The HQ is a large O-shaped building with a lawned central quandrangle overlooked by green louvred shutters. One walks, like a cloistered monk, under red-tiled, covered walkways. The offices have not changed since colonial times. As in much of black Africa, the system against which the population rebelled has merely been adopted by the new leaders. Anterooms and superfluous secretaries are given to the most minor of officials. Chaonsa had three secretaries in his outer office, who were discussing the recent outbreak of cholera when we arrived. He was unable to do anything for us on such short notice so we had a long meeting in his office, explaining what we wanted to do when we returned before Christmas. JJ Mwanza, one of his juniors, was seconded to show us around Kabwe and it was agreed that on our return they would spend a couple of days showing us around the copper belt and surrounding areas.

'We will introduce you to the people working on the track and show you the trains but we will need a four-wheel-drive vehicle.' As in Lusaka it was taken as read that travelling by rail was a waste of time.

JJ took us to the station in a company car and introduced us to the station PR man and the station master. Kabwe station, which sees a maximum of three trains a day, has its own PR and secretary. It looks like most other African railway stations – incongruously grand and very pretty – but uniquely has a pair of black gates over which hovers the eagle of independent Zambia.

It is no phoenix rising from the ashes, more a scavenging bird of prey. Zambian Railways is in a sorry state.

At the far end of the station there is a cattle kraal where farmers bring their herds to be taken to the market. We found a man there, washing himself in the trough. His cattle had already been loaded and their wagon was standing on the tracks as the sun beat down upon it. Anguished lowing reverberated around the station. As JJ showed us the sights, the mooing became noticeably quieter and by the time we left Kabwe, the next morning, there was silence. Hooves stuck out of the wagon at odd angles, where the cows had dropped from heat exhaustion. The farmer had disappeared – his year's profits having died before his eyes. When a train finally did arrived, the driver would discover that his cargo wasn't worth moving. Many hours would have to be spent removing the carcasses which would probably be eaten by ZR staff. Then, unless the wagon was cleaned, the next load of cattle would die from infection.

The British-made and -laid tracks at Kabwe are laden down with broken, rusting wagons awaiting repair. The wagons are from Belgium, Japan, Canada and almost anywhere else that makes them. Hired South African locomotives (of an advanced age) do the shunting, while Zambian engines (gift of USAID) wait for obsolete parts. A British-made hopper lay on its side where it had derailed in the centre of the station. The teak sleepers, which had been in place since being laid by Varian's gangers in 1906, had rotted away and the hopper had gently tipped over in the night. People claim that Pauling built poor railways very fast, yet here it was rotting but still in use.

JJ, who seemed to be noticing the decay for the first time, said, 'You must publicize how much we could do if only people would help us.' Our presence had brought home to him the desperation of the situation, but not the answer. Zambia Railways has had too much help.

The Indians, who have a successful steam-train operation, came to help Zambian Railways and were succeeded by the Canadians.

The Canadians ran the system for a few years and made the change from steam to diesel. The diesel trains use thousands of gallons of imported fuel and are difficult (often impossible) for the Zambians to mend. The spare parts are expensive, difficult to get and need to be paid for in rare foreign currency. The efficient signalling system, left by the British, was ripped out and replaced by a sophisticated Seimens (German) system which doesn't like hot weather. They now have to use a bastardization of the original part-destroyed British method. Called a paper order, it used to involve telephoning the control room for an order to carry on. Now that the telephones no longer work, often another train has to be sent down with a piece of paper authorizing the driver to proceed. Foreign interference combined with corruption and bad management has brought the system almost to a standstill.

JJ and the other PR man showed us around and gave us a brief history of the railway by pointing out broken spare parts.

'This is from when we were Beira, Mashonaland and Rhodesian Railways. Look at the stamp,' explained JJ as he kicked about a rusting plate which had fallen off a wagon.

'That's one of the old telephone poles but we use a microwave system now because people stole the wires and chopped up the poles.'

The one and a half hour road journey from Kabwe to Lusaka took us eleven hours the next morning, when once again we spurned offers of lifts and took the express back to the capital. Due to poor track maintenance, the trains have to travel at near crawling pace to avoid derailment. Passengers, who cannot afford the bus, have to take the trains at lunatic hours in order to fit in with this. The express from Kabwe left at 4 a.m. and arrived in Lusaka at 3 p.m.

Ginny had just returned from Chiyaba (where she lives during the week) and had a car full of condoms and 'real men avoid casual sex' bumper stickers. Robin was in his office trying to sort out the importation of some fertilizer with Martin, Ginny's brother. Zambia's desperation to hang on to foreign currency reserves makes it nigh on impossible to run a business there, since anything useful comes from elsewhere and has to be paid for in forex. The new government was trying to make life easier on this front but had not as yet succeeded. All farmers in Zambia were suffering the same problems. Unable to buy fertilizer which they need to ensure a successful harvest, they were being strangled with SAP-inspired red tape. It wasn't only the government and the IMF's fault. Fertilizer being imported through Beira was being held up because of priorities on aid shipments. Farmers in Zambia were being prevented from paying to feed themselves while Mozambique mounted up excess aid stocks.

Things were not looking good at the farm. All the countries we had been travelling through had been in the grip of a biblical drought. Maize (the staple food of Africa) had become so expensive that even the small middle classes were being affected. One of the secretaries working with Ginny at Lusaka University was unable to celebrate Christmas that year because she did not have the money to buy presents for her children. The great grey green greasy Limpopo had run dry. Headlines such as 'Game Parks Ravaged by Drought' had pricked the conscience of the west and the much more ravaged peoples of southern Africa were benefiting from the knock-on effect. Hippos and elephants were wallowing in aid, Sudan and Somalia were getting massive media coverage and therefore massive aid, and southern Africa was getting its bit too. West Africa was not so lucky but, all in all, 1992 was a good year for aid recipients.

Zambia had slightly different problems. Chiluba was following his World Bank-imposed structural adjustment programme with such dedication that his people could no longer afford to eat. Reduction of subsidies on crops and the liberalization of the parastatal system which controlled agriculture had led to a 1,000 per cent increase in the price of maize.

Aid maize and fertilizer had been pouring into Beira (our destination) but a combination of incompetence at the port and on the railways, strained foreign relations along the route, and theft, meant that Zambia, Malawi and Zimbabwe were in dire need of a good harvest. When Robin and I went duck shooting (or rather missing) that evening, the occasion was rather dampened by the fact that Robin believed he was about to lose his crops. Rain clouds had been hovering on the horizon for days, tantalizing the population and then scudding off elsewhere. We returned to the house for supper after which Robin, Ginny, Martin, Harriet and I sat on the verandah, drinking beer and feeling maudlin. It was my birthday the next day, but having opened my presents early, there wasn't much to celebrate. Then we smelt the rain – sweet and delicious and very close. It poured. Robin estimated than the rain's arrival had saved the farm twenty million kwacha. We wandered around in it, grinning foolishly, and went to bed happy.

Early the next morning, Harriet and I packed some essentials and drove into Lusaka. We were going to try to get back to Angola and take the first part of the railway. Lobito and Benguela were firmly back in government hands, so we would at least be able to visit the stations if nothing else. Some might say we were being obsessive, others that we weren't doing very well. We felt that it was ridiculous to study this railway without even going to the place where it started. By this time we knew Angola quite well but had been nowhere near our line. Offered the opportunity, we jumped at the chance.

Our only problem would be getting there. Flights to Namibia were easy, but hitching a ride up to Luanda would be more difficult. No commercial airlines were, by this time, still flying there. The road into Lusaka was awash with mud. An American aid project with a Japanese contractor had been widening the road with a singular lack of success, and drenched workers were sitting by and watching as their work was washed away. The planners had obviously assumed that the drought was never going to break and were now doing penance for false prophecy. Still working were the men and women who lined the road selling piles of stones. Like participants in a job-creation scheme at a southern jail, they spent their lives digging for and breaking rocks. They then sold them at the roadside for building work. You could buy chippings, little rocks, pebbles or boulders. The Zambian government holds this up as a shining example of the informal sector at work. Encouraging small businesses is one of the cornerstones of SAP policy. A family breaking rocks is thus categorized as thriving private enterprise in tones as laudatory as the British government's descriptions of its Youth Training Schemes. The people breaking the rocks did not agree. 'It's all we can do. Our jobs have been taken away and we have to eat so we break stones. It's hard work for sure,' I was told when I asked one man what he thought of the private sector.

We listened to Mike the Maverick's brilliant radio show as we sat in the traffic jam that had come with the floods. Lusaka was beginning to look like Bangladesh. The drains had given up and cars were driving through two feet of water in some places. Desperate shopkeepers were trying to sweep water out of their premises and pedestrians huddled under awnings, shivering and waiting for the rain to stop. You could almost see the cholera spreading. The north of the country was already suffering an epidemic and the rain would, within a few days, spread it to Lusaka.

Mike the Maverick, the man who awakes the nation, added to the suffering of the people: 'The kwacha has been devalued by forty per cent,' he said. But then he made it all seem all right: 'The kwacha is now the cheapest currency in the region.'

My birthday lunch was spent at Pete's Steak House – the site of a recent fight between Michael Sata (one of Zambia's more combative ministers) and a waiter. We spent far too long over lunch and set off to the airport feeling rather happier than anyone en route to Namibia should. We had been forced to travel business class because we had been told there were no economy seats. So when we discovered that economy was empty, we set to drinking Air Namibia's profits on our tickets. Having drunk pints of champagne on the two-hour flight, we disembarked having achieved our aim. I had even managed to wheedle a free box of chocolates from the stewardess. Namibia hadn't changed. It was still a hot and dry transit point.

CHAPTER SIX

Sitting at Le Bistro, we realized that our lives had come full-circle. We had started our journey there and three months later we were back in the same place but had only just taken our first trip by rail. While pondering which hotel to waste money on, it occurred to us that we now had friends living in Namibia. We had, at least, made some progress. Half an hour later, John Liebenberg, a good friend whom we had met on the way to Luanda the first time, was driving us home. His wife and children had gone 'down south' for Christmas and he was joining them in a few days. In the time being we could rave it up in Windhoek. That night the brewery was having a Christmas party and the country was having a total eclipse of the moon – we planned to attend both.

John is a former South African who has been living in Namibia for years. He was not a popular man under South African rule and spent an unhealthy portion of it in detention. His award-winning photographs of the brutal civil war that was fought between SWAPO and South Africa in neighbouring Angola were deemed political and therefore illegal. He now works as a camera-man for NBC, the new national television station, but is never without his stills cameras. The Liebenbergs live in a small house in a street of similar houses, close to the light plane airport, with an added dark room and office masquerading as a garden shed. At the other end of the garden was a large chicken coop housing a psychopathic cock called Savimbi and some very nervous doves, who roosted with one eye open for fear of attack from the cock.

'You have to meet my beau,' called John as he loped towards the cage, emerging a few seconds later chased by Savimbi and clutching a white dove. 'This is the Angolan dove of peace,' he told us, while the cock pecked at his bare feet. 'We made the video for the Angolan elections. Ach man, we spent hours in this garden trying to film with one hand and chuck the dove in the air with the other. It worked, huh?'

It seemed appropriate that Savimbi and the dove of peace were sworn enemies – even at the bottom of John's parched garden.

We had to arrange passage to the scene of Savimbi's wickedness and so rang Tom Wight, the head of station for UNAVEM in Angola. With a little help from friends in Luanda, who exerted pressure on that end, we managed to convince him that our presence in the city was urgently required. He authorized us to travel on one of their aid flights, as soon as there was space. We were free until then.

Windhoek had not changed much but was a great deal more enjoyable with John as our guide. He took us down to the brewery where we met some Angolans who were driving truckloads of beer across the border. Angola had been at war since we had left a few months earlier and nothing was getting through to the south and centre of the country, save an occasional aid drop of food and medical supplies. Fighting a war is bad enough drunk but the thought of doing it sober had galvanized these black marketeers into action. They were recently demobilized soldiers who had spotted the gap in the market and had set off for Namibia with a convoy of ancient trucks before they were reconscripted.

'Isn't it very dangerous?' I asked them. The MPLA had been bombing and strafing roads all over the south, since Savimbi had left the capital.

'No, we drive very slowly at night and haven't hit any mines on the way down. Now we have to drive back to Huambo while we can still get through. This is going to be the hard part.'

Huambo was where Savimbi had set up his headquarters, and although the town itself was at peace and under the shared governorship of the two opposing sides, it was also the command post for the UNITA effort. Reports of what was going on were very sketchy but it was evident that the surrounding countryside was being disputed ferociously. These young men were about to drive six 10-ton trucks 1,000 miles through a battlefield in order to make a bit of extra cash. After eighteen years of civil war, they thought this was perfectly normal commercial behaviour. That night they slept underneath their trucks and were gone the next morning.

We drove into the brewery's compound and joined their Christmas party. Windhoek Breweries, despite having a monopoly, gives a party for the press every month. John had never before attended, but thought that we might enjoy it. We were greeted by the PR and ushered into the company bar. In the corner was a thorn tree in a pot, strewn with Christmas decorations. It was another clue as to why so many Nambibian whites have appalling facial scars and squints, but no one came to sing under the tree in the two hours that we were there.

We were invited to make use of the free bar and having filled up, we started introducing ourselves. It was most intimidating. The room was full of small groups whispering together who, it emerged, worked for rival news organizations. There were no cross-party talks and our arrival caused not a stir. We were expected to talk to each other while everyone else spoke to the people they worked with every day. Under pressure, a news reporter on the *Namibian* explained to me that there was such rivalry between opposing media that it was seen as treachery to talk to the other side. This probably explains the dire state of Namibia's press. When there was something to fight against (South Africa), Namibia had quite a feisty media, but now that independence had arrived the press had settled down into humdrum reportage of the latest dispute between the miners and Consolidated Diamond Mines.

Occasionally there would be a more interesting story about loony Germans living in the bush. A recent report had detailed the death of the last scion of a hermit family. In 1941, three sisters had been offered, by their father, to Adolf Hitler, as possible breeding stock for some of his boys in grey. Hitler replied, saying that he would send out some suitors immediately, and the sisters had lived – splendidly isolated and *virgo intacta* – on a smallholding outside Swakopmund for the next fifty-two years. The last one had died just before Christmas – still waiting. Child abuse and rape were the other staples of the Namibian press, save on Sundays when the editor of one of the papers writes short stories of a sexual nature, spread over four pages, with accompanying pornographic photographs culled from South Africa porn mags.

The brewery, though, was convinced of the power of the press and continued to give its monthly parties. Large bowls of lasagne were brought out and the hacks edged towards them. A mouthful or two quickly changed their minds and sitting down became dangerous as overflowing plates were abandoned on every available flat surface. The three of us made a hasty exit and headed off to the next event. At eleven o'clock that night there was going to be a total eclipse of the moon, which it was hoped would be fairly spectacular. It wasn't. First, Windhoek Lager had failed to organized a piss-up in a brewery, and then it rained for the first time in two years. The eclipse was obscured by heavy cloud.

We set off for Luanda in an ageing Antonov with a Russian crew. Fifteen UN workers, hundreds of bottles of champagne, a few televisions and some frozen chickens competed with us for space in the fuselage. Harriet and I played Scrabble for hours as we flew against the wind, back to Luanda, where our journey was meant to have started. Jon Hsuan, who was in the capital to try to negotiate a new diamond-mining contract, met us off the plane and said we could stay with him and Speedie, his Angolan-Portuguese deputy. Luanda had filled up with people fleeing the provinces and was its usual swinging self. It was great to be back in the vibrant city we had come to love.

Bob wasn't at his diner, so we went to the Surf for dinner, where we discovered that little had changed. They still had the most surly waitresses in Africa and nothing to eat, but in a new departure had bought some pedaloes which now lined the beach. Commerce never stops in Luanda. The dollar was now 9,000 kwanza, which indicated a marked lack of confidence in the peace talks, but meant that we could live more cheaply than ever.

The British Embassy was still the only halfway reliable diplomatic source in the capital. The Americans were down to a skeleton staff of CIA men, the South Africans were sitting on their thumbs and the Portuguese always had rather too much vested interest for their comments to be trustworthy. Rafael, at the *Jornal de Angola*, was pleased to see us. The departure of the foreign press had made him feel rather isolated. Elder, our former landlord, was also pleased to see us. The *Sunday Times*, unknown to me, had not yet paid our expenses. My cheque had bounced, which had understandably depressed him. Jon and Speedie, for whom Elder worked, had assured him, however, of my good faith and an angry altercation was averted.

We did not have much time for socializing. The war was hotting up and we had to see the bits of the railway still in existence before it was once more reduced to mangled metal. Dennis, the UNAVEM flight coordinator, was unable to help us. He had no flights going down to Lobito and was getting rather nervous about sending planes to anywhere south of Luanda.

'Gunships and Su eights have been going out full and coming back empty for the last week,' he told us. 'Those gunships don't have much range so the war can't be too far away.'

Meanwhile, the government (still desperate for US diplomatic recognition) was insisting that the country was at peace for the benefit of Jeffrey Davidow, America's latest peace envoy. Anyone who lived or worked within a mile radius of Luanda's airport knew that either this was false or the MPLA were wasting all their munitions on target practice. The United States was once more in an unenviable situation. The Frankenstein they had created was no longer obeying orders. Savimbi had stormed off like a rogue elephant and was ignoring everyone's advice except that of the voices in his head. His negotiating teams continued to make peace deals, which he immediately countermanded, and his generals were being forced into a war that only Savimbi wanted. Every day the MPLA, with their new, reasonable façade, gained more credibility.

The World Food Programme, we discovered, was still flying down to Lobito so we went to visit them. Moving around Luanda was at its most difficult. Ninjas and police were on every corner and road blocks were more frequent than cars. At the WFP office in the UN building, we found their flight coordinator.

'Dennis at UNAVEM said you might be able to help. We need to get to Benguela,' I pleaded hopefully.

'Of course. We have a flight going down the day after tomorrow. When do you want to come back?'

'Great, thanks, a couple of days after that, maybe. We need to go to Huambo as well so we can't spend too long there.'

'Oh, I'm sorry. No one is going to Huambo at the moment, if they can help it. We haven't had any flights there for a while.'

'Ah well, thank you very much anyway. Can we get on that flight to Benguela?'

'Sure. Hang on a sec,' he said, consulting his timetable. 'If we pick you up the next morning, we can re-route the return flight via Huambo.'

Harriet and I reeled out of his office. He had just laid on a seven-hundred-mile diversion entirely for our benefit. Our return to Angola was going disturbingly well. We hadn't even had to feign interest in WFP's projects, normally a prerequisite for filling up seats on pre-scheduled aid flights. Neither of us had ever had a special flight put on for us.

We set off to enjoy the next couple of days with a nagging feeling that something had to go wrong. We had a barbecue at Speedie's beach hut and listened to Maria Callas booming across the bay on the car hi-fi, while the rest of Luandas's population skulked inside the city limits. We went dancing on the Love Boat and chatted with the key players, who had been too busy to see us when there were a hundred and seventy foreign correspondents in town. The British Embassy now had a close protection team, yet despite the increased military presence on the streets, Luanda seemed more relaxed than we had ever seen it. When we had first arrived in the capital, there had been an election pending and a confrontational atmosphere in the city. Posters had been up all over town. UNITA soldiers and supporters had walked around with impunity. Now that UNITA had been wiped out in Luanda, there was much less confrontation. It was an MPLA town and on that score there was no debate.

Benguela Province, when we arrived, was another matter. We drove straight to Lobito as the sun rose and checked into the Grand Hotel. I don't believe it was ever grand but it was certainly a UNITA hotel. Lobito and Benguela are second only in importance to Luanda and the MPLA rules as much of them as they can with a steely control. The population, though, are at least 60 per cent UNITA supporters. UNITA flags far out-numbered the MPLA's on the streets of the two towns. Citizens wore the T-shirts of their choice. The MPLA controlled the town centres where UNITA still had open and heavily guarded offices but the outskirts were UNITA's. The MPLA did not go there, even in pairs. They went in force or not at all. Our host was that rare thing – a Portuguese UNITA supporter – and having installed us in our rooms (no water on the fifth floor because, back in the realms of folk lore, the pipes had burst on the fourth and flooded everything below), he offered us a lift back to Benguela.

Lobito is a modern and unattractive town, built to service the port. It never really stops until it reaches Benguela, but we had plenty of time to admire the built-up road between the two. Our landlord's car was a pre-revolutionary model and did not exceed 25 miles per hour. The road runs parallel to the railway along the coastal plateau. Looming alongside are tall hills which stop about a mile from the sea. These foothills of the shrouded mountains are densely inhabited. Adobe houses, made out of the same soil as the mountains, blend in like the troglodyte dwellings of Cappadocia. They cluster round churches and are a no-go area for MPLA supporters. Benguela was dominated by the governor's mansion, from where Paolo Jorge governs with a rod of iron. The enlarged doll's house, freshly painted a delicate pastel grey, was guarded by scores of troops and military vehicles, defying the population to express their opinions too loudly. From every wall, chest and plastic bag stared back the malevolent visage of the doctor – Jonas Savimbi. We were dropped at the railway station – bustling with activity and hopelessly picturesque.

Mature trees shaded the platform. Pink and yellow warehouses, which the station master claimed had been used for slave storage but looked too modern to me, lined the tracks. We felt we had strayed on to the set of *The Railway Children* as we chatted with the avuncular station master under the eaves of the station house. The clock had stopped at five past six, a small hole in its centre. The other side had been smashed to oblivion where a bullet, having rattled round the innards, had exited at high speed. Hundreds of women and children sat in the shade of the trees, waiting for the train to arrive. Beyond them and outside the perimeter of the railway station was a shunting yard from which a burst of automatic fire could be heard.

It was from Benguela, in 1902, that Robert Williams set out to link the copper deposits of Katanga with the coast. Williams was the head of Tanganyika Concessions, which still owns and runs the Benguela Railway today. A wily Scot, he was an associate and admirer of Cecil Rhodes, who in 1899 had asked Williams to investigate the mineral deposits of Northern Rhodesia. Williams, having discovered the Kanshanshi copper mine (six miles south of the Zaïrean border), on behalf of Rhodes, entered into his own negotiations with King Leopold for the mineral rights to Katanga. Leopold, who had already prospected the area and discovered nothing except ancient workings, thought he had made the deal of his life when he sold Williams the sole rights to 60,000 square miles of what he imagined was barren mining land. But Williams soon discovered the 250-mile copper belt which spun west from Northern Rhodesia towards the Zaïrean border with Angola.

Williams realized that he could knock thousands of miles off the trip to Britain if he linked Katanga with Lobito in the west, rather than Beira on the east coast. On 28 November 1902, he was granted the concession to build a railway through Portuguese Angola to the then Congolese border at Luao. Having employed Pauling's as contractors, he completed his heroic task on 28 August 1928 and it was officially opened the next year. The vision that this must have required is difficult to comprehend.

The first hundred miles of track travel through 'thirst country' where, for every worker employed, another had to be contracted to carry water. There follows three hundred miles of 'hungry country' where there is water but nothing will grow in the soil. All food had to be carried by ox cart from the coast. Before the thousands of Senegalese and Asian workers (there was no local labour because of the hostility of the country) reached mile 208, the line had ascended 6,081 feet from their starting point on the sea. Camels had to be imported from north Africa to fetch and carry. After Kohemba and the four hundred and eighty-four miles of thirst and hunger, the pioneers were dogged by cannibals. The Great War intervened and, as happens today, every bridge and station had to be guarded. The Germans of South West Africa, hemmed in by Britain, marauded up into Angola. Williams died before his vision became tarnished, but the yard beside Benguela station would make even a man of his stature sob. His railway now stands idle while people along its length starve.

EC-donated corn was being unloaded from rail wagons on to trucks, only thirty-one miles from the beginning of Williams's great railway. Children, their parents and their grandparents scrabbled in the dust for the maize which was spilling from the ancient, creaking rolling stock. Bright yellow maize shone briefly in the sunlight and was scooped from the ballast. No one in Africa likes yellow maize, they prefer white, but starvation was the only other option. MPLA guards shot at them; they scampered away and others took their place. Long bursts of fire from soldiers with orders to kill, but no stomach for the job, failed to intimidate anyone.

'They have to do this,' explained one of the government guards.

'These are UNITA supporters. We are sending the food to MPLA areas.'

Communist dictator, Haile Mariam Mengistu, had deliberately tried to starve seven million people in the Ethiopian Live Aid famine of 1984 and succeeded with almost a million. Now a former communist regime seemed to be doing the same thing by withholding EC aid. Even their own troops were shamed into disobedience by it. Savimbi is so obviously wicked that it was difficult to remember that, in this war, there were no good guys and bad guys, merely a few power-crazed leaders victimizing a long-suffering population.

As we waited for the train to Lobito the station master showed off his new locomotive. A shining South African diesel was shunting up and down with great panache. It had never been further than 31-mile-distant Lobito where it had arrived by ship. The rest of the track was off limits. UNITA had started mining it again, after the farce of the elections, and the only functioning track was between the two ports, ancient and modern. Heavily armed soldiers and policemen accompanied every train while Soviet-supplied attack helicopters hovered protectively overhead.

'The train will leave at eleven sixteen,' said the station master.

We smirked at his precision and were shamed and awed when precisely at the time specified it did. We had encountered some difficulty buying a ticket. The fare was 150 kwanza (2 cents) return and we had never seen money small enough to pay it. The conductor had no change for our ostentatious notes and was dealing in blackened pieces of paper which, though still legal tender, were no longer in circulation in Luanda. An honourable man, he would not countenance keeping the change. When we moved off, the train was packed with people, but there can have been no more than 1,000 passengers. Caminho de Ferra Benguela was grossing just over $21 for the round trip.

Our carriage was a 1965, brown and sand Metro Cammell, built in Britain. Next door was one made in Huambo (then Nova

Lisboa) in 1944. The brass railings and polished teak shone richly in the sun. Some things had not changed on this railway. It ran on time and the carriages were spotless. It was by far the cleanest train – bar Amtrak – that I had ever been on.

A strange assortment of people was returning to Catumbella and Lobito, having been to the market in Benguela. So loyal to UNITA is Benguela's surrounding countryside that Savimbi has been known to sneak deep into this MPLA stronghold, give a rousing speech in the market, and disappear again before the government realized that he was in their midst. He had not, though, appeared in public anywhere for the last two months. Opposite us sat a family who had been to the market and failed to sell their cock. A young girl stared, fascinated by us. She was clutching a broken, plastic Chianti-type bottle which she could not, as yet, think of a use for but was not willing to throw away. In a UNITA plastic bag, she had some dried fish and a reed mat. A man opposite was reading a magazine in a hard grey folder. Intrigued, I leant over for a better look. Its cover story was Richard Burton and Elizabeth Taylor getting married for the first time. He had withdrawn it from the library, where it had been carefully preserved since a bored Portuguese housewife had donated it in 1964.

Catumbella station is where the two trains intersect, for there is only one set of rails except at that point. When the railway was first built, it was called the Benguela Railway since Benguela was one of the oldest towns in Africa. Catumbella, too, was a well-established town but Lobito did not exist and was built only for its harbour. Now the three separate towns, hugging the line of rail, merge into one. Residents of the three would disagree, for Benguela is to Lobito as Hove is to Brighton.*

Soldiers sat on the steps of every carriage and others patrolled

* Hove, although now part of the British seaside metropolis of Brighton, is considered to be a cut above the rest of the town by its more genteel residents.

up and down. A policeman wearing a police cap, an inside-out UNITA T-shirt, threadbare uniform trousers and yellow flip-flops was in charge of us. Bored of patrolling, he leant his rifle against the window and sat down by Harriet and me. He was not amused by our references to his T-shirt and later took it out on a twelve-year-old boy who was caught stealing a cake from one of the marketeers in our carriage. The boy was kicked and punched for a while by outraged traders and the policeman then hurled him from the train. He jumped up, seemingly unscathed, and ran off into a field. All along the line, as in the Benguela shunt yard, were corn pickers scrabbling in the ballast.

Just beyond Catumbella, we passed over the road and rail bridge that was built by Pauling's in 1903. A bullet-holed water pipe, which explained the absence of water in Lobito, ran parallel. Above the bridge was an observation tower which resembled a colander on legs, containing a rather nervous-looking soldier who had a tripod-mounted machine gun balanced precariously on the side. The bridge still worked perfectly. The last stretch into Lobito followed deserted docks, overshadowed by shining yellow cranes. Later that evening, I was told that the last time they had been used in earnest was to lynch a pair of thieves, two months earlier. The EC is proposing to give the Angolan government $50 million with which to rehabilitate this port. It currently serves a 31-mile railway. The other 1,269 miles of track to the copper fields of Katanga are under constant threat of destruction and it is no longer possible even to send armoured trains along them. At the height of the civil war, trains used to dare the journey to relieve besieged garrisons and feed stronghold cities like Huambo and Luena. In front of the trains would be pushed two wagons of sand which would absorb the explosion of any mines. Behind the guarded engines were pulled flat-beds of rails, sleepers and rail workers to relay the destroyed track as the train progressed. Even this method was no longer viable.

On the platform at the also beautiful Lobito station, we discovered CFB's Loco Number 1 which had pulled such luminaries as H. F. Varian, the railway's first chief engineer, George Pauling, the contractor, and Robert Williams, the man who thought up the whole idea. Feeling quite pleased with ourselves, we tried to take a run-around photograph by balancing a camera on the water boiler and standing in the cab. A boy tried to steal the camera, so we gave up and went for a beer.

We had now taken the first thirty-one miles of the railway and a bit in Zambia. We had never imagined that we were going to travel on all the railway but we had been hoping to see a little more of it than we had. Now we had at least achieved something but it dawned on me that it was going to take some extremely creative writing to gloss over the missing 1,300 miles in the middle.

Vasquinho, a former paratrooper we had met at the UN compound, skived off his afternoon's work to show us around the surrounding area. It emerged that we shared some mutual Angolan friends, so we ended up spending the evening together as well. He took us to Catumbella, the midpoint between Lobito and Benguela, where there had been recent fighting. As soon as the post-election fighting had started, Benguela and Lobito once more became key objectives. The loosening of security necessary for the elections meant that UNITA came closer to taking the two towns than it ever had before. The MPLA managed to regain control but it had been a close-run thing and the civilian population was scarcely supportive. Periodic fighting still broke out, and ten days before we had arrived there had been a fierce battle in Catumbella.

The MPLA had retained their grip but they did not have enough men to guard their gains. Although it was ostensibly theirs, the MPLA (like the LAPD in Watts) didn't dare go there for fear of inciting unrest. Most of the time, guns are kept under beds in Angolan towns, but Catumbella was a place where the 'civilians' liked to give them frequent airings. The pale pink commissariat building was topped by white plaster statues, many of which had been neatly decapitated by machine-gun fire the week before. The freshly whitewashed church hall was peppered with bullet holes which stood out like blackheads on an albino's nose. As soon as we stopped the vehicle, a group from the local neighbourhood watch scheme came to ask who we were. We were scarcely welcomed with open arms but were allowed to stay and have a drink at a bar which was decorated like a shrine to Jonas Savimbi. There was near total silence and an unhealthy atmosphere so we jumped at the opportunity when Vasquinho suggested it might be best if we left. After a quick look at some rusting steam engines, preserved for posterity by the side of the road, we headed back to Lobito, before darkness fell.

There was no longer a curfew in Lobito but everything closed early. To be on the streets too late, while not illegal, was regarded as suspicious by the forces of law and order. The street where UNITA had its offices was not a place to visit after dark. We had driven past earlier and had been tracked down the street by a sandbag-enclosed UNITA machine-gun post. We had made that mistake once before, in Luanda, and went to great lengths to avoid the street in Lobito. At least this time, the UNITA office did not face the police station but the atmosphere was far from easy. Vasquinho took us to the Tic Tac where a normal door off the street concealed the type of long formica bar that one would find in an American hamburger joint and the Snake Disco.

The bar was presided over by two men: one effiminate Portuguese in a pastel pink Lacoste, the other an Angolan, built like Mike Tyson and wearing a matching baby blue Lacoste. They should have helped with the elections as they were dressed like the ballot boxes. The white one had a barbie-doll haircut and was sulking. The black one, despite having a neck like a bull and a rippling torso, had cupid's bow lips and a voice which spoke volumes about war disabilities in Angola. They sold joints, all manner of drinks and excellent steak sandwiches over the bar but had recently been forced to close the Snake Disco. 'We close disco. Problema bang bang,' squeaked Mike while pointing a finger with a total lack of conviction.

We got the point. It soon emerged that Mike had fallen in love with a journalist friend of ours a few weeks earlier when he had passed out in their bar. Angolan grass is very strong.

Harriet was feeling ill and was still hobbling, having walked under a horse in Zambia, so we took her back to the hotel which was guaranteed to make her feel even more ill. Vasquinho and I drove on to the night-time market, where people congregate after everything else closes. Kwashiorkor-suffering children scampered around in the darkness, picking up discarded chicken bones and drinking the remains of people's beers. This was the first relaxed place that I had been in Lobito or Benguela. All sorts of people were congregated there – soldiers, policemen, businessmen and farmers. Even a few Portuguese had emerged, one of whom knew Vasquinho. Romo had a Ramboesque air about him. He was carrying no visible firearms, but a large hunting knife was strapped to his belt and a glistening, tanned and hairy chest was not very well covered by a khaki photographer's vest. Until recently, he had earned a living by taking hunting parties of Portuguese into UNITA territory. He derived great amusement from the fact that a quarter of the $120 a day (cheap by East African standards) that he charged to the rich, MPLA-supporting Portuguese went into Savimbi's coffers.

'I'm sure they know,' he grinned, 'but pleasure always comes before principles.'

I expressed amazement that there was any game left. We had spent half an hour in northern Angola trying to find game from a helicopter and had discovered only two antelope.

'No, there's still plenty,' he told me. 'You just have to know where the mines are. Where there are mines, no one dares hunt, so there is lots of game.'

It seemed insane that mines were helping to preserve wildlife in Angola. The rest of the war had taken a terrible toll. The South Africans had demanded ivory in return for arms to UNITA so there were no elephant left and everything else had been killed for food. H. F. Varian had discovered the giant sable antelope, a few hundred miles away, and I wondered if any of them still existed.

Romo knew he had never shot one and he had often hunted in the tiny area where they were meant to live. This was hardly conclusive evidence. They had been endangered when first discovered and Varian had immediately arranged for their protection from marauding Boers. But I think it would be safe to announce that *Hippotragus niger variani* is no more.

At sunrise we left for the airport. Next on the whistle-stop tour of the railway was Huambo, the headquarters of both Dr Jonas Savimbi and the Benguela Railway. Huambo became unnerving even before we had landed. We had climbed every mountain and hurtled across plateaus deep into the central highlands when we started to notice rather a lot of green hardware lying around. The countryside was littered with heavy-duty armaments. They weren't messing around with troops and machine guns down there, they could have re-enacted the Battle of the Bulge. As we came down to land at Huambo, the pilot did some precautionary circling to make sure that he wasn't flying into the centre of a battle. Surrounding a kopje alongside the airport was a battle-formation of MPLA tanks. I lost count at thirty.

Huambo is a vital MPLA helicopter base and lines of vicious-looking gunships stared, bug-eyed, at us as we landed. A group of UNITA soldiers was guarding the unmarked plane, with a yellow stripe down its fuselage, which Savimbi had been using at the time of the elections and which was also identical to the one the American Embassy had evacuated in. Well away from the terminal building, they were the only armed men visible within the airport perimeter. Unarmed UNITA and MPLA troops, carrying brief-cases and suspicious-looking holdalls, mingled on the apron. Rows of flag-poles on the roof of the terminal building flew alternate MPLA and UNITA flags. Both sides wanted to know what we were doing there so all the bureaucracy had to be done twice.

'If you're not back in three hours, we leave without you,' said our friendly South African pilot, who was not leaving his plane.

We managed to purloin a Unicef car and driver and raced off

to the railway headquarters. The airport is close to town and only a large coffee field separates it from the first suburbs. UNITA troops, hiding under coffee bushes with radios and heavy-calibre machine guns, monitored our progress as we edged past the first suburb in which Savimbi was rumoured to be staying. There was no right turn – signs were unnecessary in the presence of road blocks. Instead of the normal pole dragged across a road or an oil drum, the road blocks consisted of human walls, tensed as though they were expecting the imminent arrival of a free kick from Maradona. Instead of clutching their testicles, however, they were holding grenades and all manner of other armaments. These were Savimbi's crack guard and they made it perfectly clear that they would die to keep the road closed. The tense stand-off we had sensed in Lobito and Benguela faded into insignificance. A backfiring car, or even a dropped tray, could have sparked the death of thousands in Huambo.

It's difficult to tip-toe in a Land Cruiser but we did our best and drove through the centre of town towards the railway. Huambo is beautifully situated and constructed. The Portuguese called it Nova Lisboa, and one of their more lunatic dictators wanted to make it the official capital of Portugal before he was deposed. Looking at the town, his idea was almost understandable. It is high in the mountains and so has a much better climate than the burning coastal plain, where the icy Benguela current ruins the swimming but doesn't do much to cool things down. Wide avenues, lined by pastel-painted villas with large verandahs and tall cool rooms, form the centre of the town which is intersected by the railway. There was no hiding the fact that it had been through some pretty vicious fighting, but it was still beautiful.*

The railway headquarters had not survived so well. A key

---

* It is beautiful no longer. The most recent reports, after months of siege when UNITA took over the town, describe it as 'flat'. Huambo has apparently been shelled out of existence. Conservative estimates suggest 24,000 civilians were killed.

economic target, every warehouse and parts shop was without a roof. The area resembled photographs of shipyards after the Blitz. At the entrance was a gatekeeper's lodge, made out of the cab of an old steam train; behind it, a large rock which had mysteriously moved from Luao, where it had been planted, complete with plaque to commemorate the completion of the line.

The Benguela Railway Company
Concession granted to Robert Williams – 28 November 1902
Formation of Company – 26 May 1903
Completion of Construction – 28 August 1928
Formal Opening Ceremony – 10 June 1929

In his memoirs, Varian becomes uncharacteristically sentimental when describing the stone-laying ceremony. It was quite a ceremony though, attended by HRH Prince Arthur of Connaught, the Portuguese foreign minister, the High Commissioner of Angola and, of course, Williams and Varian.

Here, then, is the terminal point in the history of this great project, begun just after the conclusion of the Anglo-Boer War, when Sir Robert Williams obtained the concession to build the line, and ending with the final laying of the rails to the frontier nearly thirty years later. That granite boulder might well have borne an epitaph, instead of its legend of success, had it not been for the indomitable courage of Williams, and the loyal help of his Portuguese friends.

The rest of the yard *was* in need of an epitaph. The plaque and the perfectly preserved engine CFB 24 which loomed above it were the only things in the grounds of the headquarters of which anyone could be proud. Like Saint Paul's, the engine had sustained no damage while all around it went up in flames. Rows of decaying steam locomotives were lined up beyond the skeletal sheds. Grass had overgrown the lines on which they stood and in some cases had become an integral part of the rusting black engines. Frederico, a generally depressed but momentarily elated Brazilian aid worker, came out to greet us with some colleagues. They welcomed us with the joy normally reserved for relievers of beseiged garrisons. They had not seen a moving train since early October and had begun to think they were forgotten. Anyone showing interest in their railway gave justification to their labours.

In one of the sheds, a group of ageing artisans were repairing bullet holes and replacing glass in a 1929 carriage. Others were making sleepers from eucalyptus, a wood totally unsuited for the purpose, but the only one available. They were all old men – the fathers of conscripts, cripples or cadavers. This was the kind of 'never say die' spirit which Varian demanded from his gangers and which had been an essential ingredient of the pioneer railway. Then, though, there had been a goal – far away but surmountable. The men at Huambo had much worse odds stacked against them. Savimbi had decided to make Huambo his headquarters and in the event of an escalation of the war the MPLA would, and indeed did, throw everything they had at Huambo. The government had already lost its diamond fields and many other key areas, but losing Huambo would be like the French losing Lyons. In the time being, whether UNITA mined the tracks or not, the MPLA had no use for the railway.

'The government won't allow trains here any more because they don't want to send food here,' elaborated Frederico.

The possibility of sending passenger trains was not even discussed. The 1929 carriage which was being repaired before our eyes was reason enough why. Still, though, there were sixty faithful railway workers remaining. The sheds were scarcely humming with activity but the best machines from the badly shelled sheds had been moved into one of the more stable structures and work continued – when it wasn't raining.

One of the senior managers took me to admire his old engines. He had driven almost all of them and was devastated by what had happened to them. 'I wanted to give them to a museum so someone could look after them,' he told me, while lovingly stroking one of the aged hulks. 'There is no way to get them away from here but we can't just leave them here to rot.'

Images of train-spotters' charities paying millions so that the engines could be taken to safety flashed before my eyes. It was too reminiscent of other African countries, where the wildlife charities are better funded than those fighting starvation. But here was a genuine victim of the war who wanted his engines preserved for others who had not had his advantages. It was he who maintained CFB 24, the shining locomotive whose cow-catcher stood proud and straight, in defiance of the destruction in which it stood.

The resilience of the Angolans no longer inspired Frederico: 'I have given up on Angola, there will never be peace – next year I return to Brazil.'

His co-workers bore him no resentment. Frederico, after all, had proved his mettle during heavy fighting and artillery barrages. But for those who had served the railway all their lives, there was no get-out clause. They would continue to do their jobs, as best they could, until told otherwise. War is a way of life in Angola and the majority of the population has known no other. We had been drinking Windhoek lager which must have been delivered by people like the smugglers we had met in Namibia. In the absence of any faith in the future, Angolans take pleasure and profit where they can find it.

Some derive joy from the steam engines and are concerned for their future. The craftsmen, at work in the sheds, lovingly sandpapered cannibalized parts from other carriages in order to restore just one to its former splendour. It would bear its Nova Lisboa plate with pride once more. I wish I could say that it was the carriage which took the Prince of Connaught to Luao, but nobody knew. They understood the significance of the date but all their records had been destroyed in the shattered offices of railway headquarters. The passenger carriage was being restored out of love. No travellers were expected, no trains were expected, but when representatives of Tanganyika Investments next visit

Huambo, they will be able to return to London with some good news. The railway is shattered and useless; the locomotives are no longer functioning; the offices no longer have walls and roofs, but in the hearts of a few tired old men, the spirit of Robert Williams is still alive.

Our driver was impatient to take us back to the airport. Previous experience had taught him that WFP pilots keep their word about leaving on time. We raced back to the plane, leaving CFB's few remaining employees waving to us from the gates. We were frustrated by how little time we had been able to spend there but we seemed to have cheered them up. The *Guardian*'s Chris McGreal had done the same thing the week before when he took one of the last UN evacuation flights into Luao where the Angolan part of the railway meets Zaïre's. There he had met the station master who reportedly had ranks of perfect steam engines, polished and ready to go. CFB seemed to inspire fanatical corporate loyalty. Everyone we met in Huambo, Lobito and Benguela was proud that we had come to see them and their railway. They took no offence that we stayed for such a short time, yet their very stoicism made us feel guilty at our superficial voyeurism.

Back in Luanda the next morning, Harriet and I had our first and only argument of the trip. I won — one of the few advantages of looking after all the money. Having made arrangements to meet at 2 a.m. to leave for the airport, we stormed off in opposite directions.

I had always wanted to look at the fort but after two months in Luanda had never had time. Two policemen who were guarding it agreed to show me around. In the courtyard stood a strange assortment of military paraphernalia — burnt-out APCs, cannons and jeeps. An enormous statue of Portuguese explorers, displaying physiques like Holbein's Henry VIII, had obviously been moved. Instead of staring bravely out to sea, they seemed to be eyeing up a small 1950s fighter plane. Had they turned around, they would have been inspired by the view. Luanda bay was at its best. The palm trees of the Marginale cast long shadows on to the shining blue water, which from that distance could not be smelled. The sunken mine sweeper which swam in a sea of rust outside the Panorama Hotel looked like an intentional piece of sculpture. The Meridien looked imposing and progressive, merging the port area with the beauty of the old town. The Central Bank, whose interior has been ruined, looked magnificent – six storeys of pink icing sugar, topped by rounded turrets on either end. Only the closer landmarks were sullied. In the square below the fort, a UNITA house had suffered a bad attack of the measles in the post-election fighting. At the other side of the spit, ramshackle squatter's huts crowded together in squalid patches.

If they had really stretched their necks, the sailors would have been able to see the Angolan Space Project – a Cape Canaveral-style mausoleum for Agostinho Neto, the MPLA's founder. Known locally as Neto's rocket, the ten-storey monument had been built to commemorate the life of the great liberator who had died in Moscow twelve years earlier. Neto had been the first president of Angola and although he was rather more of a poet and a politician than a warrior, a few photographs of him carrying machine guns were found after his death and a legend was created around him to make up for the fact that he had no obvious successor.

His body had been badly embalmed by the Soviets and put in some forgotten morgue drawer until the break-up of the Soviet Union when it had been rediscovered. It was returned to the Angolans who were somewhat desperate to bury it before it fell apart. The great liberator of African slaves was fast turning an embarrassing shade of caucasian white. Added to this, they wanted to put him in the rocket while it was still possible. Having been built on sand, the tower shared properties with its leaning brother in Pisa. They had to get him in before the doors stuck. The next morning there was a grand ceremony at which he was finally laid to rest.

The guards changed their mind about letting me into the building, so I wandered down to the British Embassy. It was being fumigated. They had suffered an infestation in the midst of the chaos so Paul and I sat, drinking beer, on the ambassador's newly arrived and, as yet, unused armoured Range Rover. George drove up with a very frazzled-looking ambassador's secretary who had just returned to Luanda via Kinshasa. At least twenty had been killed in that day's rioting and her flight had been delayed while Mobutu made quite sure that he still controlled the airport. Luanda, the capital of war-torn Angola, was, for that day at least, a haven of peace.

I was planning to have a final dinner with Bob before we left Angola for what would be the last time, but in the time being (bereft without my faithful photographer) I went down to the beach. There I was approached by six fishermen who thought I was looking lonely. They took me back to the tarpaulin-covered hut in which they lived. One of their mothers had been a maid at the British Embassy and her son spoke a little English. Another had been a teacher. One of them was deaf and dumb, yet was accepted by the others and a key part of the fishing party. They had been sitting on the beach, drinking beer and smoking joints, for the last eight years. One of the restaurants on the Ilha provided them with free beer in return for fish. Anything else they needed, they bartered for. They had not used money for years and wouldn't let me use any of mine. I was their guest.

They took me out fishing in their boat which, although it had not seen any paint for some time and looked like a lifeboat from the Titanic, was perfectly watertight. I caught a dorado on a hand-line by way of recompense for their hospitality and had one of the best afternoons of the whole journey. I was in a foul temper when I arrived and was embarrassed into one of peace and happiness. Their lives had been destroyed by a few politicians and soldiers, fighting on their behalf yet without their sanction. Instead of giving up to despair, they were patiently biding their time and waiting for the powers to come to their senses. When it was nearly dark, we returned to shore. After eight years of doing it to survive, they still enjoyed the Hawaii-Five-O style of beaching.

After a while, Ernesto, the one who spoke English a little, leant over to me and said, 'It is not agreeable to be outside after night,' so they all escorted me to the other side of the Ilha where I was meeting Bob for dinner.

Early for dinner, I listened to the radio with Kim and Arlanda at the diner. Jeffrey Davidow, the US peace envoy, was trying to dig himself out of another hole. Savimbi was refusing to talk to the MPLA and had presented his latest set of demands to the Americans. Davidow had quickly unloaded this hot potato and passed it on to dos Santos. He then made a statement to Radio Nacional. 'It seems to me,' boomed the deep Stallone voice, 'that it is a choice between talking and fighting.'

Kim had shot and been shot at by American planes. Arlanda had American weapons to thank for half the destruction of her country. Now they had to listen to American banalities on their national radio station. Davidow did not inspire confidence.

After dinner, Bob and I went for my last visit to the Love Boat. The Cubans were meant to have pulled out of Angola in 1990. But almost three years later they were still dominating the dance-floor on the cross-channel ferry. Shady Americans and Portuguese propped up the bar. A team of fresh-faced South African account-ants sat nervously by the dance-floor, surreptitiously watching the Cubans dancing. Pelvic bones clamped together, they flew round the room like Siamese twins on speed. No one else dared compete. The accountants were on triple pay, doing a final audit for one of the now mineless mining companies. Big bucks or not, they wanted to go home. Everyone else was making deals. Anything could be bought and sold in Luanda and the Love Boat was the place to do it. The 40,000 carats of diamonds which UNITA had removed from Ode Brecht and RST were rumoured to be on the market, but then they were also rumoured to be in Jamba (Savimbi's war-time capital), Brussels, Lusaka and Switzerland. Someone else was hawking more pedaloes.

Angola was showing its resilience. Four hundred years of Portuguese colonization hadn't got them down, nor had thirty years of civil war. The next morning everyone would be on the beach: the businessmen with their radios, the politicians with their bodyguards, the smugglers and the con-men. The beggars would still be selling 1960s postcards of Angola's flora and fauna, washing cars and hawking cigarettes. The fishermen would continue to fish. There would still be a small market for lilos and beach toys and dos Santos and Savimbi would still be squabbling to the detriment of ten million people and the enrichment of maybe a thousand. For the native and expatriate rich of Luanda, life's a beach. The rest of the population will continue to die until the shells start falling on the Ilha. Then, maybe, there will be peace.

The 'chronically underfunded' UN weren't going to be much help either. Bob dropped me off at Speedie's house and Jon took Harriet and me to the airport for our 3 a.m. flight back to Windhoek. Most of the people on the flight were UN personnel going to Namibia to do their Christmas shopping. Then there was Chris McGreal from the *Guardian* who was trying to get home to Johannesburg for Christmas, and Harriet and I who were also going to do our Christmas shopping in Windhoek.

Chris stayed in Windhoek for the day so we trundled round town together, trying to buy interesting presents. The *Namibian* reported that it was taking Christmas and New Year off – the next issue of the national newspaper would be on 11 January. The town was deserted. Almost the entire population had gone to the coast for the holidays. Saddiq and Eve, friends of John Liebenberg's whom we had met when last in town, were relieved to see us. They were house-sitting for six different families and taking John's house off their hands was doing them a favour. Everywhere we turned, we bumped into UNAVEM II personnel on the same quest as ourselves. We had a few days but they had to catch the *urgent* aid flight back to Angola that night. Not everyone wants a German South West Africa shaving mug and the choice after that was severely limited.

CHAPTER SEVEN

Zambian farmers were still complaining when we returned to
Lusaka. In place of the drought had come floods, cholera and a
plague of black maize beetle. The more time one spends in Africa,
the more it seems that the biblical Egyptians had it easy. At least
you can eat frogs and locusts. Grasshoppers are a surprisingly
good and immensely popular seasonal dish in Zambia, Uganda
and many other countries.

The only reliable cure for the inedible black maize beetle is
DDT which, although freely available in most of Africa, is
expensive, carcinogenic and illegal. It also has terrible effects on
the environemnt and future crops. Zimbabwe's harvest was being
eaten up at a terrifying rate and the beetle was just starting to
take hold in Zambia. The Millers had lost fifty hectares already
and were thanking providence that they had planted some soya
that year.

Mr Chaonsa, the railway PR, had forgotten all about us when
we called, but said that we could come up to Kabwe in between
Christmas and the new year when the managing director would
be able to see us. We would spend Christmas at Lilayi with Robin,
Ginny and Martin and then drive up to Kabwe afterwards. It was
a great relief to be able to stop for a few days. By that time we
were getting rather tired of flying all over Africa in a desperate
quest for a functioning railway. Zambia, Zimbabwe and Mozambique we knew had working railways so after Christmas we
would be able to start travelling in a straight line. By Christmas
we had travelled about 18,000 miles in pursuit of the tracks and
had travelled on only about 180 of them. Fed up though we were,
we did feel as though we had achieved something. Zaïre was
going up in flames again. The army was on the rampage and

refugees were flooding over the borders of the country, telling tales of terrible atrocities. We had picked the right moment to get out of Zaïre and Angola looked as though it was about to go the same way. We had managed to see as much of both country's railways as would be possible for some time.

On Christmas morning, we went up to the big house to have a celebratory drink. As we sat on the verandah drinking Pimm's, Peter and Robin handed out Christmas presents to the massed ranks of farm labourers. All the children from the farm were in their Sunday best, playing in the bright sunshine and eating sweets and bread rolls hurled at them by Miller grandchildren from the verandah. A local band of actors and dancers, from the police college that borders the Millers' farm, sang and played drums while each worker was given a pair of dungarees and some gumboots. Those who had worked especially hard were given watches. It could have been a scene from *White Mischief* save that the watches were digital.

Harriet and I exchanged embarrassed glances throughout the spectacle, yet these were some of the few Zambians able to celebrate Christmas in a country where the price of the basic foodstuff, mealie meal, had multiplied weekly over the last few months. The farm workers also had clean water, comfortable houses, a fabulous soccer pitch and employers who were on their side. To invest in Zambia, many would say, you would either have to be insane or willing to sacrifice everything to help build the nation. Peter Miller's father was a railway engineer and he and Peter had carved Lilayi from the bush. Robin is an accountant who worked for Virgin when it was still an innovative company. Neither is mad, yet they were both investing in Zambia's press, tourism industry and agriculture. It was surely no coincidence that some of the workers queuing for their gumboots were fourth-generation employees of the farm. We had lunch at Lilayi Lodge which has become one of Zambia's most popular hotels and a valuable forex earner since the Millers built it two years ago.

Over Christmas, we met Mike, the manager of a small parastatal. He was a believer with a brain. A scholarship graduate of Birmingham University, he despaired for Zambia.

'I received a decent education under colonial power,' he said, 'but now, many children have no schools to go to. There are no teachers, no books and no curriculum.'

He expected to be fired within the next month because he had just made a hundred people redundant without waiting for government approval. 'That would take months, by which time we would have gone bankrupt. I am sure to have fired someone distantly related to the minister, but anyone can see that it doesn't make sense to have sixty-nine people in the personnel department of a small company.'

The whole parastatal system, he believed, was wide open to abuse. As part of his job, he was provided with a free house, a free car with petrol, unlimited telephone calls, and two servants, also on the company pay roll.

'People have to learn to fend for themselves,' he continued, 'but it is easy for me to say that as I fire them. With no social-security safety net, I am condemning people to no short-term hope, not even mid-term. If the country is to survive, people need to be fired and then those who actually do something useful can be paid a living wage for it.'

This is the dilemma facing all African governments and employers. The economy is the only thing about which anyone has time to care about. If you can't afford to eat, the fact that you are not represented in parliament doesn't really bother you. Years of mismanagement has led to grossly over-staffed companies (public and private), patriarchal business practices (a direct follow-on from colonialism) and rampant inflation. The companies need to be streamlined but to do that voters have to be thrown out of work in vast numbers.

Zambia, in common with twenty-seven other African countries, has the added problem of IMF and World Bank funds being tied to a strict structural adjustment programme. To receive aid, Zambia has to do what it is told, although this leads to unpopularity among an unsophisticated electorate who cannot see the connection. That is not to say that sophisticated western electorates are able to see the connection between good management and future prosperity, but the problem is magnified in Zambia. The Zambian administration's latest method of maintaining good public relations *and* IMF funding was to give people enormous pay raises and then fire them. When told to fire half the civil service by the IMF, they first tripled everyone's wages. They were, therefore, landed with tripled redundancy payments which they could not afford to meet. They had, though, complied with the IMF who had overlooked this possible escape clause. The IMF was actually getting rather nervous. No one was willing to go on the record, but a friend working for them in another African country with similar problems told me: 'We never expect people to comply with all our conditions, so go a little over the top in our demands to leave room for negotiation. The Zambian government is carrying through all our recommendations and causing the most terrible social problems. No one can afford to eat in Zambia any more.'

Another parastatal manager gave us a lift up to Kabwe the next day. He was facing problems similar to Mike's. The journey, which had taken eleven hours on the government-run railway, took an hour and a quarter by car. We scarcely had enough time to discuss the difficulties that Mark was facing.

The government, he told us, had an IMF-ordered blanket policy of not giving money to parastatals prior to their privatization. Mark desperately needed money to buy seeds, without which his state-owned farm could not plant. The government would not give him any for this essential task and the banks had none to lend. This meant that Zambia would be selling a bankrupt farm rather than a going concern and would therefore get much less money for it. On top of this, Zambia would have to import expensively rather than grow its own food cheaply.

Mr Chaonsa, who was beginning to get more than a little irritating, had once again forgotten that we were coming and was on his way to Lusaka – by car. We were left in the charge of Lizzie Chushi, Kabwe's station PR, who looked after us for the rest of our stay. The office of Hopkins Nyimbili, the general manager of the railway's central division, was our first stop. To do anything on this sector of the railway, we first needed his authorization. Railways are strategic and thus illegal to photograph without permission. His office was well protected by secretaries but we were ushered in immediately. Mr Nyimbili was sitting behind an enormous desk on which sat three small flagpoles on a single base. Everyone in the company seemed to have this arrangement but with only two flags – Zambia and Zambia Railways. I later discovered that the missing flag was that of UNIP, the former ruling party and no longer politically correct.

He warmed to us and decided to help us in any way that he could. This was a refreshing change and very useful, since everyone on that part of the railway answered to and took orders from him. Zambia Railways has such an over-staffed management that it is next to impossible for anyone to do anything. Only a few people can make decisions on their own and Nyimbili was one of them. He decided that the best way for us to see the railway would be by accompanying the pay train the next day. This train would slowly travel up the track, taking wages to all the gangers who live in cottages along its length. We would thus be able to meet the gangers, find out how they lived and also inspect the track. Before that we would be given a guided tour of the workshops and Central Train Control by the operations manager. Things were looking up.

Until 1975, almost all of Zambia and Rhodesia's trains were mended and maintained in Bulawayo, which is now in Zimbabwe. With Ian Smith's Unilateral Declaration of Independence, and the split of Rhodesia Railways, Kabwe workshops, where small jobs have always been done, became the core of Zambia's maintenance section. Livingstone in the south and Ndola in the north perform smaller tasks. The workshops at Kabwe are full of disillusioned old men, who have spent their lives on the railway and are greatly depressed by what has happened to it. Symbols of its decay lie all around them. Beaten-up old steam engines and irreparable diesels watch over their work together with comradely signs saying: 'If I don't get hurt today, no one will get hurt today', and 'Do it right the first time all the time'.

The foreman of one of the repair sheds took me to look at his old locomotives, which languished in a disused part of the station under the coal hoppers that used to fill their tenders.

'In India they have two hundred of these still working,' he said. 'When I joined the railway I wanted to work on them. They are such beautiful things. Last year we sent one to Zimbabwe to be reconditioned for the tourists. It was so beautiful to see one working again. These Japanese things aren't made any more, so when they break down there is nothing we can do. We can't make the parts for them. But all these steam engines can be repaired by us and we can even make the parts. I don't understand it.'

No one else seemed to understand it either. We had tea in the bunkhouse where crews go to eat and sleep in between jobs. A sign on the noticeboard, copied to seven different people including the managing director, proclaimed: 'We will try to provide a breakfast which will be as reasonably heavy so as to avoid starvation as much as possible.'

A couple of old drivers, who had been pushed upstairs and were now locomotive inspectors, chatted to us about the old days. Having joined together in 1963, they were important enough to speak their minds, yet still in touch with the troops. 'The British gave us a good system, then the Canadians came from Canada and gave us some more. Then the Germans came from Germany and gave us that new signalling system that no one can work and then the Indians came from wherever they came from and pulled out some wires.' They ranted on, 'Before it was British. Now there is just confusion. The British system was wonderful. You used to get green lights all the way to Lusaka. Now you could die waiting for a green light.'

Like wicked schoolboys, they egged each other on to greater criticisms of the company while Lizzie looked on nervously.

She and John Minsula, the operations manager, took us off to the central Train Control building from where the signalling system is run. It is the only part of what is meant to be the new headquarters that has actually been completed. An anonymous brick building by the station, its façade belies the glamorous interior. John ushered us into a room dominated by a massive control board portraying the railway. Six technicians sat at streamlined desks with mounted microphones and high-tech telephones. Dr No was nowhere to be seen but his presence was tangible. The white board, which showed the whole network like a lit-up Underground map, was a sea of red lights and flashing signs saying INTRUDER. There were only three green lights on the entire board. The two old inspectors had been underestimating the company's problems.

Zambia Railways is plagued by vandalism, which is one of the reasons why none of the Seimens equipment works. Thieves kept on stealing the copper telephone wires so they had been forced to introduce an expensive microwave system.

'We have to guard against pilferage by these scoundrels,' the general manager told us in the slightly Victorian manner in which British-educated Africans speak. Meetings in Africa always take place in 'fora' and soccer matches in 'stadia'.

The main reason that the control system doesn't work, however, is that it does not like dust, sun, rain or heat. All of the above come to equatorial Zambia in erratic spurts of vast quantities. The gangers routinely smother the electric boxes that control the points with mud to protect them from the sun. This has the same effect as a tandoor, but if the mud is kept wet the electrics won't overheat; not too wet, mind, or they'll short circuit.

'We are going back ninety years,' despaired John. 'We now have to use paper orders for the trains.'

Having made plans for us to board the pay train early the next morning, Lizzie took us to supper with her family. She lived in a small company house with her husband and their three children. Fortuitously, her husband manages the enormous car pool for railway HQ, so when the inevitable powercut plunged us into darkness, we opened the front door and ate by the light of his car's headlamps. The question of which tape to watch on the video recorder that they had borrowed for our entertainment did not arise. We had a delicious dinner – proper African food rather than the dreadful school dinners available at the Elephant's Head – and talked about normal things for a change: education (a worry), inflation (likewise) and soccer (a great source of national pride).

Almost the entire Zambian soccer squad was killed in a plane crash in early 1993. Tipped to win the African Cup and adored by the population, the death of the squad profoundly affected the country, which is still reeling from the shock. The mangled corpses were displayed in the Lusaka soccer statium where thousands came to mourn before the remains were buried just outside the complex. Rumours abound that the plane was shot down just after take off from Gabon's Leon M'ba airport but no evidence for this has been found and it seems incredible that even in Africa anyone would shoot down a plane in order to ensure victory in a football match.

A new team was created by Ian Porterfield, the former manager of British football club Chelsea, which stormed towards the World Cup with spiritual fervour. They failed at the final hurdle but doubts about the match will always linger due to FIFA's remarkable choice of a Gabonese referee.

Early next morning we arrived at the station and things did not go as smoothly as we had hoped. I had interviewed the managing director of ZR the previous day and he, too, had given us permission to travel on the pay train. No one had bargained on the local police force, however, who had orders to guard the train and repel all boarders. Colonel Simumba, former army officer and head of the railways, Mr Nyimbili, the general manager, and the general in charge of the railway police all tried to intercede with the one constable who would not let us on the train. His boss was in Lusaka and he wasn't going to let us on without orders from above. The combined onslaught of the managers failed to sway him. Nyimbili was outraged. These were his guests, his train and his money and nothing was going to stop him from helping us.

Occasionally – in the interests of PR – he would retreat from the argument with a beatific smile and say, 'Well, this is all fun, isn't it?' before vigorously wading in again.

Nyimbili was one of the few men on the network entitled to say 'expedite' and expect results. The constable, who was armed with an ancient bolt-action-rifle, was challenging his authority and driving him to heights of fury. After three hours of argument and consultation with third parties, while the train awaited Nyimbili's order to leave, he saw a way around the problem. Five minutes later, he had equipped Harriet and me with a Land Cruiser and driver, plus a locomotive inspector, chief track inspector and a PR officer to answer any questions we might have and help us on our way. We also had a police escort in case of bandits.

'You will have to chase the train cross-country,' Nyimbili told us, 'and get to the pay points before the train does.'

We set off like happy picnickers. Everyone in the car was getting a free day off to drive around the countryside chasing a train. All they had to do was keep us happy and their by now rabid boss would be placated. It was going to be a great day out. We raced out of town, barrelling over bush roads, and arrived at Natuseko well before the train. Twenty grizzled gangers had gathered to collect their pay. They were somewhat out of sorts since the train was apparently three days late. Groups of about twenty gangers patrol twelve to twenty kilometres of track which it is their job to keep safe – replacing sleepers and rails where necessary and keeping an eye out for wash-aways. A wash-away is what happens when a flood washes away the ballast that supports the rails and sleepers. From an approaching train, no fault can be seen on the line, yet the train will fall off the rails if it drives on tracks with no ballast beneath them. Most railway disasters in Africa are caused by them.

The gangers live in small tin huts known as cottages which are built to the same design as classical African beehive huts. They bear no resemblance to cottages. They are unbearably hot, so are generally used for storage while the gangers and their families live in huts which they build themselves out of mud. Many gangers' cottages are inaccessible by road so they are dependent on the railway that they maintain. However, when you earn 17,000 kwacha (£32) a month, the ability to go shopping in town is rarely more than a symbolic privilege. When the train eventually arrived, the constable who had obstructed us was furious. He would not let us anywhere near the peeling green caboose which was being used as the accounts office.

'How do I know you are not planning to steal the money?' he asked us. 'Do not come closer than twenty feet,' he shouted at Harriet, waving his ancient weapon at her to reinforce the point.

'Do you really think I would use a Zambia Railways vehicle as a getaway car and two heads of department as my accomplices?' countered Harriet, edging ever closer.

Harriet was entering her 'I will get this picture or die' phase which was always getting us into trouble, so I was much relieved when she was pulled back by Mr Mulenga, the locomotive inspector seconded to our team. Foiled, we beat a hasty retreat and raced on to the next pay stop.

There was a carnival atmosphere in the car as we plunged through the undergrowth on bush tracks that had not been used for years. After ten minutes, the dour driver – the only one who was doing his normal work – began to look edgy. We drove on through meadows of lilies, crushing wild mint under the wheels. The vehicle was filled with the scent of Pimm's.

'We are lost,' announced the driver.

'This is an experience,' countered the track inspector.

'Mushrooms,' bellowed Mr Mulenga.

The car skidded to a halt and everyone bailed out.

Was this slang for mines, an ambush or worse? I thought.

It had certainly produced a startling reaction from everyone else. Four grown men threw themselves out of the car and raced into the woods, where they frolicked among the trees in paroxysms of joy, picking huge white mushrooms.

'They are the first of the season,' cried Mulenga. 'We can never pick them any more because the children get there and sell them first. We are so far from a village that no one has discovered these. My wife will be so happy. Mushrooms for supper.'

Having meandered around the bush for a while, we eventually found the railway again and followed it to the next gangers' camp while Mulenga told us stories. I had asked Colonel Simumba why the railway had such an enormous police force (605 men) for one line. He had been evasive but Mulenga was more forthcoming: 'It's the theft. The bandits come and put grease on the rails at the bottom of hills so that the train slips on the tracks and slows down. Then they come and steal maize from the wagons. In 1986, my train was derailed by thieves. They thought it was going to be a freight train with food but it was a passenger train with hundreds of people aboard. Luckily we have to drive so slowly these days that no one was killed.'

At Luwashimba, there were some very irate gangers and three railway police waiting for the train. They pounced on their boss, the track inspector, demanding to know why they had no water. Many of the gangers' little villages have no water supply and rely on tanks of water brought up by rail. This one had been out of water for a week and they had been walking the four miles to their children's school to drink and wash. Their crops, which they grow in patches around the camps to supplement their income, were suffering too. The foreman of the gangers was rather nervous because, in the absence of anyone else to blame, the others had been threatening him with witchcraft. This is a major problem in many African countries, where managers don't dare to discipline people for fear of being cursed.

The railway no longer pays the gangers enough money to survive so every camp is like a microcosm of an African village. Chickens, goats and dogs wander around while the women mash maize and tend the crops. We could see the train coming from miles away when we looked back up the dead straight track. The line had been carved out of thick bush, so the cyclops headlamp of the train shone out from the dark of the forest long before it arrived. The men calmed down after they had been paid and the track inspector promised to send them more water that day.

We, though, went on to Kapiri Mposhi, 1,860 kilometres from Dar es Salaam, and the start of the Tazara railway. The Tazara railway and pipeline was completed with Chinese expertise and financing in 1975 and was a valuable life-line for Zambia when they were supporting sanctions against Rhodesia and South Africa. The closing of the Benguela Railway which came with Angola's independence in 1975 meant this was a very lucky coincidence. Tents the size of football pitches had been erected to store donor maize being delivered through Tanzania. Inefficiencies on Zambia Railways had led to massive backlogs and there was enough free food awaiting delivery to halve the price of maize overnight. The Zambians had not been helped by their neighbours in Zaïre, who had destroyed two hundred of their wagons during a periodic fit of looting. This made it difficult to move things around, but it did seem a shame that there was so much maize in Kapiri and so little in the rest of the country. On top of this, there were hundreds of unemployed wagons sitting in the sidings. Many of them were awaiting return to Zimbabwe, and it would have seemed logical to fill them with maize and send them on their way. When I suggested this to the assistant station master, back in Kabwe, he told me it was impossible.

'They want them back as soon as possible, and the train will not be able to go as fast if the wagons are full.'

Zambia and Tanzania's showpiece railway was not fulfilling its promise. It, too, had been ill-maintained and journey times were double what they should have been.

After another night in Kabwe, we bowed to popular pressure and took a car back to Lusaka. Lizzie's husband had laid on a vehicle and chauffeur for us and it seemed churlish to refuse. We booked tickets from Lusaka down to Livingstone through the head office and went back to Lilayi for the new year's eve celebrations. Once again the journey took no time and we were back at the farm within a couple of hours. The only hiccup was at a police road block. Road blocks are so common in Zambia that Bata, the local shoe company, advertises on the signs:

'Slow down. Police check point. BATA BY CHOICE.'

We had no problems, though, since every policeman in the country is trained next door to the Millers' farm and knows them by name.

That evening, we had heart-warming stew with Anne and Dave Wallace – some friends of Ginny and Robin's who worked for an Irish aid group. There was a new year's eve party at the lodge where we spent the latter half of the evening. Everything after that was an enjoyable blur until two days later when, at 9 a.m., we found ourselves waiting at Lilayi siding for the train down to Livingstone. Robin took us through the gangers' camp to Bwana Porter's house. He was the man with the microwave telephone who could find out when the train was due.

'Three o'clock,' he said, having spoken to Central Train Control in Kabwe.

Robin chuckled merrily as we loaded our luggage back into the car and returned to the farm. We made our last trip to the siding at eight o'clock that evening when a freight train came through. It was delivering aid – 'a gift from the people of the United States of America' – but had to get off the main line so that our express could come through. The mud-covered electric points box failed and the train had to reverse back into the siding. A railway policeman jumped off the train and had a conspiratorial chat with Bwana Porter. Shortly afterwards two boys appeared with an enlarged skateboard which they rushed back up the tracks at high speed. Ten minutes later, we heard a squeaking from the darkness and the boys returned with a bag of maize which had 'fallen off the train'. Money changed hands and they disappeared with their skateboard and bag of maize. An estimated 30 per cent of Zambia's donor maize disappears between delivery and distribution. This method was used with impunity, within five hundred yards of the police college. In less guarded places, aid theft is more industrial. Trucks and AKs are used instead of skateboards and bribes.

As the train pulled into the siding, eleven and a half hours late, Robin asked Mr Porter what he thought would make the trains run on time.

'Privatization,' he replied immediately. 'Yesterday it passed around midnight. Today, you might say at least it has tried.'

Despite checking with Lusaka station and having our tickets booked by the general manager of the entire system, inevitably there was no compartment for us. The train was jammed with people. We left Robin roaring with laughter at the siding and resigned ourselves to standing for the long journey down to Livingstone. We were very lucky: Patrick, the railway policeman, and John, the conductor, had both seen telexes about us and were aware that they were meant to be nice to us. Weeks earlier, Mr Chaonsa had sent a telex to all the stations, saying that we could take photographs wherever we wanted and should be offered all assistance. When a compartment became free at the next stop, it was immediately given to us. We settled down to sleep and spent a fitful night, alternating between deep slumber and panicked awakenings.

The Zambian tracks are in such poor condition that the trains have to go very slowly to avoid derailment. Simumba had told us that 70 per cent of locomotive repairs involved their battered undercarriages. The trains, wagons and carriages themselves remained relatively unscathed. It was on the journey to Livingstone that we began to understand why. At times, it was like wakening to find oneself lying on the back of a trotting horse. We discovered that wrapping shirts round our heads saved bruising them on the bunk or roof above. When we discussed the problem with Patrick in the morning, he was optimistic.

'Don't worry,' he said with a grin, 'the trains go too slowly. No one ever gets killed when they derail.'

'I've been derailed seven times in nine years and I've never been injured, touch wood,' said the equally chirpy John, rapping a Formica-covered wall with his knuckles.

On arrival, Patrick and John managed to find the Livingstone PR officer, who had not received word of our arrival but reluctantly agreed to help us out the next day. They dropped us off at the Rainbow Lodge which is a little outside town, on the banks of the mighty Zambesi and within sight of the Victoria Falls. We were in the presence of a wonder of the world and deeply underwhelmed. The drought had only just broken, so the falls were still at an all-time low. Instead of the raging torrents and roaring cataracts we had expected, the legendary Victoria Falls was doing an only slightly grandiose impersonation of an overflowing bath. Hippos lolled around in the water and crocodiles did such good log imitations that I was unable to point them out to Harriet. She has worked all over Africa and spent many months on the continent yet still never seen anything more exciting than an antelope.

Meanwhile, irritatingly good photographs and postcards of the river in flood littered the hotel. The drought had been so severe, the receptionist told us, that the falls hadn't looked truly impressive for about four years. Aeroplanes overflying the cataracts were still doing a roaring trade with expectant tourists, however. They buzzed over the falls like overgrown mosquitoes, from dawn till dusk, destroying what would otherwise have been a pleasant and peaceful scene.

Later that evening we met an extraordinary priest. Father Sean Reilly belonged to an obscure community of Irish brothers who were threatening to defrock him because of his attitude problem.

'Condoms are the only answer. I would encourage wearing them always and putting a pin prick in the end during the most fertile period,' was his radical (for a fellow Catholic) view about the Pope's latest guidance on contraception.

He openly contradicted the Church's teachings but could not be made to criticize the infallible Pope. One of the most thankless tasks imaginable must be that of the Catholic priest counselling AIDS patients in the slums of Livingstone. Say anything constructive and you get into trouble with the abbot back home; follow the Church's guidance on contraception and watch people die before your eyes. The agonizing suspension of intellect necessary to stay in the Church must be akin to that suffered by Chinese officials during the cultural revolution. Blind faith is the only way out and that is the doctrine followed by the otherwise intelligent nuns whom I had met in Lusaka. They looked after terminal AIDS patients with extraordinary dedication and passed judgement on no one.

It was an interesting glimpse into the secretive Catholic Church's internal strife. In Livingstone a monk was recommending condom use. In Lusaka, nuns were saying contraception was evil. The nuns were right. The 1994 publication of some more papal bull in the form of Veritatis Splendor confirmed their medieval views.

Daniel Simunda, the Livingstone station PR, took over our entertainment for the next day. He hadn't been too happy to see us in the beginning, but over the next few days, he and Rafael, our taxi driver, showed us a great time in Livingstone. Both in their thirties, Rafael was never without his Bible and would sit drinking squash and making caustic comments while Daniel, who shared a love of Mosi beer with Harriet and me, told us railway stories. Daniel made it very clear on the first day that if we wanted to see anything of the railway, we were going to need a car on permanent standby. He was based at Livingstone station, which had the same air of decay as Kabwe, but seemed busier because it was on the border with Zimbabwe.

All the import and export administration had to be done in Livingstone before goods could be dispersed around the countryside. The very first task when a South African wagon arrived was to whip its tarpaulin off and replace it with a grotty Zambian one. Let loose on the network, the South African ones get stolen by itinerant upholsterers and converted into three-piece suites before the train reaches the next station. I was so stunned by this information that Daniel thought I didn't believe him. He pointed out evidence for the rest of our time together.

'Look, there's a suitcase made from a tarpaulin,' he would cry as we drove through town. 'And there's a handbag.'

It became rather dull. There were hundreds of them. Zambia Railways must have spent thousands of dollars replacing missing covers before they worked out what the problem was.

We spent hours on the bridge. Harriet wanted to take pictures of a train crossing the falls, so needed to know the timetable, but since one wasn't available we just had to sit there waiting. It had been completed by Pauling's in 1906. To Pauling's chagrin, his company had failed to get the contract to build it, but they were allowed to erect it. Cleveland and Bright built it in Darlington and then it was exported piecemeal to Beira, up the railway to the falls, where Pauling's rebuilt and opened it. It is the bridge that is the wonder of the world. Rhodes had decreed that 'passengers should be able to feel the spray of the falls'. To achieve this effect, it had to be built over a yawning chasm when much shorter crossings were available. It is five hundred feet long and, although below the lip of the falls, still extremely high. Originally built as a railway bridge, there is also a thin, alternately one-way road, along which cars, tourists and black marketeers constantly stream.

Watching the comings and goings with us was Astone, a very bored soldier who sat in the shade and guarded the bridge with half an eye and a G3. The Zimbabweans were taking no such chances and had an APC stationed on their side for most of the day. Astone believed they were on a hiding to nothing: 'I've lived in Livingstone all my life,' he told me, 'and nothing has ever happened here.'

The relative wealth of Zimbabwe could be seen in the huge number of black Zimbabwean tourists. A bevy of trainee mission-

aries had come from faraway Harare to see the sights, wearing
'Get dirty for God – Go lay a brick for teen missions' T-shirts.
They checked the echo by shouting, 'Praise the Lord.' Zambians
crossing the bridge on foot did so for one reason only – maize
was cheaper in Zimbabwe so if you live in Livingstone it's well
worth the walk to buy your mealie meal. It is very rare to see
African tourists. Most children living in towns have never seen a
wild animal, as the game parks and tourist attractions of their
own countries are there to bring in foreign exchange, not for local
consumption. Zimbabwe, we perceived, still had some semblance
of an economy.

We could hear when a train was coming because the drivers
blow their whistles as they leave Livingstone station. Harriet hung
off a lamp-post to get a good view as the train rounded the corner
on to the bridge, and Daniel and I crouched below her hanging
on to her legs. Soon a diesel came into view, pulling a long line of
wagons – all empty. As part of Zambia's great export drive it was
returning empty wagons to Zimbabwe. The bridge is a bureau-
cratic farce. Zambian trains go to Zimbabwe, drop off their
wagons and go back to Livingstone, then another engine has to
pick up the wagons and take them on from there.

The fact that, due to Pauling's careful planning, the same
locomotive could be driven the whole way from Beira to Lobito,
is of no consequence. In between China and Mongolia they have
to change the bogeys on their wagons. It is not necessary here but
relations between countries along the track are so strained that no
advantage is taken of the universal 1067mm gauge. Wagons have
to be leased to the next-door country and returned as fast as
possible because of punitive rental rates. Zimbabwe doesn't like
its wagons to go to Zambia because, due to the state of the track,
they come back in such awful condition. Zambia retaliates with
equally punitive charges, for reasons of parity and national
pride. Zimbabwe gets the better deal because it has a more efficient railway system and can get the rolling stock back faster.
More Zambian foreign exchange dwindles away for no reason.

Moreover, the crossing between Zambia and Zimbabwe is the most friendly on the line.

Livingstone has three museums and unlike Victoria Falls, at the other side of the river, almost no tourists. There is the cultural village, on the site of Pauling's old camp, the Livingstone museum and the railway museum. The cultural village is just an excuse for selling tourist knick-knacks, but the Livingstone museum in the centre of town is fascinating. A picture of the great doctor himself, labelled 'Livingstone by the British photographer Anon', was part of a memorial to the explorer. Pages from his notebook and the medicine bag which he lugged across the continent are all there. The top floor is like a small corner of a natural-history museum designed by a serial killer. A blood-spattered leopard was chewing into the back of a grimacing antelope to the delight of a small school party from Zimbabwe who had skipped the Livingstonia on the ground floor. This method of taxidermy, while doubtless frowned upon by purists, makes for much more interesting viewing. Sadly, the museum was almost deserted and one of the numerous guards told me that it was seldom busy.

We were the first visitors to the railway museum for four days. It had to be specially opened for us by the stroppy curator who was trying to read a book in peace. The outside exhibits of old steam engines were obscured by torrential rain. Inside was also wet but even if you're not interested in trains (which you may have guessed by now, I'm not), it's a fascinating place. The history of the railway is so interlinked with the history of the continent that the exhibits have great significance. Large charts with excellent photographs and maps detail the past of the railway and the country. The museum is built on the site of the old Zambia Saw Mills depot which used to operate its own lines until there wasn't any wood left to saw. The company bought up old steam engines from ZR and drove them into the bush beyond Mulobezi, laying track and cutting trees as they went. The genius behind this project then sold the locomotives and engine sheds back to the government for use in and as the museum.

The museums desperately need to be advertised. Thousands of tourists visit Victoria Falls every week, but without doing some intensive research they would never know that just over the river in Livingstone there are exhibits to look at and much cheaper prices. For the white tourist in Africa, a museum can be a welcome change to the endless slog of game parks and sunbathing. In the time being, scores of people, on the Zambian government's pay roll, sit around doing nothing.

Daniel took us on a tour of Livingstone's railway clubs. As we walked under the grandiose arch of the Livingstone Railway Recreation Club, a tree fell on to the pavilion of the railway bowling club. No tears were shed. Everyone thought that bowls was a silly game. It had not been played since the whites left and the old bowling balls were used to support the scuffed brass foot-rail which lined the bar. Mr Malisase, the Livingstone station master who greeted us as chairman of the recreation club, was drowning his sorrows at the state of the railways. After twenty-eight years on the railway he was fed up with what was happening to it.

'Wait until you get to Zimbabwe,' he said, 'you won't believe that we used to be one federation. The railway has done so much for this country and we are just letting it fall apart.'

I asked, 'What has it done for Zambians? Surely the British got all the benefits?'

'No, the British may have built the railway and run the mines but we have profited too. Apart from anything else, they are the reason why Zambia is so peaceful. Tanzanians came to the north to mine, and they married the local girls. Gangers on the railway moved around the country. My tribe, the Tonga, like bossing people, so many moved away, joined the police and married local people. Now there is no tribalism. I don't even know what Mr Simunda's tribe is. Look around Africa. Everywhere except Zambia there is a problem with tribalism. We have never had such problems here.'

Kaunda is widely admired for making the country's seventy-three tribes think of themselves as Zambians. But recently tribalism has been rearing its head once more.

'What has saved us is that all our generals were educated at Sandhurst,'* piped up Daniel.

'That too, but it's the railway. Everyone loves it. In Eastern Province, where there are no trains, the women sing a song when they're pounding maize: "Let me see the railway before I die," they sing. They'd be so disappointed if they knew what was going on.'

We left the SM weeping into his beer at the bowling club but the conversation continued at the railway's tennis club.

'We were never divorced from Britain. It was only a separation,' Mr Malisase said plaintively as we left.

Rafael, who had stayed respectfully quiet in the presence of the station master, launched into a diatribe against African rule.

'The British should be our masters,' he said. 'When they were here everything worked. Now nothing does. Look at any country. Their economies go down after the colonials leave. Look at Tanzania. They used to buy food from us when the white man was here. Now we both have to buy from South Africa.'

Daniel nodded sagely while Harriet and I fidgeted. An African had voiced the things that, in the politically correct environment of the 1990s, a white man is not allowed to say. Africa doesn't work. It is pointless to pretend otherwise. There can be endless debates as to whose fault this is and what the solutions are, but until it is accepted that African management is a disaster area, no progress will be made.

'Just look at Zimbabwe's immigration house at the falls,' continued Rafael remorselessly. 'Five years ago they had flowers and green lawns, now it is all yellow and the flower beds are full of weeds. They still have good roads, but will they keep them up? The British are very kind. We fought for independence and told

* England's officer-training college.

you to go away, but still after four years of drought, you are sending us free maize. I don't understand it.'

Daniel dug into a packet of soggy Zimbabwean crisps. 'They should have bought these from South Africa. They're as bad as ours.'

He had arranged a trip up the track for us so that we could meet some more gangers and talk to the people who used the railways. We had to be at the station at 7 a.m. to take the up train, so we woke early. We listened to the radio. The inevitable had happened in Angola. Fierce fighting had broken out again in Lobito, Benguela and Huambo. Lubango had fallen to UNITA overnight.

Margaret Anstee, interviewed on the World Service, had given in to despair. 'This is a spiral of violence which no one will be able to control,'* she told an interviewer.

Patrick and John who had brought us down from Lusaka were taking the train up again to Ndola. We would accompany them as far as we could. The next day we were going on to Zimbabwe. The train did not leave until 1.30 and ground to a halt, promptly, at 1.31. Half in and half out of the station, more people had appeared. The driver stopped so they could pile into the train. There are three classes on Zambian trains – first, which we had experienced, standard, which has old, ripped vinyl, airline-style seats, and economy, which has padded benches. All classes were packed to the gunwales, the lavatories had overflowed and none of the fans was working. Many people were settling in for a three-day journey and had packed accordingly. Vast *sufrias* (beaten metal pots) of mealie meal, bags of indeterminate foodstuffs and endless bottles of murky water were shoved into every available space while their owners showed an incredible talent for sleeping under extreme circumstances.

As the train set off again, I followed John who was collecting

---

* At time of writing she has been proved right. She has retired from the fray and the war rages on.

tickets. Daniel wasn't moving from the open window next to which he had lodged himself. There was an amazing assortment of people on the train. Miners, who had been visiting their families, going back to the copper belt; market people who had been selling their produce at Livingstone market; students going to school, and anyone who couldn't afford the bus.

'It's much cheaper than the bus and you can bring as much luggage as you like,' explained a woman who had been to her father's funeral and was going back to her husband in Lusaka with the loot she had salvaged from her father's house.

The engine had to stop at every signal, where the driver had to get out and call Central Train Control in Kabwe for permission to carry on. Anyone who has to contact Kabwe carries a microwave telephone headset with them. These were plugged into the white boxes next to the signals which still work even when the points have overheated. When they don't work, the driver has to walk to the next box and try again. In extreme cases, which happen all too often, a spare locomotive has to be sent out to tell the driver he can carry on. Every time the train stopped, people appeared from the bush to fill containers with water at the tanks attached to the bottom of the carriages. Children ran up for a drink and men ran in from the fields to wash themselves and brush their teeth with twigs.

Harriet was causing chaos as she photographed people further down the train. Jardine, who was dressed for a discotheque, was furious with her.

'You are only taking photographs of people who are badly dressed,' he shouted.

He and Daniel were the only smartly dressed people on the train. I went to talk to him in the hope of defusing the situation. On his way to Lusaka for a job interview, Jardine had left three days before the event in case of train delays. He had nowhere to stay in Lusaka, but wasn't expecting to get there until the next day and hadn't wanted to chance a cancelled train.

An old woman with a deeply lined face and rheumy eyes, sitting next to him, was on her way back home. She lived six stops up the line from Livingstone and had been to the market with all her village's chickens. Jammed under her feet was a griddle and a bag of charcoal wrapped up in newspaper. A roll of notes was wrapped in a fold of the kanga she was wearing round her hips. Once or twice a year, on behalf of her fellow villagers, she takes the train to Livingstone to cook and sell the chickens in the market. They earn more money cooked than alive.

'They are too expensive to eat. We only eat them on special occasions,' she told me. 'We need the money we get from selling them to buy maize. We sold all our maize to the government mill, but now it costs many times what they paid us for it.'

Last year, the extra profit had been spent on books for the children, but there wouldn't be enough left over this time. All the money would go on food.

Moving from carriage to carriage on the wildly vibrating train was a dangerous pastime – almost a sport. The concertinas on the 1974 Japanese-made carriages had ripped and fallen apart long ago. The plates upon which you are meant to walk were often booby-trapped, so when you put any weight on them, they snapped down and let you fall towards the ballast. Crossing the gap involved timing your moment so that you were not violently hurled from the side, and then jumping the yawning gap to the next carriage. When I arrived in the guard's van, I discovered a battered red box screwed to the wall. 'Drop defect reports in slot' had been painted on the front. It was jammed full. Rafael was waiting for us at Senkobo and raced us back to Livingstone and across the bridge to Victoria Falls. We had to book a ticket for the next night's train and wanted to make sure that we would be allowed to take photographs.

Having made the necessary arrangements and returned to Zambia, we spent our last night having dinner at the hotel. It was a beautiful evening. The falls are called Mosi Oa Tunya (the smoke that thunders) by the Zambians because of the clouds of spray that rise above it. When Livingstone first clapped eyes on them in 1855, he said the sight was so lovely that it 'must have been gazed upon by angels in flight'. That night, it lived up to its press. The planes (taking tourists on the flight of angels) stopped circling early in the evening and peace reigned. Against the background of the roaring falls, crickets chiruped, hippos yawned and we sat on the terrace of the hotel, drinking beer and reading recent issues of *Rail News* – Zambia Railways' in-house magazine. We were to appear in the next issue, having been photographed by every PR officer on the network, and had met many of the featured characters. The falling sun caught the spray of the falls and a spectacular rainbow developed. For the first time, everything was as described in the tourist brochures and it was easy to forget the terrible state in which Zambia had found itself.

The Movement for Mandrax Dealing, as Zambia's ruling party the MMD is known to the more cynical members of Zambian society, was about to be reshuffled. The IMF had told Chiluba that he had to do something about his less than pure cabinet so there were a lot of very nervous cabinet ministers preparing for bed that night. In fact, they were worrying unnecessarily. The reshuffle which eventually was chosen in 1993 retained the most dubious character and got rid of the better ones. Zambia is still in crisis.

The unrestrained joy that had greeted Chiluba's election was turning to resentment. The people of Zambia had been looking for a quick fix. The world community, who had forced multiparty democracy on to Zambia, was not yet looking shamefaced. Chiluba's peaceful victory is still being used as an example of successful free elections to wave in the faces of Africa's surviving dinosaurs. Hastings Banda in Malawi was the last person to be blackmailed by this argument but his people continue to suffer. The men at the top in Zambia have been changed but the people are still living under the tyranny of crushing poverty.

Chiluba did not change the money when he gained power – a rare example of restraint. He has had to since, because of inflation, and now the notes have no one's head on them. When we were there, the increasingly blackened and worthless notes still bore the head of Kenneth Kaunda. Chiluba, however, has all KK's powers. He can force through any law that he wants without overstepping Zambia's legal framework and had recently wasted valuable parliamentary time in order to outlaw smoking in public. Everyone on the terrace was smoking and the police only stopped smokers to scrounge cigarettes. By western standards, 70 per cent of the Zambian population lives in public.

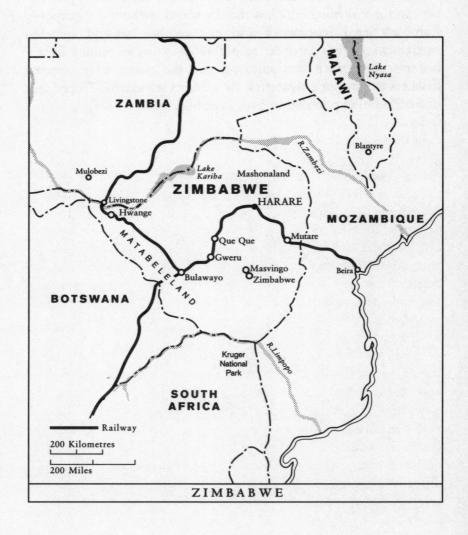

ZIMBABWE

Rafael took us over the bridge and dropped us off at the Victoria Falls Hotel. It was a startling change from the hotel in which we had been staying. It had been started as an adjunct of the railway, indeed its first dining room was a disused engine shed, but since then things have moved on. When the railway reached the falls in 1904, the bridge builders, surveyors and engineers of the BMR (Beira, Mashonaland and Rhodesia Railways) needed somewhere to stay and the Victoria Falls Hotel was their answer. Ninety years later, it is a tourist trap of magnificent proportions. Shining bright white against the surrounding forest, it is a huge hotel of one hundred and forty rooms, built round a central courtyard. Its wings frame a manicured lawn where we drank cocktails and admired the view. From the comfort of the hotel, in flood or not, the falls are pretty good. A plume of spray is in constant attendance above the bridge and an army of staff does the same for the guests.

The hotel's interior colour scheme of duck-shit green and white with chintz accessories may be better suited to somewhere cold and stuck in the last decade, but I saw no one complain. The elegant oval windows of the older buildings betray its kinship with the railway station, which is only a short stroll across the car park. The station's immaculate flowerbeds, fish ponds and well-polished signposts drove home the fact that we had entered a different country, as did the fact that a compartment had been reserved for us on the night train to Bulawayo. On a neatly typed list encased by a glassed-in noticeboard were our names: 'Mr and Mrs Bredin, coupé to Bulawayo.' We weren't taking any chances with the moral police.

An exquisite train was being cleaned in the station. It was

spotless already but the etched mirrors of the first-class compartments were being given a final once-over. The station house was freshly whitewashed with pale blue guttering. Columns supported a new tin roof under which was the station master's teak-tiled office. He was expecting us and had a photographic pass which had been sent down from Bulawayo so that Harriet could work on the journey. The station sign announced that it was 1,434 kilometres to Beira. If the rest of the journey was going to be like this we were going to enjoy ourselves.

The train itself was wonderful. After an excellent dinner in the dining car, during which one of our fellow passengers was asked to remove his hat before eating, we returned to our well-polished compartment. A railway policeman came to check under the beds to see if there were any stowaways, warned us about theft on the railways and moved on. He was succeeded by a uniformed guard who made our beds for us. After a bump-free night, we awoke to gentle tapping on the door. Steaming coffee appeared and we disembarked, refreshed, in Bulawayo.

I needed to buy a couple of books about the building of the railway and went to an antique book shop to find them. The certificates of incorporation on the wall of the office summed up Zimbabwe's recent history – confused. In the space of twelve years, the name of the company had changed from Books of Rhodesia to Books of Zimbabwe Rhodesia to Books of Zimbabwe.

The Rhodesia problem started when Rhodes's British South Africa company was given permission to make treaties in the area above Bechuanaland (modern-day Botswana). They took over Mashonaland straight away. Three years later, they overthrew the all-powerful Lobengula, King of the Ndebele. The two regions of Mashonaland and Matabeleland* made up the mass of southern Rhodesia and had been around for centuries. This was not a part

* Mashonaland is the home of the Shona people; Matabeleland, that of the Ndebele.

of Africa that could be written off as uninhabited because all the inhabitants were primitive tribespeople. There are thirteenth-century ruins at Zimbabwe (after which the country is named) which indicate that a sophisticated culture, based round an impressive city, existed when wattle-and-daub houses, coracles and woad make-up were still the rage in England. The BSA's occupation of the area was armed robbery and was reacted to as such. The *chimurenga* (liberation war) from 1896–7 was the result. It united the Shona and the Ndebele for the first time in centuries and took a massive effort to put down. Rhodes, who believed that 'we are the first race in the world, and that the more of the world we inhabit, the better it is for the human race', rode rough-shod over the local inhabitants and established the protectorate under the unassuming name of Rhodesia.

From the very beginning, Rhodesia was in constitutional crisis. Like early colonial India, the country was run by a company – Rhodes's British South Africa company. More diplomatically, Rhodes, who in 1890 was to become prime minister of South Africa, called the capital Salisbury after the prime minister of England. Britain, though, wasn't fooled, and sought to control the power of the BSA from very early on. By 1907, the white settlers had a majority in the legislative council and wanted autonomy. They became gradually more important as the power of the BSA, which had been unable to find the expected gold, waned. During the First World War the Ndebele fought for the restoration of their king. Both black and white camps, though adversaries on the ground, had the same goal of shaking off both British and BSA rule. In the 1922 whites-only referendum, which foreran the withdrawal of the BSA charter, it emerged that the white settlers wished neither to be part of South Africa nor a British-run colony. What arose was nominally a British colony, but the power of the legislature was such that it was run from Salisbury rather than the King Charles Street headquarters of the British Colonial Office.

None of the constraints of the British Colonial Office were put upon the government in Salisbury and although the British government had a veto, it remained only a theoretical one. A succession of important laws was passed before 1930 which gave the country its racially segregated structure. Pass and land laws were enacted which inhibited African development and gave vast advantages to the tiny white settler population. The whites also benefited enormously from a war and postwar boom when they were making things for the front under a protected market. In 1953, Nyasaland (Malawi), Northern Rhodesia (Zambia) and Southern Rhodesia (Zimbabwe) were united in a federation under Britain. They had a fair degree of autonomy and under their first leader – Rhodesia's Prime Minister Godfrey Huggins – made some strides towards improving the lot of the ordinary African. Internal black pressure in all three states, combined with British pressure for change, forced this upon the federation. It did not last. In 1961 Malawi was given full independence and in 1962 Zambia followed suit. Rhodesia which had the largest white population (as a result of postwar boom and white flight from Malawi, South Africa and Zambia) saw this as a threat and entrenched. The ground was laid for Ian Smith and the Unilateral Declaration of Independence (UDI).

The 1950s and 1960s saw the revitalizing of the African National Congress (the Rhodesian wing of the ANC had first emerged in the 1930s) and the emergence of the National Democratic Party and the Zimbabwe African People's Union (ZAPU) – all African parties striving for independence. White Rhodesians had to fight two battles at the same time – one against Britain, which was trying to force liberal ideas on to the settlers, and another against the blacks who wanted to get rid of both Britain and the white settlers. This state of affairs made a perfect launch pad for the Rhodesian Front – a white party which wanted to stop the 'rot'. With the support of farmers – the mainstay of Rhodesia's white population – it gained power in the 1961 election, ousting the more pragmatic government of Whitehead. In 1962 Ndabaninghi Sithole split from Joshua Nkomo's ZAPU to form ZANU. Both parties were proscribed, the press was censored and all opposition viciously put down by the hardman tactics of the new government. For Ian Smith though, the Rhodesia Front government of Winston Field was not strong enough. In 1964 he replaced Field and in November 1965 he made his UDI – the kick-off for the second independence war.

The second *chimurenga* was a nasty little war. Harriet and I had seen evidence of it in Zambia, whose capital was bombed as part of Smith's retaliation. We would see more in Mozambique. Smith's UDI was totally against the grain of everything else that was going on in Africa. The 'winds of change' were sweeping across the plains, through the jungles of Zaïre and Central Africa, and gradually eroding everything that stood before them. In 1965, the only countries yet to react to the draught were Angola and Mozambique, who were still under Portuguese rule, South Africa (where Macmillan's speech was made in 1959) and Rhodesia. Portugal was too busy with its own problems to worry about Africa. Rhodesia and South Africa closed the door and put up the storm shutters. There began a long siege which in South Africa has only now reached its climax.

From 1964 to 1974 Robert Mugabe, who had replaced Sithole as leader of ZANU, and ZAPU's leader Joshua Nkomo were kept in prison, but their parties' military wings fought ill-planned guerilla wars against the white minority. Their release and departure from Rhodesia led to an escalation of the war. Mugabe had spent his porridge doing correspondence degrees and planning strategy. He emerged with three degrees and left for Mozambique where eventually President Machel grudgingly allowed him to join the 20,000 ZANU guerillas based there. Nkomo likewise skulked off to his guerillas who were based in neighbouring Zambia. Nkomo received support from the Soviet Union and the Ndebele; Mugabe, who at that time described himself as a Marxist–Leninist, from China and the Shona. There followed a brutal civil war which by 1979 had cost a seventh of the population their homes, and innumerable lives.

Nkomo had many guerillas but did not use them extensively.

Mugabe, who had bases in both Zambia and Mozambique, fought ferociously although not a soldier himself. Appalling atrocities were committed on all sides. The notorious Selous Scouts and other bands of white Rhodesians routinely tortured. ZANU's soldiers routinely mutilated. The seemingly gentle and unassuming Mugabe was held up as a rabid Marxist terrorist. Smith, whose charm is well known, was portrayed as a psychopathic white supremacist. That there was any room for political manoeuvre is astonishing and largely thanks to Lord Soames, the avuncular British cabinet minister who was called in as Rhodesia's last governor.

When Smith lost the support of like-minded South Africa he had to cave in to the pressure which had been put on him by trade sanctions and the effects of international unpopularity on a land-locked country. UDI lasted for fourteen years during which time industries developed through necessity, farming became more essential and therefore protected for the whites and, against all odds, the railway kept going. As in South Africa who, unable to buy arms on the world market, reacted by creating their own, now envied, arms industry, sanctions actually did Rhodesia some good. Complacency and laziness often prevalent in white settler populations could not be allowed. Everyone had to strive to survive. But, although this gave the pariah nation a backbone, it was still weak enough to be broken.

Smith tried for an internal settlement with the Patriotic Front which Nkomo and Mugabe had been forced to create together, but his intransigence made that impossible. It was left for Arch-bishop Abel Muzorewa to make a deal with Smith. The resultant elections made Muzorewa Rhodesia's first black prime minister. The only problem was that ZANU and ZAPU, with majority support, had boycotted the elections and continued to wage their independence war. Nothing had changed except the name. It was now Zimbabwe Rhodesia.

At Mrs Thatcher's first Commonwealth conference that year she scored a remarkable success by getting all parties to agree to the temporary return of British rule.* In 1979, the former protectorate once more became a British colony and returned to its name of Rhodesia. Lord Soames became governor, managed to oversee free and fair elections, hauled down the Union Jack for the last time and made a dignified exit. In April 1980, the Banana Republic was born. Ian Smith won the twenty guaranteed white seats, Nkomo won the twenty seats in Matabeleland and Mugabe won fifty-seven of the remaining sixty. Canaan Banana became president. Mugabe became prime minister, Rhodesia became Zimbabwe, Books of Zimbabwe Rhodesia became Books of Zimbabwe and it has been downhill since then. Twelve years later, after massive political wranglings, atrocities by all political parties and a fairly successful disarmament of the population, Mugabe was firmly in place as the president and Nkomo was a member of his cabinet. The country, though, has lost its sheen. The government is deeply unpopular but following the merging of ZANU and ZAPU as ZANU PF there is no longer an opposition. The economy was in crisis and Mugabe was up against the ropes.

Zimbabwe retains its regional dominance but with neighbours like Zambia and Mozambique this is not a difficult task. When the Queen visited Bulawayo in 1991 she said that it hadn't changed since her last visit as a princess. The large white population of the town took this as a compliment but in fact it is a horrifying reality. To say that Bulawayo is a sleepy little town maligns it. It is wide awake, but stuck in the 1950s. In Zimbabwe's second city, the shops close on Saturday afternoons and for the remainder of the weekend the streets remain deserted. The streets were built, to Rhodes's specifications, so that a cart with a full span of oxen could do a U-turn. Today, it would not be at all surprising to see an ox cart in Bulawayo and it would be able to perform the required manoeuvre without holding up the traffic.

* This was not a success of her own making although she took the credit. She was forced by Soames and Foreign Minister Carrington to talk to people whom she regarded as terrorists.

Immigration at Victoria Falls had been rather strict with us and insisted that we produce press accreditation within twenty-four hours or leave the country. This was why we had raced on to Bulawayo and our first day was spent in frenzied rushing about, filling in forms and having our passports stamped. The chief immigration officer in Bulawayo had denied there was a Ministry of Information office in the town but we eventually found one where we were ushered into the office of Benjamin Jubane. His office looked like the bedroom of a politically active fourteen-year-old schoolboy. A poster for Azania (South African freedom fighters), a portrait of Comrade Mugabe, an ANC poster, countless magazine spreads of topless girls and bits of paper with slogans written on them, all jostled for wall space. On the door was a neatly written jingle on Ministry of Information writing paper: 'Working here is like mating elephants', it proclaimed. Another said, 'All I want is less to do, more time to do it and more pay for not getting it done.'

We explained our situation and hoped that it would not be too much trouble to arrange.

'I don't have the right forms,' he told us.

'In that case, could you call the immigration officer and ask him if we might be allowed to travel on to Harare and get our papers there?' I asked.

This suggestion was greeted with a very worried look. He didn't want another department to think he was inefficient. He jumped up and walked out of the room, returning a few minutes later with two forms entitled 'Accreditation for local journalists'. He crossed out local, replaced it with foreign and gave them to us to fill in and sign. Having claimed our tribe as European, we were rewarded with two used 1990 presscards from which the original photographs had been removed before our eyes and replaced with our own. The information on them had been Tippexed out and our names had been typed on top. They looked so much like forgeries that we were nervous they would get us into trouble rather than out of it. He was very insulted when I suggested that he write an accompanying letter and was eventually proved to be right. We encountered no problems with them whatsoever. Immigration stamped our passports and we were allowed to stay in Zimbabwe for a month.

Bulawayo is the centre of the railway system which had so impressed us, so we took advantage of this and went to see their PR people. They weren't keen on doing any PR. Grace Lupepe, a forbidding former headmistress who ran the department, had already retired but had not yet been replaced. We had spoken to her from England but were by that time over two months behind schedule. Having told us off, she arranged for us to have all the right passes and indemnity forms in case we got run over by a train, but from that point we were on our own. This was the perfect situation. We were authorized to go anywhere and didn't have to drag a reluctant PR around with us. We arranged to take a steam train the next morning and signed endless forms in order that we might be able to travel on the engine.

We were in the steam sheds at dawn. Fires under the massive black locomotives cast eerie shadows on the steam and smoke which poured from every cranny of the forty-four great engines. The clashing of fire doors, hissing of escaping steam and rhythmic scrape and clank of shovel on coal filled the sheds with noise and atmosphere. This was what it must have sounded like in a dark satanic mill. Drivers were meeting up with their crews; the men who kept the fires burning at night were just coming off shift and heading, owl-eyed and blackened beyond negritude, to their beds. Brian, our driver for the day, strode through the steam to meet us. The oily earth of the shed floor was already making its way up his trouser legs but he was feverishly cleaning his hands with cotton waste before shaking ours. The whole day long he continued to wash himself and the engine at every opportunity. When we boarded the locomotive – six big steps up to every schoolboy's dream – it was filthy. When we handed it over to the next crew there wasn't a damned spot on it.

We were to pull empty wagons down in the direction of

Hwange National Park. Despite being named after a local chief, the town has recently been renamed Hwange in a failed attempt to stop the ribald laughter and Africanize the name. Everyone still refers to it as Hwange. This has been a policy in many African countries and has produced strange results, particularly in Zimbabwe, where the border town of Umtali, which couldn't sound more African if it tried, has been changed to Mutare. Grassroots political pressure to share land more equally and give every family their own plot had been diverted by such Africanization policies. Mugabe, having realized that the country would not survive if all the whites left, has always kept them in the government and not confiscated their land.

As in the west where everyone expects a TV and VCR as their natural right, in Africa everyone demands a plot of land. By 1993, the population was more concerned about having a job, but since jobs were even more difficult to arrange, Mugabe had declared war on the landowners. As we arrived in Zimbabwe, Mugabe was gradually caving into the pressure and making forced purchase orders on white farms (and a very few black ones – for political purposes). The whites had no right of appeal and the resultant despondency among farmers contributed to the effects of the drought. The same Africanization had been happening on the railways, much to the chagrin of both the whites and the blacks working on the system who could see the railway falling apart before their eyes.

We sat down to make tea at the beginning of the journey as we were waiting for the brake pressure to rise, and Brian explained the problems he faced.

'It's almost impossible to get promotion on the railways these days if you're white,' said the blond and bearded Brian. 'There's hardly any whites working in the sheds any more. Most of them have moved back down to South Africa.'

Brian, Mark the fireman and Justin the coal trimmer ran about with their tuck boxes full of provisions for the journey. They had their own teapot which kept warm on a little shelf above the fire doors and their own water since the water in the engine now has chemicals in it and they can no longer drink it. Brian was paid 3000 Zimbabwe dollars a month which usually doubled after overtime but was down to 2800 take-home pay after tax. He and the others were finding it very difficult to maintain their lifestyle. From 1991 to 1992 the value of the Zim dollar fell by 48 per cent. Unemployment rises in line with the population explosion and the SAP-induced liberalization of the economy. Two hundred thousand people enter the job market every year chasing 7,000 jobs. Mark had taken his wife to Mauritius for their honeymoon three years earlier.

'I don't think we'll be able to go there again,' he said. 'We just don't have the money any more.'

While it was indicative of Zimbabwe's success, in comparison with Zambia, that Mark could even consider going to Mauritius, the fact that he couldn't go again was a bad sign for the future. Mugabe entered office as a committed Marxist–Leninist and he is an intelligent and able man who has reacted to the times. At the beginning of his tenure, it was essential both to retain white dominance of the business sector and to improve the lot of Africans. Millions have been spent on primary health care and education but this spending has necessitated cruel cutbacks and a freeing-up of the economy. Harsh monetarist policies, at the urging of the IMF, have been imposed. They in turn have resulted in soaring interest rates, inflation and unemployment, with a vague hope of building a solid base for the future. The foundations of that solid base are, however, being rocked by the politically necessary Africanization process.

'Whites who know their jobs are being replaced by blacks who don't,' one of the last surviving white foremen in the steam sheds had told me that morning. 'People are being promoted before they know what they are doing and then messing up everything and stealing everything when they get there.'

It took about an hour for us to turn around, hitch up the wagons and get on our way down to Hwange. It was a beautiful cool morning as the sun rose over the outskirts of Bulawayo up into the boundless, bright blue African sky. Within a few minutes we were travelling through the bush. Our class-15 engine had entered service as late as 1952, but it was easy to imagine what the railway pioneers must have felt like when they reached Bulawayo in 1897. All the same hazards apply. Elephants on the track are still a problem, as are lions. On the passenger trains the drivers play a joke on the guards. When they pass a pride of lions by the side of the track, they slow down and pull the whistle three times. This is the signal for the guard to come to the front of the train. The guard jumps off and walks to the front and into the pride of lions: laughs all round. Elephants are about the only thing that can derail a big steam engine. One of the African drivers I spoke to on our return told me about driving troops into Mozambique during the war under UDI.

'We were very lucky,' he said. 'One crew was blown up twice on one trip. They tried to derail us three times in seven years but those big engines used to just keep going. I was a fireman then, so we were pretty safe in the front because of all the metal but they used to strafe the carriages at ambushes all the time. It was horrible and I felt like a traitor.'

Brian lovingly cleaned the cab as we steamed on towards Hwange. 'In the old days everyone used to have their own engine and kept them clean themselves. We would turn up an hour early for work and go over them with Brasso. Now there is no discipline. We used to have to explain if our train was late. I haven't been on time for years,' he said. 'Fitters used to be fired for using a hammer instead of a spanner. All the spanners have been stolen now. I have to bring my own tools to work.'

So dirty was the interior of the cab that it was difficult to see that it was indeed made of brass. Small wheels on stalks, all of which needed constant minute adjustments, encircled the top of the boiler. The main brake lever had a bakelite handle which had worn away under thousands of calloused hands. The drivers speak of and to their engines in loving tones and the engines talk back.

'Listen to her,' said Brian as we ground our way up a hill. 'They groan when they're working hard.' I listened. 'I'm getting tired, I'm getting tired,' translated Brian. And when we were going downhill, 'Let me go. Let me go.'

'Sitting on a steam locomotive is like part of your body,' explained a grizzled old driver who had been a fireman for years before the beneficial effects of Africanization had allowed him to become an excellent driver of the old school. 'You can feel it right through you. It's something with life in it. These new boys don't know what they're doing. They all want diesel. Diesels are just like a moving box.'

As in Zambia, the desperate struggle to buy new and shiny but unnecessary engines is going to lead to Zimbabwe's downfall.

'Why do they want to phase out these trains when we can mend and maintain them ourselves?' pleaded the old hand. 'We have an abundance of coal which no one else wants. With diesel we have to spend forex for trains and fuel and they break after ten years.'

The only people making big money out of the railways are a private company that puts on steam safaris for tour groups. National Railways of Zimbabwe has cleaned up and painted an old engine and some carriages which they lease to the tour company concerned. In between tours it stands idle in the all but deserted railway museum. It does not seem to have occurred to anyone at NRZ that they could cut out the middle man and make all this forex for themselves.

The scrapping of the old steam engines was not the only problem facing the railway. Our progress to Hwange was interrupted every ten minutes or so by the necessity to get out of the engine at a red light and call for a paper order. The lights go to red automatically when they don't know whether it is safe to continue. Brian would stop the engine and walk to the nearest white box containing a telephone. Many of them were broken, so often he would have to walk another mile to the next box for permission to proceed. A steam locomotive is reasonably comfortable when it is moving along, but the moment it stops, the cab fills up with steam like an out-of-control sauna. Justin the coal trimmer, whose job involved jumping around on the coal making sure it flowed down smoothly to Mark's shovel, would immediately pounce from the cab and roll a joint. It's illegal for whites, legal for blacks. Mark would have to stay in the cab, adjusting the valves to keep the engine ticking over nicely. Once Brian had permission to proceed he slapped his left fist with his right hand – the signal to put in more coal – and walked back to the locomotive.

To watch Mark work was curiously hypnotic. Where the fireman put his left foot, there was a hole worn in the teak floor of the cab. In one fluid motion, he dug his shovel into the coal on the tender, pivoted on his left foot, stamped on the foot pedal for the steam doors which open to the roaring furnace, chucked in the coal as the doors opened and started the process again as the doors closed. The 'scrape, whoosh, crash, scrape, whoosh, crash' would continue as the engine, under Brian's careful ministrations, started its own rhythmic progress.

'Gyms are very expensive,' said Mark. 'This way I get paid for exercising.'

Tooting the whistle is fun and frightens animals from the tracks but the rest of driving a steam engine is hard work. The mixture of water and fire which produces the correct amount of steam is difficult to attain and control. That which is done automatically in the internal combustion engine has to be done individually on a steam locomotive. More air has to be let into the furnace, but not too much. Coal has to be added but not too often. Brian made it seem easy as he slammed the control levers up and down and then fine-tuned them by playful slaps of his enormous hands. This was all done with his head hanging out of the window in classic style. All he needed was an Osh Kosh cap. Whenever there was a spare moment, out came the steam hose to wash away the coal dust and the feverish polishing would continue. All this from a man who with his huge beer belly, lank blond hair, beard and boots resembled nothing more than a Hell's Angel temporarily separated from his Hog.

He kept us entertained between stops with stories of haunted trains. Engine 414 used to have horrendous accidents every time it left the sheds until, after numerous rebuilds, they changed its number and it hasn't had a crash since. Brian himself had only ever had two accidents. Once he crashed into an articulated lorry which had stalled on the tracks and another time he ran over a couple who were making love under some wagons which he had attached to his engine. The lines are in better condition than those in Zambia, so the safety record of Zimbabwe is more impressive, but everyone on the railways acknowledge that this is not going to last for long. The tracks are being neglected. Regardless of the condition of the track, it can still take five kilometres to stop a fully laden freight train and people and animals continue to wander aimlessly in front of them.

We changed trains at Saw Mills, halfway to Hwange, and brought a consignment of coal back to Bulawayo in a diesel. The next few days were spent in different parts of the railway. It is a hotbed of political and corporate dissent. Boilermakers, foremen, electricians and drivers were all depressed by the way the railways were deteriorating and blamed it immediately on management and eventually on the government.

'Why are they getting the Canadians to come here?' asked one man. 'We all know how the railway should work. It is just senior management who are causing the problems. There's plenty of money. It's just misused.'

I had seen what the Canadians had done to Zambia Railways and found it difficult to disagree. None of the whites can get promotion, because all the important jobs are political appointments.

'Under UDI we didn't have any of these problems. We had no aid and the railways worked like clockwork. Now it just gets worse every day,' said one black manual labourer.

Somewhat disarmed, I replied, 'Surely UDI had other problems. At least now you have the vote.'

He laughed at my innocence. 'Yes. But what's the point? There's only one party. Here in Africa once they get sat on that chair, they tie themselves to it.'

This honesty was doing no good for my already strained liberal views. It seemed that the closer we got to South Africa, the more Africans acknowledged that whites had their uses. The previous day a very old man who was, I suspect, slightly mad, had thrown himself to his knees and clutched mine.

'You have to come back. Look what has happened to our country since you left,' he pleaded with me.

Not willing to act as an emissary for my race, I extricated my legs and ignored him. But here were more lucid people agreeing with him and providing relentless proof.

'Mugabe is a corrupt bugger,' continued the boilermaker, 'but no one can prove it. Why is it that all African leaders are corrupt?'

This conversation was getting nowhere. I wasn't going to defend his president to him. It is part of the Mugabe myth that he is not corrupt. He merely surrounds himself with corrupt people who drag him down, claim the apologists. The same excuse was used for Hitler in the 1930s.

While we had been staying in Bulawayo, there had been strict water rationing because of the drought. Now that the rains had come, cholera was rife and the genteel residents of Bulawayo were using this as an excuse to get rid of the fly-pitchers who sold vegetables around the town. There is no official market there, so there was nowhere else for them to go. They were being blamed for the spread of cholera because they were selling unwashed tomatoes. The hawkers were intelligent enough to realize that cholera has absolutely nothing to do with tomatoes and were protesting vociferously. Two thousand five hundred cases of the disease had already been reported and it was getting worse. Hit-squads of colonial-style policemen in brogues, long socks and khaki shorts raced around town moving on the fly-pitchers while the white ladies of the town (all of whom seemed to be in advanced middle age) took tea in our hotel.

'It never used to be like this,' said the women. 'They always sold their food in their locations.'* Independence seemed to have passed most of the women by. They walked round town, massive arms unable to lie straight down by their sides, like fat children playing aeroplanes. Their polyester A-line dresses in floral prints stopped abruptly at the knee but stood out to each side like the bases of triangles that never reached an apex. Horn-rimmed 1950s glasses sat atop spiteful mouths that spoke incessantly of the good old days of UDI. They made me wonder if Mary Whitehouse (the vociferous and sometimes despised guardian of British morals) had roots in Bulawayo. The older men, who spent more time in contact with blacks, were less short-sighted but reached the same conclusions. 'UDI was like an IUD. One keeps sperm out. The other kept the blacks out.'

Contraception was high on the political agenda. Joshua Nkomo had just made a speech fighting against sex education and condom advertisements because they were destroying traditional values. Nkomo was acting president while Mugabe (a man accused of enough human rights violations to fill a book) received the Holy Cross of Peace from the Pope in Rome for his contributions to world peace. Nkomo's novel way of defusing the population bomb and controlling AIDS was causing outrage among the aid community which was already hard pressed by the government's insistence on making people pay for condoms. There were already 14,000 *registered* AIDS sufferers in the country yet the Zimbabwe National Family Planning Council had recently started charging ten cents for a condom. In Hwange only three had been sold in a month. In Bulawayo itself the demand had gone down from 67,700 in January 1991 when they were free, to 983 in December 1992. Prompted by the Zimbabwean SAP, which insists that even the most basic health care is paid for, this policy is causing

* Location is a white South African term for a township.

incalcuable harm. It is also rather unfair on Mugabe who had spent so long trying to provide a few basics for his people. It had been one of his few successes.

Zimbabwe's natural problems did not stop with drought, AIDS and cholera. The new threat was army worm – the same kind of pest that had been such a problem for the Millers. Thousands of acres were being lost to the voracious little beasties and once more Zimbabwe was going to need millions of tons of donor maize to feed its population. As we set off for Harare, we were beginning to worry about the rest of the world from which we had been parted for so long. Britain doesn't make the news on the World Service unless something really spectacular is going wrong. We had heard about the miners' strike and the conflagration of Windsor. Now it seemed that the royal family were about to be retired. Chuck and Di had caved in and separated. More bombs were being dropped on Iraq, Clinton was being inaugurated and we were missing out on all the fun. Harare, which is only marginally more sophisticated than Bulawayo, at least provided a blast of TV news, although the joy does not last for long when CNN is the only news channel.

I had been to another deserted railway museum in Bulawayo and had been fascinated to find a mission coach. I set myself the task of finding out whether the railway mission still existed or if it had become a heli-mission like the strange outfit that works out of Wilson airport in Nairobi. I had missed it by ten years, but while looking for it had come across another story in which I had been interested – white refugees. I had picked up rumours in England that whites had been forced to move out of their homes, having lost their jobs, and to scrape by were renting their houses to aid workers while living in camping sites. Having done the rounds of the camp sites in Bulawayo and discovered no one, I was amazed to find plenty of white homelessness in Harare. An aggressive thirty-year-old hippy was lying on the floor outside the WFP office complaining that they were willing to feed everyone except him. He claimed to be the son of a farmer from up country who could find no work in Harare. He had been living on the streets for over a year and got by on odd jobs and begging.

'I can't get anything from the state. They say I should go home,' he told me.

'They might have a point. Can't you work on your father's farm?'

'Look at me, man. Do I look like a farmer?'

No other whites I found had reasonable excuses for their situations either. They were just bums who didn't want to demean themselves. There is chronic unemployment among under-educated blacks in Zimbabwe but no white need be without a job. They may not have the job they want but their problem is that there are certain jobs which whites will not do. These are filled by educated blacks who are desperate for the work and by Asians. An Asian shopkeeper explained to me that all his sons had work which whites wouldn't do and many blacks couldn't do. 'I have three sons who are making money now and will have their own businesses when they have saved enough,' he told me.

African countries seem to act as magnets to the most impressive whites – like Rhodes and Pauling – but also to the most mediocre ones who can get better jobs in Africa than they would in their home countries. The British bank teller becomes a Zambian bank manager. The Portuguese minor civil servant became an Angolan district governor and the freelance feature writer can still become a press agency bureau chief. The occasional homeless whites that I found on the street of Harare were there of their own volition which rather took the meat out of the story. A starving refugee of whatever colour is not of much use if you discover he's trying to lose weight.

Beyond the station, there is not much railway activity in Harare. We had to spend some time there, however, to organize the next part of our journey. We wanted to travel on a freight train down the Beira corridor and in order to do that needed permission from a wide variety of companies and armies. We spent our evenings watching a succession of inexorably bad movies. Extreme violence is the main preoccupation of the African film-watching public. Martial arts, Arnold Schwarzenegger and Jean Claude van Damme are all big in Africa. As their stardom wanes in the west they become ever more popular there. If James Cameron (the director of *Terminator*) could find a black man with no brain, deformed muscles and a strange accent he could make another fortune.

After a few days we boarded our last wooden carriage and made our way to Mutare, a town which before it suffered the indignity of having its name changed from Umtali was uprooted and moved seven miles to be in the right place for Pauling's trains. It is set in stunning countryside, surrounded on all four sides by the button back-sofa fells you find in the British lake district. There are more trees and less scree but the similarity is nevertheless striking. Its other claim to fame is that it is close to the Eagle School, site of a famous massacre and now a rather sinisterly named Youth Training Centre. We were there because it is on the border of Mozambique and only 284 kilometres from our ultimate goal. Our next train journey would take us to the Indian Ocean coast of Mozambique and the terminus of the railway – Beira.

The customs house and the police station are the only buildings of any interest in the town and both owe more to a Portuguese influence than a British one. Pauling had a house there which was made into the railway recreation club in the 1940s but it had been knocked down two years before we arrived. As a desperate measure – we had to spend a while in Mutare – we went to the tourist office on the main square. We asked the sulky-looking white woman whose reading we had interrupted if there was anything we should look at in the town.

'No,' she replied. 'People just come here as a stop off or jump off. It's a passing through kind of place.'

She was paid by the government to provide this invaluable service so I felt free to press her a little. She would not be moved.

'There is nothing to look at in Mutare. I've lived here all my life,' she insisted.

Our hotel had a George Pauling bar with lots of memorabilia, but none of the staff knew anything about him. Head office had sent down all the bits and pieces and they had stuck them on the wall. Sandra Ellis met us there for a drink. She was the local representative of Manica, the freight company we had been using to ship film. Manica are based in Beira and handle most of the shipping through the port. Set up a hundred years ago, they had been feeding most of southern Africa for the past couple of years and to see the inside of Beira port we were going to need their help. She was very depressed.

'I was born here and thought I had got away,' she told us. 'Nothing happens here. There is no social life.' The best entertainment she could suggest for us was lunch at the Dairy Bar on the High Street. 'It's quite good but not up to the standard of Wimpy,'* she told us.

Sandra arranged for us to be met in Beira by one of Manica's local representatives who would get passes for us to photograph in the port. This settled we went down to the station to find out if we could take a train across the border. As on the Zambia border, there is a lot of unnecessary toing and froing as trains cross the border, have duty added then duty exempted, then swap engines and carry on. The station master was extremely helpful but he could not allow us to take a train to Mozambique. We would have to take a taxi to the border and then another to the station at Machipando. The good news was that we were expected. I had seen a director of Mozambique Railways (CFM) in Harare and she had done all that she had promised to do. We would be taking the dawn train in two days' time. He gave us the free run of the station, which like so much else in Zimbabwe was stuck in a time warp.

We found an old signpost for the Beira train in a cupboard and on the platform wall was a noticeboard saying: 'Reservations

---

* A British hamburger chain which makes McDonald's look like Maxim's.

Mutare–Beira'. None of this equipment had been used in any of the station staffs' memories. Solomon Moyo, the fifty-four-year-old railway police inspector who was in charge of station security, gave us tea and told us about his life. A tall elegant man with a military bearing and moustache, he sat at his desk under a portrait of Comrade Mugabe.

'I think the president is a good man,' he said. 'When independence came he managed not to frighten the whites away. Everyone in Zimbabwe is treated equally. Under Smith, I would never have been made more than sergeant.'

'Why do you want the whites?' I asked.

'Whites are good at organizing and discipline,' he said. 'We have a problem disciplining our subordinates because of tribalism and witchcraft. White men know nothing of these things so it doesn't bother them. I don't want to be powerful. When you have power you have no freedom. I don't need guards to walk home like the president. I just want to be free like a Hell's Angel.'

Inspector Moyo had the look of iron discipline about him. Imagining him unshaved on a motorbike with more than a quarter of an inch of hair was quite impossible. He had, however, found the Lord and wasn't going to let anything get him down. He continued to spill out his idiosyncratic view of life.

'All these scientists tried to stop the drought but all it needed was Jehova. As soon as he thought the drought should stop, it poured. I have learnt my lesson though. This year I sold all my maize and now I can't afford to buy any. Next year I will keep my crop and not send it to the state mill. Then I will be able to feed my family.'

As in many African countries, people were being forced to withdraw from the real economy because of government mismanagement. Manica employees had been receiving an extra 50 Zimbabwe dollars a month in drought relief but no such thing had happened on the railways. Inspector Moyo, despite being a responsible and relatively well-paid man, was having difficulty making ends meet. He felt most sorry for the young.

'They have nothing. There aren't enough jobs to go round and every year it gets worse. Even people on good salaries like me are having problems feeding their families.'

Back at the Manica Hotel, where we were staying, we didn't have such problems. People complain about inflation in the west, but the dollar is still a stable currency. The longer the journey continued, the more valuable our dollars became. We didn't have to eat mealie meal in all our travels and food was always cheap for us. In the restaurant that evening as we complained to each other about having to eat yet more steak and chips, we met a very disillusioned auditor. An American accountant doing an audit for Lonrho, he was eating alone in the restaurant. Despite knowing exactly who we were, he was extraordinarily indiscreet.

'I just wish they would get some new auditors,' he told us. 'They're the most cheapskate company I've ever worked for. They tried to send me down here by bus and now I'm having to stay in the house of the man I'm auditing. It's ridiculous. I had to do the same thing in Kenya and discovered that my host had stolen £2.9 million from the company. The difficult thing is trying to work out what is a legitimate bribe and what is management corruption.'

The part of Lonrho he was auditing at that point was missing £400,000. He was pretty sure that it was bad accounting rather than corruption, but none the less was refusing to put in his report until he had left the country. Zimbabwe is the birthplace of Lonrho, but its influence spreads right across the continent. It owns farms and hotels in Mozambique, newspapers in Kenya, mines in Zambia and, allegedly, politicians all over. Tiny Rowlands claimed credit for ending the war in Mozambique – few others concur but his influence is undoubted. Our friend the auditor was astonished and interested by the things he was uncovering but the political games were getting him down.

'I just want to get back home where a payment is either legitimate or not and there is no such thing as a legitimate bribe.'

We, too, wanted to get home but we were insistent on doing

the last bit of the journey properly. We had been disappointed by how little of the railway we had been able to see in Angola. Zaïre hadn't been much better. We were going to take a train down the Beira corridor if it killed us. The next morning we discovered there had been a train crash during the night – one killed, two in a critical condition – so we weren't far off the mark. We packed up our cases and got a lift over the border with an NRZ repair crew. There was a perfect road until the border and then hopeless rutted tracks as soon as we arrived in Mozambique.

'It's a cruel thing a border,' said our driver.

The people along both sides of the border speak Shona together and most have relations in both countries. In Zimbabwe there is genuine hardship but the gulf in conditions between the two countries is enormous. Mozambique is twice as beautiful due to the lack of development but people there have no money at all. Broken-down houses line the road and naked children run around in the sun while their parents try to grow crops on tiny scraps of rocky land. We headed straight for the station where we were expected. Signors Nicolau and Franco were both mestizos but there all similarities stopped. Nicolau was tall, fat and friendly but spoke no English. Franco was short, religious and wracked by malaria. He spoke good English, however, and welcomed us on behalf of CFM. They both wore smart new uniforms with scrambled eggs on caps that had a small badge of a steam engine where the regimental colours would be on a soldier's. They walked us up from the station to where the accident had happened.

On a sharp corner in the no-man's land between the two countries, three locomotives had plummeted down the side of a steep embankment into a ravine. The repair team suspected that the brakes on one of them had failed and pushed the other two over the side but was unable to confirm this. Great gouges had been scored into the wooden sleepers where the 130-ton locomotives had plummeted over the side. Rails, sleepers and ballast ripped from the track by the force of the accident mingled with the wreckage below. One of the trains had been pulling wagons filled with granite and wood so there was a rich, loamy smell of freshly dug earth and cut wood. About thirty workers were feverishly re-laying the tracks while the accident investigators from Harare tried to work out what had happened. This single-gauge line is Zimbabwe's main link with the sea and it was essential to get it working again immediately. The station master from Mutare was there, looking angry and worried.

'Come,' he said, 'you must see how we waste your aid money.'

The trains at the bottom of the embankment were from South Africa (rented), Zimbabwe and Mozambique – all of them new. The accident investigators were trying to devise a method to get them out of the ravine into which they had fallen. There was a train-mounted crane on its way from Harare, but due to the severity of the corner, they doubted whether it would be able to drag them out without toppling over itself. The most important thing to do in the meantime was to get the track open again, and to that end, the Mozambican track workers were doing a great job. By seven o'clock that evening, the arterial route was once more open to traffic.

We had to spend the night in Mozambique as the border would not open in time for us to cross it and catch the train in the morning. There was nowhere to stay near the station in Machipanda so Signor Franco took us to Manica, the nearest town with rooms to rent. The area looks very like Mexico. There are almost more churches than houses dotted around the countryside. It is easy to imagine small boys in sombreros running up the bell towers of the run-down and whitewash-flaked churches, sounding warnings to the populace below. Manica is crowned by a church whose steps crumble down into the town. Vaguely modern but neglected buildings alternated with mud huts and lean-tos on the main street where we stayed. Signor Franco had fixed us up with a room at a restaurant which didn't have any food but it did have a bed and beer.

By the time we arrived in Manica, Signor Franco looked as though he might die on us. He had gone a sickly shade of grey

and was sweating profusely. Still, he wouldn't give up his responsibilities as our host. After one drink we managed to persuade
him to go home and get some rest. We were the subject of quite
some curiosity. There hadn't been many tourists in Manica for a
while. We discovered that we were in the Saint Christopher's bar
but didn't have the heart to tell them that Saint Christopher had
been discredited some time in the middle of their war.* On the
wall was a mosaic showing the itinerant saint feeding children in
a Mozambican landscape.

Inspector Moyo from Mutare would have liked it because
Christopher used to be the patron saint of bikers. There were no
bikers in Manica. With the departure of Signor Franco, a hush fell
over the town. He had taken the only vehicle. Children played in
the ravaged street outside and stared through the window at the
new arrivals. Old men nursing local beers at the bar seemed to
feign a lack of interest and, our advances rebuffed, we soon went
to bed. Our imported beers had cost seventy-five cents each. The
room cost only fifty-two. We had changed money at the border
and were able to pay in meticais although it was sad to part with
such interesting bank notes. It is real communist money with
plenty of noble-looking workers labouring in the fields, heroic,
white-coated scientists and teachers depicted upon it. In the centre
of every note is the symbol of the country which has been so
ravaged by war that money is not used by two-thirds of the
population – an open book crossed by a hoe and an AK47.

Just as we were preparing for sleep, the disco started up next
door. There we were, thinking we were somewhere really cut off
from the world – interesting and unspoilt – when Elton John
started booming through the floorboards. They were still dancing
when we left at 5.30 the next morning. Signor Franco was looking
much more healthy when he came to pick us up. Since there are

---

* The Catholic Church has officially admitted that Saint Christopher
never existed. However, in a handy get-out clause, it is still OK to pray
to him as all his calls are automatically diverted to God.

no vehicles in the area, he gives lifts to everyone. There were about twenty people in the Toyota by the time we arrived at Machipanda. I had been on the back of the pick-up truck and was given a pointed guide to the ravages of the war. My fellow passengers pointed at wrecked buildings and gateways, said 'Boom' and laughed. I don't speak Shona and they didn't speak Portuguese so that was as far as our conversation could go. Harriet, meanwhile, had been fighting off attempts at conversion by Signor Franco.

The train was leaving behind schedule so we had breakfast with the two station masters before we left. We still couldn't believe that everything was going so smoothly. It wasn't in keeping with the rest of the journey and it should have been the most difficult part. There were three armies working round this corridor. Countless different authorites and mercenary groups also had varying degrees of influence.

The train was taking empty wagons and a broken-down engine to Beira which meant we could sit in our own locomotive. There was a traffic jam of donor grain in the station because of the derailment and the station master from Mutare had come back to try to sort out the mess. He took us to one side and whispered: 'Don't get sick in Mozambique.'

The whistle on the lead locomotive blew and we jumped on to the footplate of ours. A Zimbabwean army guard threw his gun up into the final wagon and jumped up after it. We had already stowed our luggage and we stood on the footplate to wave goodbye to all the station masters. As we started to move, Signor Franco shouted out, 'You are the first passengers on this line since 1965.'

We smiled and felt rather pleased with ourselves. This unlikely fact was too good to check – 1975 maybe, but 1965? We left it at that.

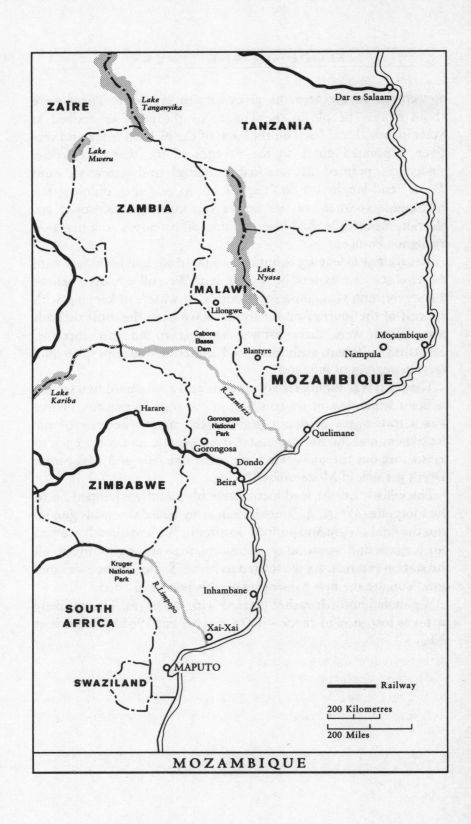

MOZAMBIQUE

Mozambique jostles with places like Cambodia, Angola and Somalia for the title of the world's most unfortunate country. Centuries of Portuguese rule have been followed by a horrendous civil war, richly spiced with drought, famine and ceaseless outside interference. Its luck has to change some time but it certainly hasn't yet. The calmest places are the corridors from neighbouring countries to the coast which are fiercely guarded by parties interested in their own future rather than Mozambique's. The Maputo corridor is patrolled by the Zimbabwean army and leads directly to Zimbabwe. The Nakala goes to Malawi and is guarded mainly by DSL, the private security firm that we had come across in Angola. We were on the Beira corridor which is protected by Zimbabwe and is their most essential link with the coast.

Our train had a tired guard riding shotgun at the front and a rather more alert one riding AK at the back – this for a train which carried nothing of value. Large shipments of aid are protected by whole patrols on board but the main work is done on the ground. Zimbabwe's troops don't let anyone near the tracks. As we travelled down to Beira, Zimbabwe claimed to have three thousand troops operating in the area. At every station we passed, tents had been erected across decommissioned tracks, camps in the empty car parks, and temporary radio towers alongside the defunct communications equipment of CFM. Beira is an essential port for central southern Africa and Zimbabwe takes no chances with it. Its troops are there to make sure that the artery remains unclogged and unsevered.

That anyone ever built a railway along this route is testament to the fact that it is essential to the interior. Just outside Mutare in Manicaland, the railway reaches 2,400 metres above sea level.

Before it reaches the sea, only two hundred miles distant, it has to cross more mountain ranges and then plummet to the coastal plain where swamps and floods are the problem. Started in 1892, as a narrow-gauge railway, it wasn't finished until 1903. On certain parts of the line it was estimated that one man died for every sleeper laid. Lions, mosquitoes, floods and dysentery all conspired to kill the workers. The death rate among the gangers and engineers on the route from Zimbawe to Mozambique is claimed to have been as high as 75 per cent. A mournful little poem called 'A Ballad of the BMR' remembers the workers who gave their lives to build it. It starts:

> Down in the land where heathens are,
> Down in the swamps where white men stew.

It was written in the days before malaria was discovered to be carried by mosquitoes. Varian, who was in charge of rebuilding the bridges when the track was widened, believed that he survived only because of his hatred of buzzing flies. Years before the connection between malaria and mosquitoes was made by Ross and Manson, he always slept with a net. While all around him died like and by flies, he continued to work on. The bridge that crosses the Pungwe river, thirty miles outside Beira, was his first big break. When the engineer originally contracted to do the job arrived from England, he took one look and boarded the next boat back to England. Varian had to fill his shoes through necessity, triumphed, and began his career of building pioneer railways.

The first part of the journey down to Beira follows passes through the mountains. At times, the combination of violent curves — to avoid hills — and steep slopes when the hills are too big to avoid causes the train to slow to walking pace. It was at these points that the most terrorist attacks on the railway were made. Bits of wreckage lined the tracks as a reminder.

The struggle for independence in Mozambique started in 1964, three years later than in similar Angola. There had been Portuguese settlements in the country since 1524 but it had been heavily exploited only since the end of the Second World War. Portuguese peasants emigrated to their colony and started farming. They enjoyed great success with the fertile and beautiful land – something which is difficult to believe now that the country is famed for famine and starvation. Elder, our landlord in Angola, had owned a duck farm near Beira until 1975 and had considered himself a Mozambican. From 1964 to 1973 Frelimo (Mozambique Liberation Front) fought a continuous guerilla war against the Portuguese authorities. They met with marked success in the north of the country which was less colonized than the south. Following the assassination of Eduardo Mondlane, Frelimo's founder, in 1969 they received even more support. The Soviet Union, China and Czechoslovakia provided them with arms. Sweden and other liberal western countries became interested in their struggle. Their great success, however, was in winning the hearts and minds of the people.

The early beneficial stages of communism proved a great hit with the *povo*. Frelimo concentrated its early attacks on the northern provinces, away from the Portuguese-dominated areas on the coast and in the south. Where they managed to oust the local administration, they set up liberated zones with their own political committees which reported up to the party leadership. Foreign aid was used to build schools, provide water pumps and dig bore holes. All Frelimo had to do after they had taken over an area was offer to provide a better life. Since the Portuguese had never provided anything and had given the local populations no say in how they lived, Frelimo was able to generate enormous goodwill by doing very little. Anything was better than nothing.

Portugal, meanwhile, was suffering badly. Internally, its political system was falling apart. A large percentage of the male population was conscripted into armies fighting wars in far-flung lands. All Portugal's mainland Africa possessions – Guinea Bissau, Angola and Mozambique – were fighting wars of independence.

Following the 1974 Portuguese coup, General Francisco da Costa Gomes said, 'The armed forces have reached the limits of neurophysiological exhaustion.'

It was the end of their colonial history. The home-based Portuguese people had given up. In Mozambique, though, they hadn't yet. The local Portuguese population tried to stage a coup themselves. They failed, and by the time independence was handed over to Mozambique in 1975, almost 200,000 of 240,000 resentful Portuguese settlers had fled the country. Before they left, many of them destroyed their own property. Cement was poured into the engines of tractors, buildings were burnt down, cars driven into the sea. Bitter and furious at their mother country's betrayal, they became a wandering tribe. Some went to South Africa, others to Brazil. Very few returned to Portugal.

Beira today is full of half-finished 1970s buildings that twenty years after they were started are no longer worth completing. All the old merchants' houses along the filled-in river have been taken over by impoverished and displaced Mozambicans. Families live in single rooms and have boarded off the verandahs to provide more living space for others. These are the fortunate. In 1991, it was estimated that 1.9 million Mozambicans were living in neighbouring countries as refugees and 1.2 million were displaced within their own country. The country has had a truly dreadful time since it gained independence.

Frelimo was the only effective opposition group when independence was offered and it quickly assumed power. Samaro Machel became the new president and set up Frelimo as the ruling party. Mozambique became a freewheeling, idealistic kind of communist state. Bob Dylan even wrote a song about it. The party had evolved throughout the 1960s from a mish-mash of people who wanted independence. Guerilla fighters and budding politicians united against their common enemy. Frelimo's power base stemmed from a northern tribe – the Makonde – but they had to assume power in Maputo, far away on the South African border. There, the population was more sophisticated and had more contact with the outside world. The Mozambique coast is incredibly beautiful and had been a popular holiday destination for tourists from Rhodesia and South Africa. In 1972, 91,000 tourists were visiting Mozambique yearly. By 1981 the figure was down to a thousand – many of whom were probably journalists and spies lying on their immigration forms.

Maputo's local tribes made good money labouring in the gold mines of South Africa. Although the trainloads of Mozambicans who worked the mines have been held up as one of the more disgusting facets of apartheid, this was a trade that Frelimo has always encouraged. Mozambique has had so many problems that it needed the money, whatever indignities had to be suffered to get it.

In the 1970s, it seemed as though everything was conspiring against the quixotic fledgling government. The departure of all the Portuguese was a crippling blow. No one in the country had ever been taught how to use any of the equipment which survived and only a very few had been educated. 1976 saw a terrible drought, followed by a year of floods. In order to combat UDI in Rhodesia, out of principle, the border had to be closed. This meant the loss of earnings on transit exports and imports through Beira and Maputo. Retaliatory raids by Rhodesia on Mugabe's ZANU camps in Mozambique led to further destabilization. The final blow was the emergence of Renamo (Mozambique National Resistance Organization). Smith's Rhodesian secret service, in collusion with Boss (now the NIS), South Africa's infamous intelligence service (with a bit of help from the Portuguese), were responsible for the creation and supply of Renamo.

To this day, Renamo has no real reason for existence – no political platform and no ideals, save the pursuit of power. When Frelimo retrenched in 1977 – the grooviness ousted by reality – it purged the party and the army. At its 1977 conference Frelimo set itself up as a harsh communist state. Re-education camps were opened and the idealistic early days were destroyed by the mountainous bureaucracy and inefficiencies that one normally associates with communism. Land was nationalized and state farms set up on the Soviet model. As one would expect, everything stopped working. The informal agricultural sector refused to give up its food because they knew they wouldn't be getting any from the state sector. The early Renamo groups, which were principally a cover for Rhodesia-backed attacks on ZANU camps within Mozembique, were reinforced by disaffected Frelimo members who had been purged from the party or escaped the re-education camps. Both Alfonso Dhlakama and the late André Matzangaissa – the head and former deputy of Renamo – were refugees of the Frelimo high command. Renamo was soon a force to be reckoned with.

Throughout the late 1970s and the 1980s, Mozambique was a battlefield. Two guerilla armies fought each other in the bush. Frelimo, with all the responsibilities of being the government, fared badly. Frelimo was supplied with Soviet weapons, but only those needed to fight a conventional war against South Africa, and nowhere near as many as Angola and Ethiopia who got first bite of the roubles. Machel supported the imprisoned Mugabe's ZANU guerillas by allowing them to have camps in Mozambique. Smith reacted by sending Rhodesian troops in after them. Renamo groups moved around the country (often in South African army transport), targeting convoys and then disappearing into the bush. Jet fighters and tanks were no use against such tactics. Like UNITA in Angola, Renamo succeeded because it had no land of its own for Frelimo to target. Renamo were financed by Rhodesia, South Africa and later Kenya and were encouraged to behave as badly as possible. Appalling atrocities were the result. Civilian women had their breasts cut off, men were emasculated and dismembered. Frelimo, in retaliation, didn't behave too well either. Tens of thousands died and the country, under the auspices of war and communism, rapidly disintegrated.

Renamo followed a scorched-earth policy. Ostensibly Frelimo towns were destroyed, their inhabitants massacred and their children conscripted and trained as fighters. Frelimo reacted by doing the same to Renamo areas but caused greater resentment because Renamo, who neither had nor valued the hearts and minds of the people, just moved area when under threat. After Zimbabwe's independence in 1980, South Africa continued to finance the war in return for tons of ivory which ironically were smuggled into South Africa through herds of protected elephants in Kruger National Park. The elephants in Kruger have to be regularly culled to keep their numbers down. Mozambique used to have endless forests and some of the densest populations of game in the world. Two hundred and forty thousand square kilometres of forest, an area the size of Belgium, have been destroyed since the railway was built. We saw no game in the time we were there. There is none left.

Frelimo reacted to the threat within its borders by becoming more authoritarian. Lunatic laws resulted: the semi-nomadic people were not allowed to move around the country because they had to man the state farms; all children had to exercise at 5 a.m. and many were conscripted into both armies; it was made illegal to put your underpants on the washing line; black vehicles were only allowed to be driven by government personnel. The war continued.

The Beira railway was one of the main targets. To travel along it was like seeing a history of the war. Every station was riddled with bullet holes. Wherever there was a siding, scarred carriages and twisted wagons attested to recent violent activity. Since the Zimbabwean army arrived the Beira corridor has been well protected and hundreds of thousands of people, displaced by the war, have flocked to the narrow strip of land which is the corridor. All along the line, humble shacks surrounded by small patches of maize have sprung up. More people live on the corridors than in any other part of the country.

Thousands of displaced people also live in the cities. In Beira, at the Grand Hotel, we discovered an entire community from around the country who had moved into its four hundred and one rooms. One family would occupy a room, another the balcony and another the bathroom. We entered through the main doors where a grand double-sided staircase swooped down to the enormous lobby. Billiard tables lay under inches of dust as hundreds of children raced around playing games. Soon after independence, the hotel was taken over by Frelimo. The great wrought-iron gates which led to the tea rooms and the billiard tables are padlocked shut and have the crossed AK47 party symbol welded on to them. Since then is has been an army barracks and a police barracks. It is now overflowing with refugees from the provinces. Everyone we spoke to came from a different area.

Dardino and Camilla were the leaders of the gang of breakdancing children who followed us around. They had come from Zambezia province when their father was killed by a Renamo group that then overran the area. Others were orphans or had just lost their parents. This was not through lack of care – even Lady Bracknell would have sympathized. When your village becomes the focus of a battle you just run for your life and hope to meet up with your friends later. They spent their days breakdancing to traditional tribal songs, which, in the absence of tape recorders and radios, they sang themselves. Michael Jackson (who would have liked them), however, was their hero, although they seldom heard his music. The other entertainments were hide and seek, which in a four-hundred-room hotel is good fun, as is sliding down six floors' worth of banisters. The older children dragged their younger siblings around with them, while their parents were out trying to find work. By day the hotel is like *Lord of the Flies* – the children rule. By night the prostitutes, beggars and scroungers who are their parents return and normal family life resumes.

The families group together every evening. The cooking pots come out and whatever they have found that day gets eaten. There has been no running water for years, so they have to walk to the nearest pump and then carry pails back past the slime-filled olympic-sized swimming pool and up to their fourth-floor balconies. The night after we had discovered the hotel we had dinner with a Zimbabwean aid worker whose parents had taken him there as a child.

'I still remember that swimming pool. It was the best I'd ever seen.'

He also remembered Signor Britto who had built the hotel in 1955 – a friend of his parents. He could not bear what had happened to Beira and blamed it on Frelimo.

'This used to be such a beautiful, cosmopolitan city. There were restaurants all along the beach, hundreds of hotels, nightclubs and bars. Now look at it.'

He was right. Beira was in a terrible state. Our hotel, the Ambassador, was the only one in town and it wasn't nice. The owners claimed to have recently renovated it, yet it did not give that impression. Entire floors were out of bounds: due to renovation, claimed the manager, or imminent collapse as the more candid staff explained. Cockroaches were the least of our worries. I did manage to find an Asian shopkeeper with a bank account in Leicester but Asians have always been the real pioneers of Africa. The Portuguese population was tiny – almost all involved with aid. Our hotel lay adjacent to the Chinese club which had been set up by descendants of the coolies who had built the railway but there were no Chinese left and it was deserted. Beira was still cosmopolitan but only because it was full of aid workers.

The streets were cracked and deteriorating fast. Buildings oozed sewage and rubbish lay everywhere. Homeless young children sifted through the garbage and did tricks in return for money while their slightly older sisters turned them. The shops were like those in the former Soviet Union – few and far between with long queues and nothing on the shelves. There were a few good restaurants to feed the aid community but you had to know where they were as they were invariably hidden from the street. To celebrate our arrival we went to an air-conditioned restaurant concealed down an alleyway. It had no windows on the street and you had to knock to gain entry. Inside were various aid workers, a few ship's captains and us. Even the waiters were not

Mozambican. Dinner of Beira prawns and spaghetti cost $95 with a few beers – twelve dollars more than Mozambique's last recorded per capita GNP.

Apparently the whole town was sinking because Frelimo had redirected the river. This made for an odd walk from the hotel to the port. The balustrade along the filled-in river no longer had any function. What had been built as an elegant promenade was now redundant. There was nothing to look at save a rubbish-filled riverbed. The elegant old merchant houses which lined the prom had not only been deprived of a view, they were also falling over.

Mozambique has the highest per capita aid budget in the world as the massed non-governmental organizations (NGOs) and UN throw money at the country's problems. They are not being very successful. A lack of coordination means that while some NGOs provide free food, the government, under the terms of its IMF-imposed SAP, has to charge the population for clean water. The *povo* therefore die from drinking dirty water. All the aid could be seen most clearly on the roads where there are thousands of cars. We didn't see a single vehicle built between 1975 and 1991. They were either pre-independence rust buckets or brand new aid wagons.

Without the port of Beira there wouldn't be much point in having the corridor. In the years after independence, the harbour fell into disrepair, silted up and decayed. In the late 1970s, a plan for the port's future was argued over and then discarded for lack of funds. Much wrangling later and with the involvement of many different aid groups, a project was agreed upon and funded. It came to fruition in 1991. The EC use Beira as an example for what they want to do with Lobito at the other end of the line. This is a mistake because Beira, although it looks very impressive, doesn't work too well.

At the gates of the port is an imposing Portuguese building which is the newly renovated headquarters of the Manica freight company. Manica handles 80 per cent of the freight on the corridor. Philomena Lopez, an Indian who married a Mozambican

Portuguese, has been working for Manica and living in Beira for twenty-two years. She was there throughout the war and knows everybody. With her help, we were able to gain access to the port and talk to the people we needed to at the state-controlled Beira Corridor Authority. Through Philomena we received the official version.

Lars, who was working for the BCA, took us on a tour of the docks. It is an impressive sight. There is a new container terminal which is meant to put Beira in competition with South Africa's Port Elizabeth, a new oil terminal which via the Lonrho-owned Beira pipeline will supply Zimbabwe, and a fully functional port with eleven deep berths. The railway is umbilically attached to the port so grain can be loaded straight on to wagons and taken up country or over to Zimbabwe. Glistening new cranes stand proud on the docks. The real story is a bit more worrying. We met one captain whose ship had been anchored offshore for two months. He was carrying urgently needed grain for neighbouring, starving Malawi, but was being jumped in the queue by ships with aid for Mozambique. At that point Mozambique had a massive surplus of donor aid – distribution was their problem.

'You have to bribe your way into a berth and I don't have authority to do that,' said Captain Lothar. 'There is one man who has to OK everything – the deputy harbour master – and he won't let me in.'

Pedro Junior, the aforesaid deputy harbour master, whom we had met that morning, had seemed charming enough to us, but he was the most hated man in Beira. The town was full of disgruntled captains, unable to offload and get away. A Sikh captain who was trying to unload emergency grain had left a pregnant wife at home and promised to be back for the birth. When we left Beira, his ship was still half full and he was the father of a three-month-old daughter. Some shipping companies had sent in special managers with the authority to bribe but there was still a massive backlog.

I put this to the BCA. 'We are doing the best we can,' explained their spokesman. 'Beira was not set up as an import port. We are meant to be exporting but the drought means that we have been overrun by aid imports. Since April, nine hundred thousand tons have come into this port and almost nothing has gone out. I spend most of my life trying to get empty wagons back from the affected areas. Beira has always been an export harbour and we renovated it to do the same job.'

The exports that had made it through to the port area were not receiving top priority. Zimbabwean steel rusted in trailer parks and everything was covered in bitumen. Barrels of bitumen awaiting export had been unloaded and left in the sun. The barrels had burst and now most of the port area was covered in sticky black tar. The affected corner had been closed off, but before that had been done, cars and trucks had carried the goo all over the port where it had crept into the machinery and ruined vehicles.

The port is an obvious terrorist target so endless papers (or a white skin) are needed to enter. This explained the lack of labour. When a ship did manage to berth, the captains found that in a country with millions of unemployed desperate for work there was no one to unload the ships. The few labourers that there were spent much of their time sleeping while wearing attractive chef's hats made out of aid bags. Outside the gates, hundreds gathered but were refused admission because they lacked the necessary papers. Many of them had fled the war with no possessions and no ID cards. Without them, they could not get the authorization to work in the port and will have great difficulty voting in the forthcoming elections.

The BCA had pointed out with pride their fine new tugs – the Pongwe and the Buzi. 'They have Russian crews who do not want to go home,' explained Lars. We later discovered that the two tugs were next to useless since they had been designed for inland waterways and were not equipped for the sea.

There was a clear lack of direction in the port. The aid donors were furious with the Mozambicans for charging duty on the import aid, yet one of their conditions for financing the port's rehabilitation was that it made a profit. Different wings of the same organizations were demanding conflicting things of the Mozambican government. The populace was desperate for work inside the port yet once they got there didn't do any. The WFP was paying its stevedores double the going rate thus messing up the internal economy of the port. The workers who thought they weren't paid enough reacted by sleeping all day and stealing grain. They would arrive in the morning as emaciated refugees and after tying string round their wrists and ankles would fill their clothes with grain and leave in the evening looking like Michelin men.

USAID, the World Bank and various NGOs had called in the investigators to find out where all their aid was going, because it certainly wasn't arriving where intended. Highly paid consultants called 'aid and donor-fund managers' snooped around following aid from the ships to its destination. Over dinner one night, we had the process explained to us.

'I've been following the shipments from Beira right up into Zambia,' Roger told us, 'and you wouldn't believe the places where it goes missing. My favourite is right here in Beira. There are so many delays in the port that the truck drivers just shack up in the local brothels while they wait to load their trucks. When they eventually get loaded, they go back to the brothels and pay the girls in maize. The longer the delays, the less maize we have to deliver.

'We noticed that lots of bags were getting ripped on the way up country. What was happening was people were gathering by the sides of the road as the trucks went by. They tie *pangas* [machetes] to the end of long sticks and then slash the bags as the trucks drive along. Then all they have to do is pick up the grain that falls on the road.'

In Zambia one of the big problems was that grain was being rattled out of the near-derelict wagons they used. In Mozambique this wasn't the case. We visited a repair shop that was reconditioning the old wagons and doing a magnificent job. The loco-repair shops, however, were a disaster. The old steam engines had been mostly withdrawn from service and replaced with glistening, polished, bright red diesels which were repaired and maintained in the old steam sheds by people who knew nothing about diesel and everything about steam. Four years earlier the track on the corridor had been repaired by NRZ as part of an aid project but hadn't been properly maintained since. Dependent on aid donors, the successes of the railway and the port were being overshadowed by the areas for which there was no funding. The wagons were great but the locomotives and tracks weren't. Someone had bought the railway employees smart new uniforms but the telephones were always breaking down.

'Our biggest problem has been in running the port as a customer-driven enterprise. The only people who have been properly educated here have been trained in places like the USSR and Cuba. This elite is entrenched in old communist ways which we have to try and overcome by forcing Beira port to make a profit,' explained Lars. 'On the other hand, the NGOs complain that we are charging duty on aid. Nothing is coming into this port except aid. We don't have the money to run it for free.'

As with many other massive aid projects, there were too many cooks using shoddy ingredients. The new cranes were wonderful for a while but they were obsolete when installed. No one makes spare parts for them and although they still look new, they no longer work. The railway needed new locomotives to take wagons up to Zimbabwe. They were given new engines, but shunting engines for use in the port, where they weren't needed. The shunting engines were being used on the main line which is not good for either the trains or the track and the wagons in the port were being push-shunted by fork-lift trucks which isn't good for the fork lifts or the wagons. Once again misdirected aid was causing more problems than it was solving.

Not everything looked so dismal though. There were a few success stories, but even the people who were responsible for them knew that much more needed to be done. Roger Rufi, the ICRC head in Beira, gave me his overview.

'Mozambique is teetering on the edge. The UN is trying to save money and it could be fatal. There is meant to be a peace-keeping force here at the moment. I think there is one man,' he told us. 'They borrowed twenty-five people from other missons when it was first announced and when they had to go back, they were not replaced. If they want to avoid another Angola they have to send lots of blue berets now and they have to listen to the people who are already here.

'I told the WFP last year that if they wanted to work here, they would have to bring everything with them, but they just will not listen. They still haven't got any long-wave radios and we have had to lend them some of ours. For the demobilization, the UN set up lots of concentration points and gave the soldiers six days to arrive and hand in their weapons. Because there were so many points the UN believed that it couldn't take anyone longer than five days to get there. In Angola they had a year and they still didn't do it. Thank God they didn't take the Zimbabwean troops out in November. The Italian blue berets have still not arrived.'

When the blue berets eventually did turn up, many had to be sent home again after it was discovered they had been visiting child prostitutes. In the report of the investigation it was noted that all wasn't as black as it had been painted: 'The investigation found no evidence of any homosexual sex involving [UN] personnel and Mozambican boys.'

The lack of any UN presence was Roger's main worry but it was by no means the only one. He was very concerned that Mozambique was going to become totally dependent on aid.

'Renamo have really got the hang of satellite communications,' he explained. 'They trade off all the NGOs against each other, by saying that "you are the only people who can help us". It is important that we stop food aid in April. We have given people seeds and they must learn to feed themselves where it is possible. The only people who should need food are the soldiers but no foreign government ever wants to give anything to soldiers. It's not a vote winner. We have just persuaded the EC to give food to the WFP to distribute. Until then they were demanding that all these soldiers hand in their weapons, go to concentration points and then wait there with no food.'

Roger arranged for us to visit one of his distribution points on the road to Maputo – in the heart of Renamo country. On our journey along the railway we had passed through Gondola where acres of shot-up steam engines and wagons had crowded the sidings. The stations themselves were all shot up too. Renamo's tactics during the war had been disruptive. They concentrated on making life difficult for the government rather than fighting over territory and managed to achieve a great deal by keeping key routes closed. Until the introduction of the Zimbabwean army on the corridor, they had managed it there, but the jewel in their crown had been control of the Maputo-to-Beira road – nine hundred miles of crucial importance. We set off early one morning with Carlos, a Salvadoran refugee who worked for the ICRC, to drive up the corridor and then down the Maputo road to an ICRC distribution point.

The Mozambican peace process got off to a shaky start in 1990. Frelimo, in its sixth congress, agreed to the introduction of multiparty politics and pledged itself to democratic socialism. Frelimo had made a deal with the South Africans in 1984 in which Mozambique agreed to stop supporting the ANC if Pretoria would stop supplying Renamo. Pretoria reneged on these Nkomati Accords and that was the closest either side had ever got to a deal. In July 1990, Frelimo and Renamo met in person for the first time and agreed to the setting up of the JVC, a joint monitoring commission to be presided over by the Italians. By the end of the year, after countless delays, it was agreed that if Zimbabwean troops were pulled back into the corridors, Renamo would stop its attacks. The deal signed and the Zimbabweans safely in the corridors, Renamo launched an attack on the provinces of Nampula and Zambezia and continued to disrupt the rail routes. Their actions spawned a monster. The Napramas, a band of spiritual rebels, joined forces with Frelimo and wiped out Renamo in the two provinces.

Spiritual rebel groups are an African phenomenon of awesome power. Alice Lakwena in Uganda nearly overthrew a government with hers and in Mozambique the Napramas have similar influence. Members of a secret society, they oil themselves with magic potion and, contrary to all evidence, believe that bullets cannot harm them. In conjunction with Frelimo they destroyed Renamo (who fatally believed in their powers) in Zambezia and brought the rebels back to the negotiating table. Frelimo had already promised free elections and had to face an internal party coup by its left wing who longed for the old days. Renamo had one card and has kept up with the negotiations by using it. A fragile ceasefire has existed since then. They have the ability to cut off all the roads in the country. By allowing them to be opened, they showed their goodwill and the threat of once more closing them keeps them in the game.

We followed the corridor from Beira towards the Gorongosa National Park which after years of war boasts about seven wild animals. It had been Renamo's main base inside Mozambique during the early stages of the war and as such was used as a source of food before becoming a battlefield. Frelimo launched a successful raid on Gorongosa in 1979 which killed Renamo's deputy leader, André Matzangaissa, but the rebels continued to use the park as a source of ivory with which to pay their South African sponsors. The road follows the railway so we drove past miles of burnt-out carriages and perforated wagons. It wasn't difficult to see why CFM operated no passenger services. Tica station had seen a massive fire-fight and reminded us of Savimbi's shattered house in Luanda. Once again blue and white shepherds painted on tiles had been obscured by bullets and blood. Someone had filled in the holes on the front of the station with plaster but no one had painted over it. The back looked like Emmenthal cheese.

The recent rains had caused much destruction along with the prospect of a decent harvest. Because of the war, people were living where no one should. Drawn to the sanctuary of the corridor, thousands had come to live on the Pongwe river flats. A vast area of land around the Pongwe appears as swamp on maps. They are the 'swamps where white men stew'. When Varian had been building the Pongwe river bridge and the tens of other small bridges and embankments that keep the line running above the swamp, he had been forced to bring in outside labour because nothing and no one lived there except strange web-toed antelopes and ducks. As we drove along we passed thousands of newly built huts that were fast submerging. Their shattered owners lined the road, begging for help and dying of malaria and cholera as millions of swamp-loving insects swarmed around their heads like personalized clouds. The rice which had been planted at the first sign of rain was being swept away by the excess water. Maize does not grow in paddy fields. It rots.

As we turned off the corridor and on to the Maputo road there was an immediate change in atmosphere. The corridor had always been a Renamo target but it had never been held by them. The road to Maputo, though, had been their private property since 1976. Carlos had been one of the first people to drive along it after the October ceasefire and the ICRC were still the only people who dared use it. Carlos told us about the first exploration. 'It was very frightening. There were trenches dug across the road and trucks pulled out to stop the cars.'

When someone who has spent his formative years in El Salvador describes anything as 'frightening', I begin to worry. Burnt-out trucks pushed to the side of the road proved his point. Renamo had shot at anything that dared to come down this road and then used the destroyed vehicles as road blocks. Deep bush came up to the tarmac on either side, so in some places we were scraping vegetation with both wings. We knew that all around us there were guerillas watching our progress, yet none of them were in the open. I was very thankful for the ICRC flag waving from the back of our Land Cruiser. 'They don't like the UN but they do like the Red Cross,' Carlos told us.

A few months earlier, he had come along the road with a work party to fill in the trenches and now it was one of the best roads in sub-Saharan Africa. So little traffic had been along it since it was last resurfaced in 1974 that it seemed brand new. All along the sides of the road there were dull green pebbles, which on later inspection turned out to be oxidized bullet casings. We went only a few hundred miles but apparently they line the route's entire length. Where the road crosses the Buzi river, we came across a large tank and a few soldiers guarding the bridge. We were six miles away from the official Renamo lines on the edge of Renamo country. The leader of the Frelimo soldiers had the jitters. There were seventy miles and half an opposing army between him and reinforcements if the ceasefire broke down. Banditry was the new problem, however. In the absence of UN peace keepers, bored soldiers from both sides were making nuisances of themselves. We stopped for lunch and discovered that one of the aid lorries that had preceded us had been shot at and held up but then allowed to continue when the driver proved his affiliation with the ICRC.

This would be the last food stop before our destination, where there wasn't going to be any food either. We had taken the precaution of buying a live chicken and some bread on the way. Supper stoically awaited its fate in the air-conditioned comfort of the car while we went to the small bar which overlooked the bridge. A soldier was bathing in the river, his uniform neatly folded on the bank. His AK was closer to hand, resting on the rock around which he swam. The bar itself was a hut the size of a squash court with a few tables and benches, an electricity meter and a wooden bar. We were the only customers but beyond the chicken wire, which served as walls and windows, a mob of children fought to get a view. The meter was for show. There had been no power here since 1975 and the goat, rice or goat and rice which graced the menu was cooked over an open fire outside. The *casserole au chèvre* was disgusting but we had to eat it with pleasure since the multitude who ground their faces into the chicken wire which caged us in were people to whom goat was an unheard of luxury. We didn't want to add to their wants, so saved our warm beer until we were back in the car.

As we left the bridge behind us, we officially entered Renamo territory. Alfonso Dhlakama, Renamo's leader since its creation in 1976, was born there. To distribute any aid, the ICRC needed Renamo's permission. They were first allowed in the area, four months earlier in October when we were still in Angola. Still every distribution had to be approved by countless different people and groups. Harriet's and my presence further complicated matters because although we had permission to be there from Beira, we also needed the local commander's approval.

We continued down the road past miles of monotonous bush, occasionally interrupted by the shattered ruins of a house or a burnt-out vehicle. It became obvious that we had arrived when we came across thousands of people gathered around a ten metre-square red cross which had been painted on parachute silk. Normally used as targets for air drops of emergency aid, the massive flag was a rallying point for the aid recipients, some of whom had walked a hundred miles to the distribution point. Seventy thousand people from both sides of the road were being given beans, maize, cooking oil and soap. The ICRC had given them seeds a few months earlier and were giving out their last batch of food so that the recipients would not have to harvest their crops too early in order to eat.

This project had been a great success. In only four months they had brought the local population back from the brink of starvation – at their first distribution people had crawled to the site – to the point where next month they would be able to feed themselves. As we had driven up the corridor, we had passed many small fields of maize which a few months earlier had just not been there. The Red Cross had achieved this by doing their distribution miles away from the nearest water. People had to come here to get their food and seeds and then go home to plant them. It was impossible for them to stay and become professional aid recipients because they would die of thirst.

Fellipe, the sole delegate in charge of the distribution, strode out of the mêlée and introduced himself. Tall, tanned, handsome and just the tasteful side of hairy, he seemed pleased to see us. 'There's rabbit for supper tonight,' he said. 'I got it with the Land Cruiser on my way home last night.'

We followed him back to his house where we would be able to get permission to be in the area from the local Renamo leader. Fellipe's house was a former restaurant which had no roof, no windows and extremely battle-scarred walls. At one end of the sole room was a vast pile of cashewnuts, at the other was a mosquito dome in which Fellipe slept and a battered table that he had brought from Beira.

He introduced us to Signor Cinzano, an old man who lived in a hut in the garden with his wife and a few young children. This was his restaurant and, although he was the only one with a roof over his head, we were his guests. He had only recently returned from Beira, where he had fled during the war. The restaurant had been blown up and looted in 1976 and all that remained to identify its former function were the brick bar against which the sacks of cashewnuts leant and the *maître d*'s manner. He behaved as though we were ambassadors staying at the George V and would not allow us to do anything for ourselves. A snap of his fingers and one of the innumerable children would unload the car, another and we were presented with the only plastic mug, heat distorted and full of cashew wine, to share betwen us. We discovered that Signor Cinzano had earned his monniker because of a large yellow sign which used to run across the front of his restaurant. Seventeen years after the advertisement's destruction, he had returned to his former home. The locals who hadn't fled or had recently returned still knew him as Signor Cinzano and the wrecked building was still known as Cinzano's.

'I have all my children out picking cashewnuts,' he told us. 'I will sell them in Beira and soon this place will be the best restaurant on the Maputo road again.'

His optimism seemed admirable, if a little ambitious. Cashews used to be one of Mozambique's biggest crops but with Beira in such a state they would be difficult to export. As we looked back at the house, I was seeing a derelict building which needed knocking down. He, however, saw a pretty restaurant with Cinzano umbrellas, gingham tablecloths and a Coca-Cola fridge. He was by no means the only optimist in Mozambique. It is, according to the International Index of Human Suffering, the most unhappy nation in the world – there is 35 per cent infant mortality – but through a wonderful coincidence, the *povo* did have some hope. The ceasefire had coincided, almost to the day, with the end of the worst drought in living memory. For the time being at least, the people of Mozambique would not tolerate another war. They were too happy with their new lives, which to us seemed pitiful and sad but for them were near paradise.

For the first time in eighteen years they were allowed to move around the country in accordance with their semi-nomadic way of life. There was a bountiful harvest on the way and above all there was peace. The UN might, through negligence, be conspiring to end that peace but the population was too busy enjoying itself to go back to war. In Angola everyone had worn opposing armies' T-shirts. Here many of the women were wearing kangas with the heads of both Frelimo's Joaquim Chissano and Renamo's Alfonso Dhlakama printed upon them. The fact that they had been woven at all was astonishing and to see people wearing them was a real hope for the future.

It was extraordinarily hot. Away from the coastal breezes and outside the air-conditioned car, it was difficult to move around in the shade, let alone the sun. Lungs burning, we had to wait for the Renamo leader, who we were assured already knew we were there, and would arrive at his leisure. Fellipe had not been surprised by our arrival. The bush grapevine had informed him that we were on our way half an hour before we arrived. Renamo were indeed making good use of their sat comms because we had been travelling at sixty miles an hour and the car's UHF radio was broken. As predicted, after about twenty minutes of sipping warm quinine-laced tonic water, a sinister figure in a baseball cap appeared from the bush with a couple of henchmen – Renamo's political leader for the area, Fabien Josef Antonio. It was difficult to see his eyes which were in the shadow of his cap, but those of his followers spoke volumes. One of them had a milky left eye, the other's settled on nothing, darting from face to face without making any contact. Although none of them had visible guns, the long machete-like knives which they carried seemed perfect weapons for performing the atrocities for which Renamo are so famous.

'Where have you come from?' asked their leader.

'We've been following the railway from Angola,' I replied, 'and we have come from Beira most recently.'

'Why are you here?'

'We wanted to see where the food that was coming on the railway was going.'

He turned on his heel, left us and, surrounded by his body-guards, went into conference with Signor Cinzano. We sat tight until, without another word to us, he left. Fellipe told us that we were allowed to photograph whatever we wanted but not to go too far from the road. No one carries guns around in public any more in Mozambique, but neither have they handed them in. Behind every bush, we were told, were guns and fighters willing to use them. In the deep bush around us, the quickest way to get around was by mountain bike. No car could make it through and on foot it would take a long time. In the vicinity, the ICRC told us, were 70,000 people awaiting their food aid yet we had seen only a couple of thousand. Mounting Fellipe's bike, I set off in search of them. Labryinthine paths led off into the hinterland, and everywhere there was a clearing, families had set up their temporary homes. Occasionally I came across groups of edgy-looking young men who did not wish to be interviewed. More often, though, people were smiling and welcoming, yet very few spoke Portuguese. By this time I could understand and make myself understood in Portuguese but my Shona was non-existent.

The surrounding area had been totally cut off by the war. They still used mangy old pre-1975 Portuguese escudos when they were not bartering. Meticais, the country's legal tender for the last thirteen years, had only been circulating recently and was still greeted with suspicion. The introduction of aid was helping disperse the new currency, since people were buying and selling again – swapping maize and oil for cash or queuing twice in order to make some extra cash. There was no way of stopping people from queuing twice but the gratitude and honesty of the people worked as a natural check. People caught were beaten by their compatriots. None of the children had any form of education. Official figures show that 70 per cent of the country's schools have been destroyed by the war and there were never very many in the first place. Most of the people I spoke to had lost children and husbands to the war and, although I have no empirical evidence whatsoever, I believe that there aren't many men left in Mozambique. Wherever we were in the country, there were always lots of women and children but few men. The ratio of the sexes seemed to have changed.

By the time I returned to the distribution point, Fellipe and Carlos had been joined by two more ICRC delegates. They had accompanied the oil that was needed before the distribution could commence. Signor Cinzano had announced earlier: 'There will be a revolution if there is no cooking oil,' so Fellipe had held off until it arrived.

The new arrivals were not so pleased to see us. We had come across quite some hostility from the aid community, due to an upset which had happened after the ceasefire. Earlier in the year, the donors had sent out apocalyptical press releases claiming terrible famine, so the international press had descended in a mob. Things were not as bad as had been suggested and the journalists had been infuriated by the lack of thin people starving and other people shooting each other. Without one or the other, no story from Africa ever makes the papers or the TV news, unless, of course, there is a furry animal angle. The journalists had wasted their time and money so they shouted at the aid groups. The aid groups had been horrified by this lack of sensitivity and had ignored journalists from that point on. Usually there is a better relationship between the two groups because they are often mutually dependent. Mozambique was different because it was so well funded. In Angola WFP flew us all over the country because they needed the publicity in order to solicit more funds. In Mozambique, they were loaded anyway and didn't need to help journalists.

We had to fight against this attitude and prove what jolly good chaps we were. Having failed at most of the other agencies, we had been lucky to find a friend from Somalia working at the ICRC, who had vouched for our good behaviour and sincerity. We had to prove our sincerity all over again with the two who had just arrived. It was not difficult since they were so obviously doing a very good job. For a start, I had never seen aid workers living in such poverty. They were genuinely eating the same food as the people they were helping and living in equal discomfort. The evidence of the success of their projects had been all along the road. We had travelled through fields of maize grown with seeds which the ICRC had provided. We did not have to feign admiration. Neither of us had ever seen a truly successful aid project before.

The chicken had been reprieved at the last minute in case it was a good layer, so that night we devoured the rabbit. Great preparations were made and delicious smells wafted from the garden as we drank cashew wine (which sounds a lot nicer than it is) and set up the table in the shattered remains of the house. Signor Cinzano had even found an old tablecloth and some candles. We won our spurs by beating their horror stories from the flea-pits of the world and ate the shattered remains of the rabbit. A two-and-a-half-ton Land Cruiser does a lot of damage so it was rather more like bone-splinter soup but we all enjoyed it. Signor Cinzano enjoyed it so much that he sat in the garden, staring in at the window and sobbing inconsolably.

'It's just like when the restaurant was open,' he said. 'Everyone used to stop here on their way. Soon it will be like this every night.'

Twenty-seven years of endless fighting may have destroyed the infrastructure of Mozambique. Years of famine, followed by devastating floods and war, may have depleted the population, but nothing could dampen their optimism. If only because of this, Mozambique still has hope.

That night we broke a record. Having set off from England equipped with enough foreign correspondent's kit to boost the share price of the Survival Shop, we had managed to sleep in a bed on every night of the trip. Some of them weren't very nice and we had used our mosquito nets and repellent but none the less we had been quite proud of our comfort record. That night, only days before the end of the journey, we had to sleep in the back of a Land Cruiser. We had presumed that we were staying with comfortably lodged aid parasites. Instead we were staying with people who were doing a genuinely good job on a very small budget and we'd left all our camping kit at the hotel. Chastened, we left the next day and returned to Beira with Carlos.

As we drove back, we passed a steady stream of women and children walking back to their homes, laden with spoils. Fellipe had just received a truckload of donated clothes so it was a brightly dressed procession. Many were wearing peace kangas but also they wore an amazing assortment of hippy jackets, flared trousers and shirts with vast lapels. It is fascinating to see what people give away. All these clothes were part of a recent shipment from Britain which had been given to the ICRC in an aid swap. There were some normal clothes among them – notably Madonna and Michael Jackson T-shirts – but the vast majority was pure 1970s gear. Why had people hung on to their Bay City Rollers trousers and Grateful Dead T-shirts only to give them away just as they came back into fashion? However unattractive the clothes were, they caused great joy. Most of these people had been cut off from any sort of manufactured goods for almost twenty years. It seemed right that they were wearing 1970s clothes again. A few months earlier they had been wearing aid bags and rags, now they were dressed in period outfits that were fashionable when the world had forgotten Mozambique.

When we had first arrived in Beira we had done so by train. After twelve and a half hours on board, we had slowly pulled into town – through Dondo where there was enough scrap metal to finance the rehabilitation of the railway – and into the decaying outskirts. We had spent the journey sitting on the running plates of the locomotive, waving at the amazed children whom we passed along the way. For us, it had been a momentous occasion. We had travelled twenty thousand miles trying to follow the railway and the last leg had been one of the most remarkable parts of the journey. With all the innovations of the late twentieth century, we had been hard pushed to follow the line from Angola. We had travelled by jet and propeller planes, speed boat, four-wheel-drive car, truck, bus, JCB and even helicopter yet there were parts of the railway we had not got anywhere near. We had the satisfaction of taking a train for the last part of the line but basically we had failed. Pauling, Varian, Rhodes, Williams, Lawley and all the other people who had been involved in its construction had managed to do it with none of our advantages.

A few miles from Beira there were mud flats to cross, then every geological and geographical obstacle known to man and some which they discovered. A century ago, they built a bridge over the Victoria Falls. Varian travelled most of the way on foot, and power was provided only by beast or steam. As we drew into Beira's engine sheds, we had felt too awed to celebrate. The last fifty miles of our journey had been through a lily-filled, insect-infested bog. When Pauling started building the railway across it, his goal was not the other side of the swamp but the Atlantic Ocean at the other side of the continent. To have such vision is rare enough. To have actually pulled it off – we now understood – had been an astonishing achievement.

CHAPTER TEN

Unable either to take a train or to fly direct to Johannesburg from Beira, we had to go via Maputo. Despite the fact that LAM – the Mozambican airline – has been restructured by Aer Lingus, it has taken on board the Africa effect and doesn't work very well. When we had first arrived at the Ambassador there was a group of businessmen staying there who were trying to do some deals in the port. Having failed, they spent every day out at the airport or in the crumbling LAM offices in town – trying to buy a ticket out. The LAM office was in a dilapidated building which had become permanently damp due to the dripping of ill-maintained air conditioners. Inside there was always a ruck of angry people crowding a temperamental computer. By the time we left, the businessmen had given up and were trying to organize a charter from South Africa. Luckily, we were able to fly Aid Airlines. ICRC flew us via Xai Xai down to Maputo where we awaited our SAA flight to Johannesburg. It is the only flight for which I have been allowed to pay at my destination. SAA didn't even want to *see* a metical.

The Cardoso Hotel, where we stayed, has a commanding view of the bay and the port. Built high on a hill, you can lie by the pool and see the whole of Maputo stretched out before you. Set on the Indian Ocean with a distinct Portuguese influence, Maputo is very beautiful, so we lay by the pool and looked at it. For the first time in six months, we weren't trying to catch a train. I didn't have to write my diary and we had no deadlines to worry about. Doing nothing was bliss.

The Cardoso is a Lonrho hotel and was charging absurd prices for reasonable service. It had a very dubious accounting system whereby it quoted prices in dollars yet charged at a Lonrho-invented exchange rate in rand. Meticais were not welcome. Lonrho is one of the few firms that bothers to invest in Africa and because of this has preferential status in many African countries – particularly Mozambique. The Mozambicans allow Lonrho to run its own private army. This is what African countries have had to resort to in order to encourage investment, yet it still doesn't work. Foreign companies charge customers as much as they can in dollars which are then sent outside the country and only their local currency earnings are reinvested. Decades after the end of colonialism, western business practices on the African continent are still much the same. Rape, pillage, remove.

But why shouldn't they? They do it everywhere else. Surely some investment is better than none? The west has invested a great deal in Africa. Why should it be deprived of a return on its investment? The usual answer to those questions is that we have also taken millions out in money and souls. I believe this argument no longer works. Africa has to learn to help itself and is not going to until the west stops coming to the rescue. We invariably cause more problems than there were in the first place. A few African leaders have realized this and their countries are leaping forward. Uganda was destroyed under Obote and Amin. Its current president, former rebel leader Yoweri Museveni, has accepted that many of Africa's problems are its own and has fought to sort them out. Uganda is now far from perfect and many of its citizens are dissatisfied but it is moving forward for the first time in decades.

Individual western countries have proved that they cannot divorce politics from charity. France supported the child-eating Bokassa in the Central African Republic and even helped pay for his Napoleonic coronation as emperor. Giscard D'Estaing was only forced to intervene and overthrow him when his eating habits – already well known to his countrymen – became public. Still, D'Estaing will always remember his hunting trips and as we all know: diamonds are for ever.

Belgium has allowed Mobutu to remain for decades. Britain

continues to prop up Moi in Kenya and the less dangerous Mugabe in Zimbabwe. Supping with the enemy has become an essential part of the western diplomat's diet. America, when it has intervened, has been even more disingenuous – Angola, Somalia, Ethiopia. The bungled attempts of the United Nations – particularly now that the Americans are in charge – to solve African conflicts have provided more evidence that the west should leave the continent alone. Somalia has been so ineptly handled that it makes Vietnam look like a success story.

Africa, however, hasn't exactly helped. The Organization of African Unity is a genuinely sad joke. It was founded in 1963 'to promote unity and solidarity among African states'. Since then it has put out an annual statement against apartheid and achieved precisely nothing. Its most notable *success* has been the Rwandan peace-keeping force. Based in Ethiopia's captial Addis Ababa, which from 1974 to 1991 was a city at war with its provinces, the most damning statement against it was made recently by its newest member. President Isseyas Afeworki of Eritrea, who had to earn his seat by overthrowing Ethiopia's dictator Mengistu and entering Addis Ababa on a tank, said in August 1993: 'Although the OAU has often championed the lofty ideals of unity, cooperation, economic development, human rights and other worldly objectives, it has failed seriously to work towards their concrete realization.'

He blames neither the cold war nor colonialism – both of which he has experienced personally – but African leaders.

There is no doubt that colonialism had a devastating effect on Africa. In Mozambique, the Portuguese forced blacks to walk on the roads rather than the pavements so now that the cars have returned there are frequent accidents. Whites are still treated with automatic and unjustified respect even in the most rabidly anti-colonial countries. Every time that an aid worker or a journalist is killed in an African country it is brought home to the residents how unimportant the west regards African lives to be. When the aid worker Sean Devereux was killed in Somalia there was a

Somali death rate of one thousand a day. John Maathai, Hos Maina, Dan Eldon, Anthony Macharia, Hansi Krauss – all journalists killed when covering recent African conflicts – are better remembered than the countries in which they died. As colleagues and friends I am glad they are remembered but if I was a Somali or an Ethiopian I would be outraged by the attention their deaths engendered when the deaths of thousands of Africans go unacknowledged every day.

This attitude was first proved to Africans of the modern era when the UN's predecessor, the League of Nations, betrayed Haile Selassie in 1934 and again in 1936. In an impassioned speech to the League of Nations in Geneva, the emperor of Ethiopia – ruler of one of the most ancient civilizations in the entire world – begged the international community to stop Mussolini from taking over his country. He was turned away and his country was overrun: 'Outside the Kingdom of the Lord there is no nation which is greater than any other. God and history will remember your judgement.'

Post-colonialism has been even worse. Having taken all it wanted from Africa, the west pulled out and left the continent in the hands of people whom they had never trusted even to help run it. Europe and America have never invested in Africa out of altruism and still don't. In Somalia and Ethiopia, America and the USSR changed their allegiances overnight in order to continue fighting their own cold war. The two countries were picked up and discarded like pawns and the residents of the Ogaden consequently had to endure a very *hot* war. From 1992–4 America had to suffer the effects of having 366 million dollars' worth of weapons (the admitted figure), which it supplied to Somalia from 1982–92, turned against its own army.

In Kenya, Britain was pushing Moi towards multiparty democracy well before the Gulf War but quickly changed its mind when it realized that it would need the deep port at Mombasa to supply the Persian Gulf. In 1994 the status quo has not changed. Still, *l'etat, c'est Moi.* In the 1980s, one side of the American administration worked with the communist Angolan government to negotiate terms for oil drilling while another part was supplying and training UNITA. Now that UNITA have gone beyond the pale (eighteen months since we were last there), America is giving satellite information to the MPLA on its former puppet's troop movements. Under the guise of helping Africa, the west has always put its own interests first and has probably done more harm than it did in the brief colonial period.

It is indisputable fact that Africans are 'more sinn'd against than sinning' but their leaders are also often 'ungrateful wretches'. All the beneficial effects of colonialism have been lost. The road systems that the colonial powers left behind have been left to decay, the farms and factories destroyed and looted. African leaders have merely assumed the mantles of their former colonial masters and continued the tyranny of their countrymen. In most cases they have been worse than the colonizers. Through a combination of western duplicitousness – military aid masquer-ading as charity – and African corruption, the continent has been all but destroyed. The dilapidation of the Benguela to Beira railway is only one manifestation of a continental malaise.

Britain supplies weapons to Kenya, which uses them to fuel the civil war in Somalia, which in turn means Kenya receives aid as the policy guarantees it remains the only stable state in East Africa. British officers still train the Mozambican army months after the time when there should no longer be one. American troops went into Somalia to do a quick PR job (do something nice for some black Muslims) which would shine up their image after the farcical end of the Gulf War. Months later they were bogged down, suffering increasingly heavy casualties and trying to kill Mohammed Farah Aideed, one of the most powerful leaders in the country. They chose to negotiate with a hotelier who had proclaimed himself president rather than Aideed who was once an ambassador. Their actions united Somalia behind a psychopath and killed countless innocents. By the end of 1993 they had changed their minds again and were flying Aideed, under their protection, to peace talks in Addis Ababa. In the spring of 1994 they gave up completely. The name of their mission was Operation Restore Hope.

The Americans have become an international menace. Angola was nearly invaded because the United States was stupid enough to have an insufficiently protected consulate a few doors down from Savimbi's house – a consulate in which all the communications equipment had been blown up by its own staff. The United States is not the only offender, it is merely the richest. The former Soviet Union was even worse. Britain, France and Belgium are scarcely blameless but this is not the point. It is easy to prove that the west has harmed and continues to harm Africa but Africa has also damaged itself. While the west insists on helping out in times of genuine need, none of this is going to change. The aid business has been spawned from international guilt trips. European electorates feel guilty about colonization, Americans about slavery and the cold war.

Africa is used as a source of profit – both political and financial. Much that I respect Jane Perlez, it is somewhat terrifying that George Bush invaded Somalia because of one article she wrote in the *New York Times*. Western governments, aided by the media, manipulate liberal views to make aid a popular policy then administrations follow their own outrageous agenda under the guise of charity. Only a minute proportion of aid budgets actually goes on feeding refugees. The majority goes on aid deals like road-building projects. Vast percentages go on kick-backs to African politicians.

The countries we had travelled through had the ability to feed themselves and the infrastructure to help them in the railway. If Angola was not at war, and the government was not so inept, the starving population could live on state handouts from McDonald's and still have a healthy balance of payments. Angola has oil stocks comparable to some countries in the Gulf. Texaco makes bundles of money from drilling there. Angola loses all its profits to corruption and weapons buying. It has some of the richest diamond fields in the world yet – for short-term political reasons – the government allowed independent prospectors to mine in the area. The miners have destroyed the geology of the diamond fields and millions of dollars' worth of stones have been smuggled into other countries – lost for future generations. Even the UN were smuggling diamonds out of Cafunfo when we were there. The UN team before we arrived had been pulled out because of corruption and the next team were being used without their knowledge.

One of the smugglers there told me: 'Whenever a UN helicopter flies in, it leaves with a load of diamonds' – hidden in a mobile air-conditioner going for repair or given to a maintenance man.

It is economical to mine copper at 12,000 feet in Indonesia yet it is no longer viable at sea level in Zaïre. The railway leads to the very gates of the mines. That, after all, was why it was built. Mobutu and his cronies have allowed their greatest natural resource to disappear in order to line their own pockets. The railway is only being used for ethnic cleansing. Most of the trains and wagons have been lost to state-sponsored looting or neglect. Even if they could get the copper out and on to trains, they wouldn't be able to send it to Lobito because there's a war in the way. Pre-independence the Angolan and Zaïrean part of the railway carried three million tons of freight from Zambia a year. It now carries nothing. The only option for Zaïre is to send goods down through Zambia but the railway there is so inefficient that it couldn't handle any increased capacity.

In Zambia farmers are unable to grow their crops because they can't get any fertilizer through the hapless port of Beira, even when the government has allowed them the foreign exchange with which to pay for it. Zambia's own industries are being neglected and mismanaged. Corruption plagues all business life from having to pay a bribe to have your telephone connected to the big percentages necessary to negotiate government contracts. Zimbabwe is in a slightly better state yet has Mozambique to negotiate before it gets to the coast. At the time of writing there is still only a fragile ceasefire in Mozambique and the country is nowhere nearer to a lasting peace. In the interim, the country's few remaining assets are being sold off by and to unscrupulous con artists. Mozambican army helicopter pilots are encouraged to fly their gunships out to ships off the coast where they are given $500,000 and a new identity.

The west is further destroying Africa by its bungling attempts to help. When aid is delivered late, as it was to Zambia in 1992, it distorts the real market. African countries beg for aid when they need it but it often arrives after the demand has died. Just as the country is beginning to find its feet once more, a massive excess of food arrives on the market, drives down prices and leaves farmers in need of food aid. Soon eaten, all it has done is cause more problems and stifled growth.

It is easy to sit in a comfortable London flat encouraging the world to stop sending aid to Africa. It is more difficult if you have actually seen starving refugees, watched villages being bombed and heard the wailing of wounded children. But I have also seen the damage that aid has done to Africa. However well meaning the NGO, it is always manipulated by local or foreign powers. It is wonderful to feed starving children in Somalia, but to do so it is necessary to pay mercenary guards who in turn pay their political masters. To enjoy the privilege of stopping one child from starving involves fuelling the war effort which caused the child to starve in the first place. Flying food into Sudan makes for great TV pictures when bales stamped 'Gift of the EC' hurtle out of the loading bays of Hercules transport planes but in Sudan food is used as a weapon. Food landing behind the lines of the Garang faction of the SPLA will never get through to the Machar faction. If the Muslim north had to spend any money at all on the Christian and animist people of the south, it wouldn't be able to afford to fight them.

Despite all the altruistic noises from the likes of Britain's overseas aid minister, Baroness Lynda Chalker (speaking in early 1994 during the Pergau Dam affair and the 'arms to Iraq' inquiry:

'We do not and while I am a minister we will not link our aid programme to arms sales'), Britain is only involved in African countries where it is useful to be there. Even then Britain is not giving as much as anyone else but just enough to be able to exert influence. I have witnessed spontaneous riots in Kenya complaining at Britain's continued support of Moi despite his human rights abuses. Chalker retaliated that at least Moi was trying.

The west has crippled Africa with unmanageable debts which Africa can never repay and never will. Writing off debts is merely a political concession – no one can possibly imagine they ever will be repaid. All Africa's debts could be paid off without denting the World Bank and IMF's coffers, yet they insist on rescheduling its debt repayments. To Africa they are enormous, to the west – paltry. Bradford City Council (a small town in England) owes more than Chad (a large country in Central Africa). Rwanda's third biggest foreign-exchange earner was the money it received from tourists visiting two families of gorillas in the war-ravaged highlands. America and Europe may be going bankrupt but at least we have a little more income than that which we receive from Disneyland and Windsor Safari Park. If the citizens of Zambia gave every single penny they earned to their western creditors, it would take them more than two and a half years to pay off their country's debt. Ten billion dollars of Africa's paltry earnings go to the west in debt repayments every year. With that sort of standing order it can never hope to start developing independently.

Africa's problems have been made worse by the west but it is a shared problem. An estimated 80 per cent of Africa's income disappears in capital flight. Dictators, soldiers and government officials become millionaires while their countries starve. A secret but substantial percentage of the world's Mercedes cars goes to Africa. Lonrho – of course – supplies all Zambia's. Nearly 50 per cent of African countries suffer from some sort of ethnic conflict yet as we saw in Zaïre and Angola it is often fuelled by the politicians who claim to abhor it. On a continent that has straight-line borders – courtesy of the colonial carve-up – there is a great deal of resentment for the Savimbis and Mobutus of the world to stir up. On the borders of Zimbabwe and Mozambique, members of the same family live in incomparable conditions. The Mozambicans have nothing; their Zimbabwean kin are some of the most fortunate people south of the Sahara.

Africa has been ravaged by the west for centuries. We do have a responsibility towards it but all help is pointless when the motives behind it are dubious and Africa still has political leaders willing to fill their own pockets while their countries starve. There is nothing we can do about that. The west has tried forcing western-style multiparty democracy upon Africa. It has been proved over and over again that it doesn't work. Kenya, Nigeria and Angola have all had multiparty elections which have left the same monsters in power. Tribal loyalties, cash and force are all employed to retain the status quo. When new governments have been installed as the result of multiparty elections, the old behind-the-scenes figures retain control. Only the faces in the cabinet change.

The west has also tried to force economic change. Twenty-seven African countries now have SAPs forcing free-market economies upon them. None of them works. The west has to accept that it has failed and allow Africa to advance at its own pace. A few centuries of superficial civilization – in most cases less than one – have been forced upon Africa and it has yet to adjust. In the main cities along our route we met well-educated, well-heeled Africans who lived in air-conditioned houses, used computers and telephones and drove cars. Also, however, we met people who had been living in the same manner for many centuries – tending small plots and existing by barter. The latter are the vast majority. Sixty-two per cent of sub-Saharan Africans live in absolute poverty.

There is a yawning chasm between the empowered and the powerless and until that inequality is addressed Africa will not be able to advance. We cannot address that problem for Africa. It has to do it on its own. Multiparty politics is not the answer. Freedom of speech is not too useful when – as happened with the Turkwel Gorge in Kenya – you are dying of thirst and hunger because someone in the capital has built a hydroelectric dam and cut off your water supply.

Colonialism left the countries of southern Africa with an admirable road system, thriving industries and a railway to serve them. It was not the west who destroyed what it left behind. Recently, the west has spent thirty years alternately following its own ends and trying to help. Until it frees Africa of its debts and leaves it alone to sort out its own problems, nothing will change. We have proved that we can't be trusted to meddle in Africa's affairs. To pull out will contribute more untold misery – maybe for decades – but we will no longer be interfering and adding to the problem. Until we stop propping up corrupt governments because they're better than the immediate alternative and prolonging civil wars by feeding the refugees that we have helped create, there will always be blood on the tracks.

The railway has survived for a hundred years. It can survive a hundred more if we allow Africa to develop at its own pace and in its own way. Given a chance to rid itself of its abhorrent leaders without outside funding and direction, there could be hope for a twenty-first century Africa.

Zaïre produces uranium. It would be foolhardy to allow a continent with such resources to continue under the guidance of the men who run it today. Mobutu has the funds to buy a Pershing for every day of the year. Impoverished uranium can be enriched. All he has to do is put the two together. Africa has a history of strong leaders from Lobengula to Sierra Leone's Valentine Strasser – men who have been willing to fight against tyranny. There are many more where they came from but while the west conspires to keep corrupt, vicious men in power, there is nothing that the true leaders – from tribal elders upwards – can do.

Africa is bursting with intelligent men and women who are beaten down by the system which we have helped to create and we continue to maintain. The Angolan space mission is not such an extraordinary concept. Allowed to enter the twenty-first century under its own steam, Africa might surprise us all. Neto's rocket could become the natural successor to Stephenson's. The Benguela Railway could see another century and the men of the BMR could rest in peace.

The Ballad of the BMR

Each bolt, each nut, each metal bar,
Could tell a story – grim but true –
And where the gangers' houses are
Maybe are ghosts of dead men too –
Ghosts of the men who worked and knew –
The fever-swamp, the sickening jar
That came when life was rusted through
Upon the lonely BMR.

Lo! – we may scoff – we often do –
And jest at engine, truck, and car –
But – must we then forget the few
Who made for us the BMR.

Cullen Gouldsbury